Dharma Then Moksha

The Untold Story of Swami Kripalu

Compiled, Edited, and Narrated by Richard Faulds

Peaceable Kingdom Books
Greenville, Virginia

Copyright © 2019
Richard Faulds

All rights reserved.
No part of this book may be reproduced without
written permission from the author. Yoga
teachers may duplicate sections of this book to promote
the learning and growth of their in-class students provided
they include the title, author, and e-mail address
where a copy can be obtained.

ISBN: 978-0-9859196-1-0

The archival materials upon which this book is based are used by permission of
Kripalu Center for Yoga & Health, Stockbridge, MA, kripalu.org,
with all photographs (unless otherwise noted) from the
archive of Umesh Eric Baldwin, swamikripalvananda.org.

The photographs from *Asana and Mudr*a by Swami Kripalvananda (December 2017)
are reprinted here by kind permission of Monkfish Book Publishing Company,
Rhinebeck, New York.

Cover design by Nathan Lawton. Internal book design by Derek Hansen.

Copies of this and other books by Richard and Danna Faulds are available
by e-mailing yogapoems@aol.com

Printed in the United States by Morris Publishing ®
3212 East Highway 30
Kearney, NE 68847
1-800-650-7888

By studying the biographies of great masters, saints, and people of extraordinary ability, I have gained insight into truths I might otherwise have overlooked or failed to understand even after reading many scriptures. By examining their life stories it becomes clear that all such people have endured the pain of not finding any easy solution to their problem without yielding in order to make their discoveries. The most extraordinary of these torchbearers are the spiritual masters who have gazed unflinchingly at human suffering and seen that it has a cause and reason for arising, that it has remedies, and can even be removed. The true paths they discovered should not be neglected by society because they are not meant only for a few special individuals. These paths have the power to bring happiness to everyone.
—Swami Kripalu

Dedication

This first of two books in the Swami Kripalu Fellowship series is dedicated to Urmila Desai (Mataji), whose impeccable service to Swami Kripalu enabled him to live happily in America for the last four years of his life. It is not widely known that after Swami Kripalu's death in 1981 Mataji commenced an intensive yoga and meditation practice that she carried on without interruption until the time of her own passing in 2006. It is a loss to everyone in the Kripalu community that her spiritual stature was never adequately recognized during her lifetime. With gratitude for Mataji and all she contributed, I take the opportunity of this book's publication to send blessings to her soul.

Mataji Desai serving Swami Kripalu his daily meal.

Table of Contents

A Note to the Reader 7

Author's Preface 9

Chapter 1. Kindly Write Your Autobiography 27

Chapter 2. Treading the Path of Dharma 45

Chapter 3. A Wandering Swami 52

Chapter 4. Pranotthana 64

Chapter 5. Twelve Years of Silence 84

Chapter 6. Rebuilding the Temple 100

Chapter 7. Coming to America 112

Chapter 8. Return to India 127

Epilogue 136

Appendix of Teaching Stories 140

Bibliography 191

Additional Resources 192

Photo Credits 193

Acknowledgments 195

About Kripalu Center 197

About the Author 198

A Note to the Reader

While teaching, Swami Kripalu often recounted incidents from his past to illustrate whatever principle he was trying to convey, but he never told his life story in a comprehensive fashion. Perhaps this was to keep the attention of his students squarely focused on their own practice, inner work, and self-discovery. Maybe he was side-stepping all the dangers and shadowy dynamics inherent in cults of personality. It's possible he was steering away from having to explain events central to his self-development but guaranteed to strain the credulity of any rational listener. He could also have been following in the footsteps of his guru, who from the little we know about him appears to have been singularly tight-lipped about his past.

Regardless of the reason, Swami Kripalu's restraint had the effect of reverse psychology on me. While imbibing his principles, I took special note of these biographical snippets and pondered them in an attempt to fathom how he'd become the person I encountered in 1981. This inquiry started the day we met when I began reading his first book available in English. It carried into my four years as an ashram resident, when I had access to rough translations of his written works and an archive of transcribed talks. It continued during the two decades that I served as a staff member of Kripalu Center for Yoga & Health and only came to completion while writing this manuscript. In the pages that follow, I compile these biographical incidents to let Swami Kripalu tell his own story, while providing a narrative text that fills in the gaps and shares some of my own reflections.

All the quotes, anecdotes, and teaching excerpts that follow remain as close as possible to Swami Kripalu's words. With his self-references sprinkled throughout a great many talks and writings, it was often necessary to combine material from different sources to shed light on a particular topic or time in his life. While every effort has been made to retain his distinctive voice and subtlety of expression, these quotes have been edited and excerpted to make their meaning clear. They are also presented in a manner meant to cast light on the telling of his life story. As a reader, it's important to know that any material depicted in *italics* is sourced in Swami Kripalu's legacy of written works and transcribed talks unless otherwise noted. That includes the quotations that open each chapter, shaded text sections, and margin quotes. I've also presented the seminal legends of the yoga tradition into which he was initiated, most of which appear in the appendix of teaching stories, so interested readers can see the mythological milieu and cultural ethos in which he was steeped. The photo credits provide additional information about the images appearing in this book.

As you'll find out in the pages that follow, Swami Kripalu died before I had a chance to thank him for setting me on the path of yoga at a pivotal moment when I was crossing the threshold into adulthood. As the recipient of a profound gift from a man who exited my life as quickly as he entered, I am left no option but to pay my debt of gratitude forward. May the remarkable story of Swami Kripalu's rise from poverty and despair to renown and Self-realization preserve his memory in the only way he would have wanted: by inspiring readers to explore the power of yoga through personal practice.

Richard Faulds
Greenville, Virginia

Author's Preface

My story of meeting Swami Kripalu is like many I've heard over the years, although to me it remains a singular and astonishing event. After striding across the stage to receive my college diploma in the spring of 1981, I got in my car and set out for the Kripalu Yoga Ashram, a young man on a spiritual quest. Much to my parents' dismay, the impact of four years of academic study on my developing psyche paled in comparison to my forays into the burgeoning world of post-1960s American spirituality. Something in me was waking up, and I was drawn to anything that promised to expand my horizons. I scanned bulletin boards for workshop flyers, joined meditation groups, and visited communes. My backpack always held a paperback on some unconventional topic or another. More than anything else, I was fascinated by the teachings and techniques of yoga.

Yoga had entered my life in high school, when I learned the classic poses from books to increase my flexibility and pursue a teenage dream of becoming a professional golfer. It accompanied me to Vanderbilt University, where I took an eight-week series of instructional classes and my posture routine became a morning ritual that helped remedy the side effects of my young-adult lifestyle. Yoga remained a physical exercise until my sophomore year of college, when I encountered the countercultural manifesto *Be Here Now* and the East/West teachings of its author and former Harvard professor, Richard Alpert. It was Alpert, better known by his spiritual name of Ram Dass, who helped me see that yoga was also a doorway into new realms of consciousness. Despite the mind-altering power of the psychedelic movement led by Ram Dass and others, something in me pulled back from its directive to "turn on, tune in, and drop out." I had lots of friends living alternative lifestyles, but none of them had what I was searching for, which I began to suspect could not be found in temporary highs or the choice to live outside the confines of mainstream society.

I needed to step onto the spiritual path via another door, which swung open the second semester of my junior year, after I'd completed most of the required credits for my dutiful economics major. Paging through the course catalog the first week back on campus after holiday break, my eyes grew wide as I noticed the classes in Buddhism offered by the religion department. All it took was a phone call to the Registrar's office and a drop/add form to get my name on the roster of Buddhism 101 in time for the first session.

It's hard to describe the effect that studying the teachings of the Buddha and later the exploits

You are a seeker. Follow the way of truth. Reflect upon it. Make it your own and it will always sustain you. You are a seeker and however young have been called to set out upon the way. Quiet your body. Quiet your mind. Want nothing. By your own efforts, awaken yourself and live joyfully. You are a seeker, called to come out from behind the clouds and like the moon shine bright over the world.
—Buddha, Dhammapada

of Zen masters had on me. I entered a world entirely new to me, but it was one that felt familiar. As a young child, I'd sensed there was more to life than what appeared on its surface, some hidden vein of deeper meaning that adults never discussed but whose presence I could intuit. Sheltered by childhood, I was interested in everything and inhabited a world bright with possibility. This sunny disposition accompanied me through the storms of adolescence but turned decidedly dark as I approached the precipice of college graduation. Facing career decisions that would define my future, my intuition began to call out like a siren's song, urging me to resist conformity and find a way forward aligned with my authentic self.

Learning in my Buddhist studies that sincere men and women had been setting out for millennia in search of life-transforming truth was tremendously important. It reassured me that I was not crazy in holding strong convictions. It clarified that what I was looking for was not a way to avoid or escape my problems but rather a disciplined system of self-development. It gave me hope that somewhere there must be a path to walk that would end my inner confusion and enable me to live with real purpose and joy. A chance comment by my Zen professor connected the dots. Upon hearing that Buddhist monks on intensive meditation retreats were referred to as "yogis," my next step came clear.

I submitted a proposal for an independent study in yoga to the chairman of the department. As a non-religion major, the odds of its approval were slim, but I didn't let that stop me from compiling an extensive reading list. Impressed by my choice of Mircea Eliade's classic work *Yoga, Immortality and Freedom* as a course manual, the chairman was won over by my desire to read yoga's traditional texts. It seemed fate was smiling on me as the proposal was approved, enabling me to spend the final semester of my senior year immersed in the primary Upanishads, Vyasa's *Bhagavad Gita*, Patanjali's *Yoga Sutra*, Shankara's *Crest Jewel of Discrimination*, and Svatmarama's *Hatha Yoga Pradipika*.

The literature of the yoga tradition is diverse and often inconsistent, but there was one topic all my sources agreed upon. In order to truly embark upon the path of yoga, an aspirant needs a teacher. That's what was driving my quest. Exiting the interstate and making my way along the country roads that pass through the Perkiomen Valley of northeast Pennsylvania, I approached the village of Sumneytown. Knowing it was only a stone's throw from the 55 acre farm that had been converted into the Kripalu Yoga Ashram, I began to wonder what it would be like to meet a yoga master in the flesh. Looking back, no amount of study or practice could have prepared me for what was about to happen.

Turning onto the winding gravel road that led to the ashram, I quickly found my rusty old Plymouth Duster in a caravan of Volkswagen vans and other vintage vehicles, most of them piloted by smiling young people. Stepping out onto the grassy parking area, I was taken aback to see that everyone else was wearing white Indian clothing and prayer beads. Despite my blue jeans and T-shirt, people were friendly and I learned the majority of them were resident staff coming from a second and larger retreat facility located a little northwest of Reading, an hour's drive away. Within a short time, I was sitting cross legged on the carpeted floor at the back of a second-floor chapel with the afternoon light streaming in through stained glass windows. Surrounding me was a hushed crowd of about a hundred gathered to have the audience of an Indian man widely acknowledged to be a yoga adept and saint.

Musicians and drummers took their places up front, engaging the room in a Sanskrit chant that started softly but swiftly built to a rousing call and response. I closed my eyes and tried to meditate, only to find myself a few seconds later open-eyed and staring at the young women who'd gotten up and were now dancing freely, their midriffs exposed by Indian saris. Clamping my eyes shut, I tried again to concentrate only to have this cycle repeat. It was from this divided place that my mind was catapulted into a state of one-pointed awareness deeper than anything I'd ever experienced. I was dumbstruck by the abruptness of the shift, and a few moments passed in

Let a person struggling hard for illumination seek out a teacher who is himself a knower of light. Once instructed, let this seeker become absorbed wholeheartedly in the right-teachings shown to him.
—Shankara, Crest Jewel of Discrimination

Ashram welcome sign.

> *Go to a teacher who is established in the Absolute, who is learned in the scriptures, whose mind has been tranquilized, and who has reached peace. Such a teacher, if approached properly, will bestow the sacred knowledge.*
> Mundaka Upanishad

wonderment at the depth and spaciousness of my newfound consciousness. The first thought to move across the suddenly wiped-clean screen of my mind was that this must be what Zen masters work so hard to achieve in sitting meditation. A second thought followed on its heels: something outside of me must have galvanized this sudden change.

The crowd stirred and I turned to see that Swami Kripalu had entered the room and was stepping out of his sandals a few paces to my right. The chanting stopped. As I watched Swami Kripalu slowly make his way to the front of the room with the crowd parting before him, there was not a doubt in my mind that it was his presence that had somehow elicited this shift in me. As the 68 year-old Swami Kripalu turned to greet us with hands in prayer position, my first impression was that he looked surprisingly like my grandfather, who was also bald and pencil thin. But the similarities ended there. The energy emanating from Swami Kripalu was palpable, an amalgam of brightness and warmth that seemed to flow from an inner reservoir of sheer spiritual power that I registered as almost frightening in its immensity. In the brief time it took him to greet us, bow to the altar, and take his seat, a second and more accurate impression formed. Swami Kripalu was a lightning bolt wrapped in an orange robe.

Another chant started and Swami Kripalu inaudibly sang along, keeping time with a gentle tapping of hand on thigh. His facial expressions and gestures were mesmerizing to watch, shifting back and forth between child-like playfulness and stern seriousness. Most of the time, he sat smiling, making faces, and laughing in a way that conveyed genuine sweetness and put everyone at ease. Just watching him, the door to my heart creaked open without me even knowing it. Inhibitions gone, I was on my feet and moving to the music. A few times, Swami Kripalu raised his right hand, index finger pointing skyward. Holding this gesture, he looked at us with a strict expression as if to say, "No ego shenanigans here, absolutely none allowed." Feeling the steely resolve underlying this nonverbal communication, everyone held their breath until his face softened and we all were laughing again. In this way, Swami Kripalu captured the attention of everyone gathered without saying a word.

Swami Kripalu near the time I met him.

The room gradually became drunk on his energy. Most people got giddy, singing and dancing with abandon. A surprising number seemed unable to maintain wakefulness and fell asleep despite all the noise and activity surrounding them. A few sobbed quietly, while still others assumed strange postures or sat in trance-like meditation. Swami Kripalu was not doing anything to make this happen. He appeared relaxed and happy just to be with us. It seemed self-evident to me that his years of yoga practice had somehow rewired his body, mind, and heart in a way that allowed the full force of his being to flow through him and into the room. The result was mind boggling.

Standing at the rear of the chapel, I chanced to catch Swami Kripalu's eye and a second event occurred that still mystifies me. For a moment, we were just two attentive people in a crowded room making eye contact. The next thing I knew, I was coming out of a swoon. My loss of consciousness was brief, as I came back to my senses in time to notice the instant he turned to look elsewhere. Alert again, I struggled to piece together what happened in those intervening milliseconds. There was a fleeting recollection of something passing between us, a condensed energy or intelligence. Accompanying the recollection was a felt sense that I had blanked out because his ability to transmit exceeded my capacity to receive. These were the best words I could come up with in 1981 to describe what today might be likened to a download of a magnitude that crashed my operating system.

Swami Kripalu receiving a line of people in the blessing ceremony called *vandana*.

A line formed and people began to approach Swami Kripalu two-by-two on their knees to receive his blessing. I stood spellbound, watching the impact of his presence on each individual. Eventually a white-clad ashram resident named Vijay tapped me on the shoulder and invited me to go up with him. Joining the long line, he whispered a simple instruction, "Just do what I do." 20 minutes later we were knee-walking our way to the front of the chapel. That's when I noticed the two assistants, one on each side of Swami Kripalu's seat, whose job was to keep the line moving when people tarried too long at his feet. "Imagine that – spiritual bouncers," I thought to myself.

Finally it was our turn and I bowed before Swami Kripalu, placing my forehead lightly on his orange socks. Out of nowhere an idea popped into my head, "His feet smell like anyone else's feet." What I was referring to was the nylon scent of his brand new socks, but it was too late. As I looked up, Swami Kripalu was laughing out loud, pointing at me with that right index finger of his, left hand resting on his belly. "Oh no," I thought, "my first meeting with a saint and I think his feet stink." Swami Kripalu's eyebrows shot up and he laughed even harder, as if I'd spoken my thoughts aloud. I felt completely exposed and was startled by the hand of a bouncer shunting me off to one side before I could compose myself. Vijay went the other way but quickly found me to utter these words, which I've never forgotten. "Yo bro, that wasn't any ordinary response. My advice is to move right in or get on down the road." All these years later, I still appreciate that Vijay refrained

The stone Sumneytown building that housed the second floor chapel.

The energy emanating from an adept yogi is much like the rain; it pours out everywhere and falls equally on all. Those already practicing yoga have prepared themselves and are thus more affected. After receiving this energy, an aspirant must work hard and do the practices in order to progress. Otherwise they will not derive much benefit. It is this same energy that is gradually released from within by postures, pranayama, meditation and other yoga techniques.
—*Swami Kripalu*

Note: From this point forward, any italicized material is from Swami Kripalu unless otherwise attributed.

from any effort to recruit me into ashram residency, recognizing that only I could determine my right response.

Soon it was over and everyone exited the chapel into a spring evening. Senses heightened, I took in the beauty of the gardens, trees, and stonework that bordered the chapel and its walkways. It was truly a peaceful setting. I was surprised there was no follow up activity of any kind. Everyone seemed purposeful with somewhere to go. I had noticed earlier that Swami Kripalu had written a book entitled *Science of Meditation*. The card table and glass display cabinet that comprised the shop was open and I bought a copy for $10. Placing it carefully in a brown paper bag, the smiling sales lady included a packet of materials about the ashram.

Within an hour I was back on the road, feeling uplifted but also struggling to make sense of everything that had just transpired. Aware of the power of projection from my psychology studies, my first thought was that I had made all of this up. But that didn't withstand scrutiny because the first and most potent experience occurred before I'd even known Swami Kripalu was in the room. I certainly could have read more than was there into the moment we locked eyes. Yet when bowing at his feet, what would motivate me to imagine him knowing that I thought his feet stink? Swami Kripalu had definitely reacted to me. Vijay pointed that out without any prompting on my part. Trying hard to remain objective and avoid magical thinking, I didn't want to go too far in the other direction and negate the simple truth of my experience.

One thing was absolutely clear. Swami Kripalu was the first person I'd ever met who had what I was seeking. It wasn't his spiritual power, the esteem and adoration showered upon him, or his overpowering love. It wasn't the sense of confidence and self-mastery he exuded, his innocent mirth, or the subtle artistry of his actions. While all of these were compelling, it was something more basic. Swami Kripalu had found a way to actualize the potential of his soul. That was what I wanted – to do that myself – to whatever degree possible. My parents lived outside of Philadelphia. Speeding down the Northeast Extension of the Pennsylvania Turnpike lost in thought, I was flying high on borrowed energy. I can say in retrospect that Swami Kripalu affected me like a powerful magnet. All the iron filings of my being came into immediate alignment when I entered his force field. While in his presence and for hours afterward, I functioned at peak efficiency so easily that it felt entirely natural. Leaving his magnetism, I was destined sooner or later to crash, but all this was unknown to me at the time.

Arriving home as darkness fell, I was immediately confronted with the loose ends of my life. Two law school acceptance letters were waiting for me, each requiring a prompt response. "Are you going to Dickinson or Villanova" my mother asked, knowing full well that I was far from sold on the idea of becoming a lawyer. "Let me know and I'll write a check." To her my interest in yoga was just a phase I was going through, rather than the defining life purpose it would prove to be. Opting out of a discussion that would only lead to an argument, I went to bed early and dug into *Science of Meditation*, intent on learning more about Swami Kripalu's approach to yoga.

The book began with a brief life sketch of the author, the first paragraph of which was four short sentences. After reading them twice, I had to lay the volume down on the bed. Swami Kripalu had practiced yogic meditation 10 hours a day for the last 28 years with 12 of those years spent in total silence. Up to that moment, I'd been proud of the hour-a-day posture practice I'd sustained through college. I watched my arrogance simply evaporate; it couldn't survive the heat of the book's opening lines.

Chapter one swiftly brought my psyche to a second boiling point. Swami Kripalu started his treatise by drawing a clear line separating householders from monks. He referred to householders as *samsaris*, the Sanskrit term for worldly people driven by desire to seek comfort and material well-being. Monks were *sanyasis*, monastics who renounce desire to walk the spiritual path to enlightenment. Swami Kripalu delivered the punch line in his third paragraph, which consisted of a single sentence set out by itself for emphasis: *Only one who has detached himself from all worldly concerns is capable of treading the path of yoga.* Thus began my descent into a full-blown existential crisis that lasted an agonizing two weeks.

After my independent study, I wasn't surprised to find Swami Kripalu distinguishing between householders and monks. What irked me was his upfront insistence that a seeker had to choose one of two paths with householders relegated to a decidedly second-class rank. Vijay's either/or

Yoga teaches that there are numerous energy centers lying inactive within us. A person who studies the yogic texts or comes in contact with an adept ignites a strong desire to awaken these centers, develop their personality, and obtain various advantages. Such a lover of yoga must ask an important question: Am I a great yogi able to do severe penance like that done by the torch-bearing sages of the past? Can I offer my whole life to the pursuit of yoga? Only if their heart says "yes" should a person undertake the difficult pilgrimage of renunciation. Otherwise they must accept the easier householder path. The renunciate path is like a hungry elephant; no householder can afford to maintain it. For them a goat in the form of the householder path is more useful.

proclamation played back in my mind, "move right in or get on down the road." While contemplating my future, I had run into similar dichotomies before. I heard an overpowering spiritual call but couldn't see any way to answer it. Loosely raised a Catholic, I felt no pull to participate in the church let alone join the priesthood, nor was I drawn toward any particular profession. Mostly, I felt boxed in by my mother's often repeated menu of acceptable career options: doctor, lawyer, politician. With college over, life was demanding an answer. Right there in bed, I squared off with the issue of occupation versus vocation, supercharged by my time with Swami Kripalu.*

It was not hard for me to sort out the strength of my desires. Money held little interest for me. I was willing to forego status. What I wanted most was spiritual growth and time to do yoga – that's where my passion flowed its strongest. Renunciate students of Swami Kripalu made a vow to pursue yoga, and only yoga, for the rest of their lives. Then they were free to immerse themselves in its practice. There was only one thing holding me back from such a leap. I also wanted a life partner with whom to share the path. I could not renounce this longing because it felt less like a desire and more a natural part of my being. Deep as I could delve, this drive to organize my life around the home base of a loving relationship did not feel at odds with the best interests of my soul. If this stamped me as a lowly householder, so be it. But regardless of what Swami Kripalu or anyone said, I refused to believe this ruled me out for enlightenment.

---

*Swami Kripalu called the householder path *pravritti marga*. The word *vritti* means *thought waves* and the prefix pra means *with*, making the householder path *the way that utilizes the thought waves of the mind*. He called the renunciate path *nivritti marga*. The prefix *ni* means *without*, making the renunciate path *the way that eliminates thought waves*. Not understanding these subtle distinctions, it was easy for me to jump to the conclusion that Swami Kripalu did not respect the householder path, which was incorrect.

I read into the night, finishing four chapters before tiredness began to tug at the edges of my awareness. Chapter three presented a method of meditation, and I studied its fifteen pages carefully. It was interesting that Swami Kripalu did not look at meditation narrowly as a tool to calm, concentrate, and still the mind. A much broader view was reflected in his technique, which included prayer, yogic breathing, plus guidance on how to release physical tensions and introvert the mind. Along with sitting in stillness, Swami Kripalu embraced active techniques that used movement and sound to free up the flow of energy and life force. Thinking back to my afternoon, the chanting and dancing now made sense to me.

Swami Kripalu saw yogic meditation as a time-tested way to activate the evolutionary drive that lies slumbering within us. He believed that an authentic spiritual path cannot be followed by rote. It has to emerge from inside a faithful practitioner, who will naturally pass through a progression of bodily healings, energetic openings, and non-ordinary mind states. While doing this inner work, a practitioner attains good health and develops a host of positive mental qualities that boost performance and bring external success. Only after harmonizing every level of the human organism does yoga's ultimate goal come into view. As meditation becomes an all-absorbing experience of spiritual attunement, a practitioner can step beyond the limits of the animal body and egocentric mind to realize the divinity within. Swami Kripalu minced no words in saying that a practitioner intent on making this journey should meditate for at least an hour a day without opening the eyes once during this time.

The very first line of the book had used a word that I'd never seen before: *sadhana*. By this point in my reading, I'd come to understand that it meant *the systematic practice of spiritual disciplines for self-transformation.* This was the journey and life path I was called to follow. I felt certain of that. Before turning off the light, I took heart from some guidance offered specifically

Yoga has two paths. There is the householder path for those seeking worldly fulfillment and the renunciate path for great masters seeking liberation. The householder path of dharma (right living) is meant for those engaged in an active life in society. It builds character, bringing success and spiritual growth. The renunciate path of moksha (liberation) is meant for extraordinary individuals who have abandoned worldly life and want only to free themselves from the bondage of birth and death. These paths are entirely different. A yogic aspirant should understand both of them perfectly.

> *Yoga, meditation, and sadhana – these are practically synonymous terms. By properly understanding the word sadhana, all of an aspirant's problems can be resolved. Sadhana is the means for making spiritual progress. It is the discipline of regular, methodical, continuous, and uninterrupted practice of any one or all of the techniques of yoga. To an aspirant, their sadhana is everything and thus he or she never hesitates to sacrifice elsewhere to ensure continuity in its daily performance.*

to householders: *Yoga is a universal path accessible to all. Householders should walk this path in a way that does not create disharmony between them, their family members, and others with whom they interact. They should practice yoga and meditation systematically, adjusting their schedules based upon their duties and responsibilities in life. While fulfilling these duties, aspirants must dedicate ample time to their practice to make genuine progress. It should be sufficient for them to practice for two hours every day.*

Waiting for sleep to come, I knew something important had happened to me that afternoon, an energetic quickening of some kind. But lying in the bedroom of my parent's house, it was easy to doubt its significance. Reflecting on Swami Kripalu's words, it occurred to me that an hour of yoga postures was already part of my morning routine. I could get up an hour earlier to meditate first thing, while my mind was still quiet. I resolved to start in the morning and was surprised to find my depression lifting. A fiery determination took its place. I would make spiritual practice the bedrock of my life, always giving it top priority regardless of my circumstances. I would do my part and let the future determine if Swami Kripalu's belief in the power of *yoga sadhana* was true.

Over the next two weeks, I read the remainder of *Science of Meditation*. While its concluding chapters soared high above the limits of my comprehension, finishing the book served to catalyze a final ego confrontation. Along with distinguishing between monks and householders, Swami Kripalu sorted spiritual aspirants into three grades: extraordinary, exceptional, and ordinary. According to his definition, there was no doubt as to my standing. I belonged in the bin marked "ordinary," which meant that I needed to start the path of yoga at its very beginning.

Instead of concerning myself with enlightenment, Swami Kripalu was directing my attention to the primary goal of householders: *dharma*, a far-reaching term most simply defined as *a right way of living*. As I read and re-read certain sections, his guidance became clear. My first task as a student was to ground myself in a healthy lifestyle and begin the slow process of character building that over many years would render me fit to practice the more advanced disciplines of yoga. The idea that a foundation of physical health, ethical integrity, and success in daily life is what makes higher realization possible was central to Swami Kripalu's teaching.

Once instructed, an aspirant should commence the practice of yoga in close accordance with the path set out by his teacher.
—Svatmarama,
Hatha Yoga Pradipika

This was not a message my young male ego wanted to hear. It ran contrary to how I saw myself, a heroic figure making a solo ascent of the summit of spirituality. While resisting the label of "ordinary" tooth and nail, I allowed Swami Kripalu's words to make me think. I considered the path he'd walked to arrive at his current state: living in seclusion, strict vows of celibacy and silence, eating a single meal, meditating ten hours every day. Was I being called to that vocation? Should I give up on my longing for love and join Vijay in the ashram? What ultimately humbled me was not the fabled austerity of Swami Kripalu's lifestyle. It was my experience of being in his presence. It felt preposterous to imagine a path that could pole vault me over all my problems to his level of development. Swami Kripalu was right; I was an ordinary seeker who needed a gradual approach. In retrospect this humbling was a great gift as it replaced a measure of my self-importance with a willingness to learn from others further along the path.

Getting clear spiritually broke the log jam holding me back from practical action. It would be nice to say that I made a mature choice to go to law school. The truth is that I continued to grumble, blame things on my parents, and nurse a back-to-the-land fantasy of building a stone house and becoming an organic subsistence farmer free to pursue my yogic studies. But even a reluctant decision to enroll at the Dickinson School of Law engaged me in a flurry of positive activity. My generous parents agreed to pay the tuition, but I was responsible for my living expenses, so I found a job on the grounds crew of a nearby golf course. Soon I was cutting grass all day and getting paid time-and-a-half to water fairways and greens a few nights a week. After reading that jogging was a daily discipline at the ashram, I resumed the running routine that helped me keep fit in college. I'd already left my pot-smoking past behind but suffered occasional lapses when I got in with the old crowd. Even if it meant losing friends, it was time to end that phase of my life. Meditating, doing yoga, working overtime, cooking my own vegetarian food, jogging in the evenings when time allowed – it was September before I knew it.

The intensity of the first semester of law school is more than a *Paper Chase* myth. It took everything I had to keep up with coursework while maintaining my yoga lifestyle. My thoughts often turned

The regular practice of yoga is useful to both renunciates and householders. Through walking the yogic path of dharma, a householder develops health, good character, and the following worldly powers: personal strength, determination, clear and logical thinking, good memory, creativity, and decisiveness. By learning how to direct the life energy with the mind, householders can act skillfully to fulfill their noble desires and achieve wealth, pleasure, status, and true virtue. Only after health and success are established can the door to Self-realization be opened. Unless an aspirant succeeds on this with-mind path of dharma, embarking on the no-mind path of moksha is like trying to jump from the earth to reach heaven.

to Swami Kripalu and going back to Sumneytown to see him again. Regrettably, I let the fear of flunking out stop me from setting my books aside for a weekend and making the trip. Exams carried into the third week of December, and I went home for the holidays to recuperate. Grades were posted and it was a big relief to find that I'd not only passed but done well.

It was early January of 1982 when I called the ashram. Relaying a bit of my story to the friendly reservationist, I asked when it would be possible to see Swami Kripalu. Silence followed and I noticed she took a deep breath before replying, "Swami Kripalu went back to India in October and died just a few days ago – on December 29th." It was my turn to be speechless as I struggled to comprehend how the

The Summit Station Yoga Retreat.

person I'd registered as a human lightning bolt just six months ago could possibly be dead. Several seconds passed before the perceptive voice on the phone said, "We're still trying to accept this too." I thought our conversation was over when she added, "Since you're already practicing yoga, you could come to the disciple's retreat next month. It's at Summit Station, where most of us live." Thus began my relationship with the nonprofit organization that would soon move to Stockbridge, Massachusetts and operate under a new name, Kripalu Center for Yoga & Health.

The way life unfolds is mysterious and it's seldom accurate to see any single event as causing another. Yet I can say with certainty that those brief hours spent in Swami Kripalu's presence shifted the trajectory of my entire life. Arriving at the disciple's retreat, I entered the dynamic community of yoga practitioners led by the Indian-born Yogi Amrit Desai, a student of Swami Kripalu since boyhood and the first to bring his teachings to America. It was there that I met Michael Carroll, better known by his Sanskrit name Yoganand, and our yoga kinship was instantaneous. Yoganand had come to the ashram with a background in martial arts and quickly earned a place among its foremost yoga practitioners. For the next fifteen years, he lived the life of an aspiring renunciate. Whenever I visited, Yoganand made himself available to answer my questions. Ignoring my non-resident status, he went out of his way to photocopy bulky binders of Swami Kripalu's unpublished works for me, which I carted home and studied assiduously.* I gratefully acknowledge the pivotal role Yoganand played in my yoga education.

In my second year of law school, I met Danna Spitzform, a law librarian already taking Kripalu Yoga classes. Quickly joining forces and marrying two years later, we did yoga together each morning and frequented Kripalu Center, where we trained as teachers, started a support group in our home, and otherwise served as active members of its extended community. We found practicing yoga in the crucible of a committed relationship a potent vehicle for growth and felt driven to deepen our connection to this spiritual organization that was helping us transform our lives. In 1989 we applied for ashram residency. Undaunted by the prospect of quitting jobs and selling our home, we were excited to cast our lots with the likes of Yoganand and many other residents that we'd come to know and grown to respect.

We took the monastic vows required of all residents to heart and strove to deepen our practice in the most supportive environment we could imagine. After six months at the kitchen's scrub sink, and a year in the Resident Life department organizing administrative policies and personnel files,

---

*All of these written works have since been published and are freely available online – see Bibliography and Other Resources. Yoganand left Kripalu Center in 1995 as its ashram community was disbanding and eventually married. He remains a yoga teacher.

Kripalu Center for Yoga & Health and its ashram staff in its new Stockbridge, MA facility; gathering with Swami Kripalu in Sumneytown, PA; volunteer work crew in Stockbridge.

I was assigned to the legal department. While we only remained residents for four years, I ended up serving as Kripalu Center's nonprofit lawyer for a quarter century. Alongside my legal duties, I was asked to play leadership roles at pivotal junctures in the organization's lifecycle and also given opportunities to teach and write. Danna's involvement followed a similar arc; she eventually found her niche as a member of the marketing team editing the course descriptions that appeared in two decades of program catalogs. Although we enjoyed our jobs, what kept us serving through the thick and thin of Kripalu Center's many transformations was not the outer work. It was being in a setting that supported our ongoing study and practice of Swami Kripalu's teachings.

Swami Kripalu was an old-school teacher who didn't spoon feed his students, who were expected to diligently practice his foundational teachings while studying the traditional texts. In his discourses and written works, Swami Kripalu provided commentary on these texts to give aspirants a next level of instruction. In addition, the personal guidance he gave close disciples in private talks was often transcribed, translated, and circulated more broadly. These were the materials that Yoganand made available to me, which became my primary source of inspiration on the spiritual path.

It would take me years of practice and a master's degree in human development to understand the intricacies and right relationship of the householder and renunciate teachings. When Swami Kripalu stated in the introduction to *Science of Meditation* that householders were not fit for yoga, he was not saying they should not practice postures, breathing exercises, and meditation. Much to the contrary, householders were to practice these and other disciplines daily. However the goal of practice at the householder level was not attaining "yoga" in its strict sense as a steady state of unity consciousness. It was vibrant health, abundant energy, a resolute mind, and a wealth of positive character traits.

These are the attainments of *dharma* that define the first leg of the yogic journey. In the process of developing these qualities, householders were sure to become self-disciplined, skillful in their actions, able to create a secure and loving family environment, and achieve what Swami Kripalu called *success in life*. Psychology recognizes this same quest for personal growth, creative expression, and human fulfillment, which it calls *self-actualization*. While strongly dissuading new students like me from bypassing the real work of dharma in favor of spiritual fantasy, Swami Kripalu acknowledged that an accomplished householder was free to take up the practices aimed at Self-realization and the progressive levels of *samadhi*. Samadhi or *joining together* is the meditative means to unity consciousness and yoga's ultimate goal of *moksha* or *liberation*, which defines the second leg that completes the yogic journey. Where this book tells the story of how Swami Kripalu traversed both legs of this journey, it's my hope to write a next book in this series, *Awakening in*

Compared to the rigorous renunciate path, the householder practice of dharma may seem ordinary, but in truth it is extraordinary. Even the great rishis of ancient India practiced dharma for many years. Only through dharma does an aspirant qualify to tread the path of moksha. Dharma is the first rung on the ladder of yoga and moksha is its last. How can one reach the last rung without firmly grasping its first?

Daily Life: Swami Kripalu's Path to Success and Self-Realization, presenting my interpretation of his householder path.

Despite my decidedly imperfect practice, these trustworthy teachings have delivered exactly as Swami Kripalu promised. While I stayed focused on doing my yoga, they carried me through the developmental stages that undergird the householder stage of life, bringing me health, high energy, synergistic relationships, a fulfilling career, and a cornucopia of direct spiritual experience. Best of all, my travels are far from over. On the threshold of retirement, I am only now entering the time where the yoga tradition would say that one-pointed practice is appropriate. As a student of Swami Kripalu, I feel fortunate to have a firm foundation and maybe even a running start.

While I can't adequately explain the connection that formed between Swami Kripalu and me on that eventful day now so long ago, I can faithfully recount my experience of following his example, which began with my eagerness to learn more about his past.

CHAPTER 1

Kindly Write Your Autobiography

We are all travelers on the same path of yoga and life, so your questions are my questions too. The only difference between us is that I'm old and may have gone a little ahead, so it is appropriate for me to share what I have found as it may be useful to you.

When the disciple's retreat ended, I bought all the books and pamphlets available in the gift shop. Returning to law school, I was disappointed to find that each one parroted the same skeletal life sketch of Swami Kripalu I'd found in *Science of Meditation*. There was an exception: a pocket-sized paperback written by a close student entitled *Light from Guru to Disciple* that chronicled the history of Swami Kripalu's yoga lineage in mythic and sometimes supernatural terms. It described how a powerful yogi had intervened at pivotal junctures of Swami Kripalu's life to guide his practice. On first reading it reminded me of the juvenile readers on the lives of saints I'd encountered in Catholic school. But even studied closely this recounting raised many more questions than it answered, and I noticed right away that there was hardly any mention of a 20 year period right in the middle of his life. An aura of mystery seemed to surround Swami Kripalu. Not much information was available and the little that did exist was more hagiography than biography.

One by one over my law school years, Kripalu Center published a three-volume series compiling the talks Swami Kripalu delivered in America. I studied these carefully and especially liked whenever he illustrated a point by narrating an incident from his life. I also enjoyed a set of autobiographical anecdotes passed along by Yoganand that were prepared for this series but for some reason never published, as well as the transcripts of a few speeches delivered in India on special occasions where he'd spoken about his past. These first-person accounts of Swami Kripalu intrigued me. They conveyed a down-to-earth humanity qualitatively different from the austere and other-worldly figure portrayed by his students. The disparity left me wondering, "Who was this man who had affected me so powerfully that spring day in the chapel?" I had to laugh when one of the anecdotes addressed my gripe about the lack of a good biography.

> Kindly Write Your Autobiography: *My students have asked me over and over, "Tell us more about your life; it will inspire us." In recent years it has become, "Kindly write your autobiography." During my public talks, I sometimes mention incidents that come to me spontaneously, which I do not hesitate to share. But as a rule I am not interested in discussing my life.*
>
> *Autobiographical writing is an intricate process. The writer has to leave the present and drift back into his dark past. He must dig up the cadavers of long-dead events, raise them from the coffins in which they were buried, and not hesitate to reveal secret faults. Objectivity is the soul of any autobiography and if even a drop of ego is retained the result will be mere self-aggrandizement.*
>
> *Sometimes a close associate can write a worthy biography, but if that person has an overly sentimental temperament actual life events will be adulterated with exaggerated instances of the biographical hero's sublime character and spiritual powers. Worse yet, if the biographer has his own selfish motives the image of the subject will be magnified entirely out of proportion.*
>
> *Genuine spiritual teachers direct their students' attention to truth or God rather than themselves. If they write anything, they write what we call scripture. It would be appropriate for me to write about my life only after completing the yogic cycle. At this time, my experience should be considered incomplete. For all these and other reasons, I have given up any idea of writing an autobiography.*

Danna and I moved in together at the start of my last year in law school. I was ready to set a wedding date but Danna wanted me to experience life as a monk before making that commitment. So the summer after my graduation we enrolled in Kripalu Center's *Spiritual Lifestyle Training*, a residential work-exchange program. Although engaged, we were expected to live separately and immerse ourselves in the gender-segregated life of the ashram. Even talking with one another was strictly off limits. As our two-months in the program neared its end, Danna's parents came to visit and we got permission to spend a day with them. Together again, our rightness as a couple was apparent. Affirming our relationship meant foregoing the option we had to stay on as single ashram residents, so we headed out to make our way in the world. When our wedding day dawned on April 27, 1985, we were joined in matrimony by two ministers from the Integral Yoga community, Bhagavan and Bhavani Metro, and walked hand-in-hand into our married life as yogic householders.

We returned to Kripalu Center six months later to be initiated as disciples of Yogi Desai, which was the accepted way to join the lineage of Swami Kripalu. All of Swami Kripalu's successors venerated the example set by their teacher during his last three decades. These were the years in which he kept silence and practiced 10 hours a day. Swami Kripalu's earlier life was dismissed as time in which "he exhausted the small amount of worldly karma that remained following his initiation into yoga by his boyhood guru". I regarded Yogi Desai and all of Swami Kripalu's senior students as my teachers. While working hard to be a good husband and provider, I strove to embody the renunciate ideal they held as the highest expression of yoga. This mismatch of my householder life with a monkish mindset caused me considerable distress. It left me dogged by a feeling that there was a higher path than the one I was following. Instead of helping me channel the energy generated by my practice into my career and marriage, it was an archetype at odds with my actual circumstances.

Still feeling the lack of a biography, I began to mentally stitch together Swami Kripalu's personal accounts into a chronological narrative and made an important discovery. There was a different ideal for householders to emulate, one that celebrated life and embraced its challenges as opportunities for growth, and it was encapsulated in the untold story of Swami Kripalu's early and midlife. At the time I was assembling this patchwork quilt, I was simply following my curiosity and had no idea how important it would prove to me in the years to come.

Swami Kripalu held fast to a principle espoused by the yogic sages: an authentic teacher could only prescribe to others what he'd earnestly practiced, found true, and woven into the fabric of his life. When I came to understand this, it transformed Swami Kripalu's biography into a clear reflection of everything he taught. More than anything else, it was the story of Swami Kripalu's struggle to overcome the adversity of his childhood and achieve his midlife ambitions that enabled me to discern in his teachings the spiritually-potent householder path I needed, one that not only supported my health and effectiveness but took me on a journey into the mystical depths of yoga.

The next few chapters tell of that struggle, employing the format used throughout this book of emphasizing his first-person talks and writings. Swami Kripalu liked to spice up his talks with all kinds of jokes and stories. This quip from one of his birthday celebrations is among his shortest. *Once a visitor entered a village. Looking around, he asked a child standing nearby, "Have any great men been born in your town?" The child responded, "No, sir. In our village, only small babies are born."* No matter how lighthearted, Swami Kripalu's parables always bore a message and the moral of this one is clear to me. Even revered yoga masters have humble origins.

> *Truly, I am fortunate. I was born into a family with tremendous love. Through my mother and father I was given a basic religious training that inclined me toward health and spiritual upliftment. Even as a child, I loved chanting mantras and meditating. In my youth, I suffered many sorrows but eventually met my guru who taught me yoga. Yoga gave me a vision of the ideal life, along with the power to materialize it, and it is on that basis I have lived. For a time, I was an artist and taught music. After becoming a swami, I advanced as an orator and in a way became a great worldly man. Now I am 65 and there is no attraction left for money, name, or fame. I want only to go as far as yoga will take me. Liberation is the sole aim of my life and I am very much contented with this fact.*

Early Years

Swami Kripalu was born on January 13, 1913, in an impoverished India just waking up from the spell of shame and subordination cast by 150 years of British rule. His given name was Saraswati Chandra Majmudar, and he grew up in what's now the state of Gujarat, near the small town of Baroda, in the rustic village of Dabhoi.* Swami Kripalu's parents were devout members of the Brahmin caste. His father, Jamnadas, started out as a clerk in a lower court of law and advanced to hold the position of Secretary in the Department of Revenue for the Baroda government. He also owned a small plot of agricultural land that he rented out to farmers. While discharging his householder duties, Jamnadas spent most of his spare time in religious worship. Swami Kripalu's mother, Mangalabahen, ran the household and cared for their two sons and seven daughters. By all accounts the family was loving and close. Fifth-born and the youngest son, Swami Kripalu was doted on by his mother and older sisters.

---

*There is uncertainty surrounding Swami Kripalu's birth name, as he was also called Haridas and Hariprasad by his family. Saraswati Chandra is the name of a well-known scholarly saint and it's possible he was given that name only after entering school where his studious nature became evident. Baroda is currently Vadodara.

Disaster struck in 1920 when Swami Kripalu's father died from a sudden illness. The responsibility for the family fell to his mother, who as a high-caste woman was unable to work. Despite the attempt of Swami Kripalu's affable older brother to step into the role of provider, the family slowly sank into debt. Eventually their home was repossessed and their belongings put out in the street. Life became a daily struggle to survive and stay together.

Food was scarce, and Swami Kripalu was chided for his growing-boy appetite and inability to refrain from eating on the religious fast days observed by the rest of the family. As his sisters reached maturity, they had difficulty finding suitable husbands as there was no money to pay a dowry. Swami Kripalu was a promising student but had to leave school after sixth grade to work. At 14 years of age, his only option was to conform to social expectations by pursuing a line of work similar to that of his father. His first job was as a tollbooth operator for the township. Eventually his sharp mind and exquisite penmanship enabled him to hold more responsible positions as a municipal tax clerk and later a bookkeeper in a law firm. While industrious and eager to help provide for the family, his inability to pursue an education was a source of great anguish.

> *A swami cultivates a feeling of love for the entire world by keeping the same affectionate relationship with others that he had with his intimate family members. I have been able to extend the scope of my affection only because of the love I received from my natural family.*

The Blessings of My Father: *When my father passed away, I was seven years old. On the day before he died, my mother and I were alone in the house. My acutely ill father was lying on a mat on the floor. My dejected mother sat nearby in the doorway to an adjoining room and was attending to him constantly. I was dear to my father and sitting close as he affectionately caressed my hand. He was in intense pain, vacillating between consciousness and semi-consciousness, and it was difficult for him to speak. All of a sudden, he became alert. Tears began to flow from his eyes, which my mother wiped away with her sari. Father spoke in a choking voice, "I am without wealth, and since there are lots of debts you will suffer even more. I am helpless and unable to do anything. Nonetheless, the God to whom I have prayed day after day is omnipotent. He will protect you." Then looking at me, he said to my mother, "I think this child will bring good fortune to the family."*

When I was very young, my appetite was notorious and I used to volunteer to distribute the prasad (blessed food) at the temple. Afterwards, when nobody was looking, I used to finish up the leftovers. Truly it was for this special benefit that I took on the service. One might ask if it was by eating all this prasad that I became so religious. If so, there may be very few self-made devotees like me.

Well-wishing and blessing may appear to be one and the same thing, but they are not. Well-wishes come from the surface of the mind. A blessing comes from the depth of the heart. Where good wishes are like stones thrown by a weak arm, blessings are like stones shot from a catapult. I sincerely believe that with these words my father conveyed all his spiritual wealth to me. After his death, our family came under great financial pressure. This pain I could not bear. Even though I was only seven, I gave my life to God and firmly decided to do whatever I could to make my family happy. Because of our financial condition, it was not possible for me to continue in school. In my youth, I used to think that had my father been rich, I would have not only been able to get a formal education but also develop my aptitudes and interests in various areas. During that period, I was not able to appreciate my devout father and the blessing he bestowed upon me.

Coming of Age in a Modernizing India

The village of Dabhoi was in a progressive region organized as a princely state. Instead of being controlled by the British, it was governed by the ruling prince of Baroda, a man named Sayaji Rao Gaekward III. As a boy, Swami Kripalu was undoubtedly influenced by this popular leader's efforts to improve education, establish public libraries, promote Western science, ban child marriage, expand women's rights, outlaw untouchability, foster economic development, and patronize the Indian cultural arts. Respected for its self-rule and forward thinking, Baroda is still remembered as the first district in India to provide free and compulsory primary education. Looking back, it seems certain the seeds of Swami Kripalu's progressive views in all the above areas were planted during his years in what today would be called elementary school.

Swami Kripalu did not let his forced departure from school end his education. He was an avid reader and developed a love for all genres of literature. In the evenings he would retire to a quiet spot to study. At thirteen, he began writing stories, poems, and essays. By seventeen several of his pieces had been published in respectable magazines and he'd written a captivating who-done-it detective novel. At only 18 years of age, he'd become a known writer and a thousand copies of his first collection of poems entitled *One Bindu* were printed for sale to an established audience. Alongside his bookwork, Swami Kripalu had an ear for music and learned to play the harmonium and tamboura from his talented older brother. He also listened to the discourses of the many saints, yogis, and religious leaders who passed through the area.

> **My Love of Books:** *I have loved literature from my early childhood. There was a rule at the library that you could borrow one book and keep it for ten days. But every morning I would be waiting at the front of the library before they opened the door to get a new book. Walking down the library steps, I would start reading. There was a marketplace in-between our house and the library, and I used to bump into many people on the way home. When I was eating, I would have my book open on the side of the table until my mother would give me a slap on the cheek and make me put it down. At night, I read with a kerosene lamp into the early morning, which caused my sister to get angry and blow out my lamp. This is how I finished a book of a few hundred pages every day. I took out so many books that I helped sweep and clean the library so the librarian wouldn't feel irritation towards me because I was coming so often. So much love I had for books! It was at that time I learned to study in a methodical manner, holding the mirror of my mind steady so I could observe the subject properly and dwell deeply upon it. All these years later, I still consider myself a student.*

As a youth, Swami Kripalu must have been enthralled by the towering political and religious figure of Mahatma Gandhi. Gandhi returned to India in 1915 as a national hero after his successful civil rights campaign in South Africa. The ashram he established in Gujarat on the outskirts of Ahmedabad to serve as his headquarters was only 90 miles from Dabhoi. Swami Kripalu was seventeen in 1930 when Gandhi was in the thick of his struggle with the British, writing India's declaration of independence and marching to the sea to oppose the salt tax.

About this time, Swami Kripalu joined Gandhi's movement to serve the cause of independence. His nephew Dinesh Majmundar recounts an incident in which Swami Kripalu was dispatched to a nearby village to calm tensions. Unnerved by the religious rancor and vociferous threats of violence, Swami Kripalu was unable to prevent a fracas from arising. When

After the death of his father, Swami Kripalu had to grow up quickly.

Gandhi arrived to personally quell the disturbance, the youthful Swami Kripalu confessed his failure to the 61 year-old leader and resigned his post. Although his direct participation in the independence movement was short-lived, Swami Kripalu went on to display a Gandhi-like candor and interfaith religious orientation throughout his life.

Meeting His Teacher

Anyone familiar with the yoga tradition knows that it is rife with tales of miracle-working gurus or *siddhas* and their occult powers or *siddhis*. Until meeting his teacher, Swami Kripalu was certain these powers did not exist. After seeing them exhibited repeatedly, he was forced to conclude that the laws of material science did not preclude the existence of a complementary set of spiritual laws able to transcend them. This view of his was bolstered by respected texts like the *Yoga Sutra* and *Hatha Yoga Pradipika*, which catalog the paranormal abilities attainable through intensive practice, with the greatest of these *siddha yogis* praised as god-like beings who have overcome death and roam the earth bent on doing good. While easy to dismiss as symptomatic of India's mythic culture, the miracle stories told by Swami Kripalu about his teacher are puzzling given the intellectual rigor and honesty exhibited elsewhere in his life.*

In my childhood, I used to read about magic. Later in my youth, I came in contact with many saints and sadhus who experimented with mantra, Tantra, and other methods of gaining various powers. Despite having seen the best in the field of magic, I never had the slightest belief in it. I was a lover of science. There could be nothing without a material basis, this was my firm belief.

That was before I met my guru and lived with him for more than a year. Every day two to three hundred devotees visited the ashram, but he never asked anyone's name. Whenever he spoke to someone, he always knew their name along with the details of their life. He talked to the Hindus in Hindi, the Marathis in Marathi, the Panjabis in Panjabi, and the Tamils in Tamil. How he learned all these language was a question I often asked myself.

---

*Swami Kripalu rarely spoke publicly about the miracles performed by his teacher but it appears that he conversed freely with his close student, Rajarshi Muni, whose books *Light from Guru to Disciple* and *Infinite Grace* recount that Swami Kripalu witnessed his teacher heal the sick, walk on water, make himself invisible, appear in multiple places at the same time, communicate telepathically at a distance, foretell the future, and otherwise demonstrate inexplicable mastery over the material universe.

My guru could read minds as easily as most people read books. Everyone in the ashram knew this from experience. It was during this time that I became acquainted with the innumerable siddhis residing within him. Today I can say that if any yogi were to perform before me an unusual miracle I would not bat an eyelid for in my guru I have seen far greater powers. Before parting from me, he told me countless times: "My son, until you complete the cycle of yoga, do not write my story." This wish of his is still respected, but were I to do so the reader would be forced to conclude that it was a product of my imagination.

Swami Kripalu met his teacher soon after attaining the age of majority, when he left home for Bombay (now Mumbai) where he'd been told it would be easy for him to secure a full-time position sufficient to support himself and his mother. Staying with family friends, he wandered the streets of the teeming city in search of work. Unable to find even day labor, he quickly ran out of money. Weeks passed and he was ashamed to return hungry night after night to the home of his gracious hosts. To lessen the strain he was placing upon their household, he started skipping meals and eventually going without food for days at a time. After three months of futile effort, he began to suspect that his inability to find a job might be a result of his dark skin color. Incapable of providing for his mother and now feeling himself a burden to others, Swami Kripalu grew depressed and resolved to end his life. It was in the midst of enacting his suicide plan that Swami Kripalu encountered the mysterious swami who became his teacher.

Meeting My Guru: *When I arrived in Bombay, I was young, only nineteen years old, and extremely ambitious. Yet my heart was filled with darkness because I saw no avenue to attain what I wanted. Unable to find work, I began to feel an intense contempt for my purposeless existence. In despair, I decided it was preferable to die rather than lead such a pathetic life. In the evenings, I used to go to a small temple of the Divine Mother for the arati (offering of light) ceremony. It was near the Chowpatty Sandhurst Bridge, beneath which electric trains ran swiftly. Possessed by extreme thoughts of suicide, I had a vision of my body being crushed by these trains and with firm resolve decided to make the vision come true that night at midnight.*

As soon as I entered the temple around nine o'clock, the tears started rolling down my cheeks. The ceremony was underway and I went in front of the deity and bowed down. I had not come to get anything or ask anything, but simply to say goodbye. When the arati ended, everyone left but I stood there crying. The priest knew me and tried to console me, but my tears would not cease.

At that moment an unknown swami wearing only a loincloth entered the temple. Approaching me he uttered a single word, "Son." I cannot describe the sweetness of that word. He lovingly placed his hand on my head and said, "Come with me." Although he was a total stranger, his kindness brought peace to my mind. Following him out of the temple, we came to the veranda of a closed shop. He sat down on the wooden planks and motioned me to do the same. Then in a serious voice he said, "My son, remove the thought of ending your life from your mind. Suicide is contemptible." Hiding my astonishment, I replied, "This idea of yours is false. I have no thoughts of suicide." His eyes filled with pity and looking downward he said quietly, "My son, you are a seeker of truth. It does not become you to take refuge in an untruth. Tonight you were planning to commit suicide by throwing yourself under a train at the Sandhurst Bridge."

I was tremendously affected by this statement. That a stranger could know another's innermost thoughts was something beyond my understanding. After he exposed the secret of my mind, I immediately asked his forgiveness. He instructed me to meet him at his ashram the following afternoon. By the time he'd left, I was looking forward to the next day and all thoughts of suicide had vanished.

When I arrived at the ashram, everyone was waiting expectantly. Entering the darshan (audience) room, I saw the swami sitting in front on a platform, and he motioned me to come and sit down by his side. I'd spent the few rupees I had on a garland, which I put around his neck. Only later did I learn that four months earlier he had told everyone a penniless youth would arrive that day whom he would train to be his foremost disciple.

He again placed his hand lovingly on my head, "Swami, it is good you have come." Being addressed in this way made me nervous. Many people from Madras are dark-complexioned and have last names ending in "swami." I contradicted him, "Pardon me, but I am from Gujarat. I am not a swami, nor have I the inclination to become one. A swami is dependent on others. Rather than begging, I prefer to work." He responded, "My son, I have not called you swami because I imagine you to be from Madras. It's because you are going to be a swami in the future. Swamis are not beggars as you understand it. They give as well as receive." While I could not accept this statement, the exchange allowed my nervousness to disappear. He ended the conversation, "If you wish, you can stay with me here."

With these words, the door to my future flew open. The idea that I could serve this powerful swami and acquire the knowledge of yoga aroused within me a feeling of boundless confidence. I felt like one coming from the dead into heaven. Even after these events, the wish to be his disciple arose only later. I had seen many holy men, saints, and magicians but never had trust in any of them. I was confident of my intellect and therefore obstinate; nothing could influence my mind suddenly. Arriving the next day with my trunk of clothes, the word "guru" was not in any corner of my mind.

I stayed with this swami for 15 months. Being his favorite, his entire assembly treated me with respect, regarding my pleasure as his pleasure. While a dozen of his devotees were millionaires, his compassion fell on a poor fellow like me. He hardly spoke a word to anyone yet would spend hours with me explaining the meaning of the Vedas, Upanishads, Puranas, Ramayana, Mahabharat, Tantras, and other yogic texts. He also taught me yogic rites and even made arrangements for me to study Ayurveda and Western anatomy, physiology, and psychology with local experts. He not only modeled the holy life; he gave me the strength to seek it for myself. Such was his greatness.

A Year and a Quarter in the Ashram

Arriving at the designated address, Swami Kripalu was amazed to discover that the ashram of the loincloth-clad swami who had saved his life was a multi-storied mansion overlooking the ocean. The stately house was encircled by a privacy wall that enclosed a beautiful garden. The lavishness of the surroundings was not limited to the real estate. When his teacher took him to the dining room the morning after his arrival, Swami Kripalu fell into a swoon when his breakfast was served to him on a gold-covered stool with matching plates and cups. Once at the ashram, his studies began immediately. He was told to keep a diary and schooled in yoga's classic texts for an hour each morning and afternoon. It appears his first lesson was an explanation of the eight-limbed path as codified by sage Patanjali in the *Yoga Sutra*.* He was also given the practical job of administering the ashram's activities under his teacher's direction.

At 19, I was fortunate to serve my guru in his ashram for 15 months. Only the two of us resided there, but many devotees longed to serve him and it was my job to oversee the ashram's affairs. Women contended with one another to prepare his food, so I divided up the tasks. One made the dhal, another the rice, still others the vegetables, and someone else the chapatis. Even in shining the utensils and washing the clothes, there was a struggle. Outside, the men stood by the front and back gates day and night to admit guests. On certain months, the first floor swelled with people chanting or practicing meditation. Other months, the ashram was unoccupied and peaceful. Everyone was able to work together efficiently because of the set schedule and my insistence on punctuality. Truly the

---

* Scholars believe the Yoga Sutra was written between 150 and 450 C.E. Patanjali's eight limbs of practice are accepted by virtually all contemporary schools of yoga. They are: 1. *Yama* or *moral restraints*; 2. *Niyama* or *ethical observances*; 3. *Asana* or *posture*; 4. *Pranayama* or *breath regulation*; 5. *Pratyahara* or *withdrawal from the senses*; 6. *Dharana* or *one-pointed concentration*; 7. *Dhyana* or *the flow state of depth meditation*; and 8. *Samadhi* or *bringing together into unity*. The first five limbs are often referred to as *hatha yoga* and the last three limbs as *raja yoga*.

> *disciple absorbed in the cycle of ashram life and service is fortunate, as this is the best way to digest the universal principles taught by the guru.*

Along with yoga philosophy, Swami Kripalu was taught the pillars of a healthy lifestyle. All of these things provided Swami Kripalu with a learning environment in which his basic needs were met, he was esteemed by the ashram community, and could step beyond the limits of his traumatic past.

> *Even today my guru's advice comes to mind: "Chew your food properly." He taught me this lesson early in my ashram training by asking me not to eat vegetables with my chapattis (flat bread) for three days. Hearing his instruction, I wondered how one could swallow a dry chapatti. However the next day I started eating a chapatti all by itself, taking care that no one would see me to avoid ridicule. I chewed each morsel and as I kept chewing found that it tasted sweet. This was the first time I had enjoyed the true taste of a chapatti.*
>
> *Continuing this practice for two more days, I came to understand why Guruji had asked me to conduct this experiment. A person eating a chapatti with vegetables tends to swallow it without much chewing. This becomes habitual and leads to indigestion and poor health. Food that is chewed well is eaten in smaller quantities and digested properly. This keeps the body and mind happy. I discovered all this by experience.*
>
> *Happy to hear the results of my experiment, my gurudev revealed a yogic secret. "Chew your food properly and it will mix with saliva and become amrita, the nectar of health. There is another form of amrita that advanced yogis can drink in meditation that enables them to glimpse divinity. But first you must learn to chew your food and drink the stream of nectar present in the mouth while eating. Doing this you won't be troubled by physical or mental problems, and over time your body and mind will be purified and become fit for yoga. Thus you can court both health and yoga by chewing your food properly.*

The inquisitive Swami Kripalu wanted to know more about his teacher and was frustrated by the fact that he never spoke about his past. Even his closest devotees only knew him as *Mahatma*, an honorific meaning *great soul*. When a chance visitor to the ashram recognized the swami as one of his schoolmates, Swami Kripalu learned that his teacher had grown up in the East Indian city of Calcutta as a member of a prominent family. After completing his education, he married and took over the family business, which prospered under his leadership. Wealthy but childless, the couple embarked on an arduous religious pilgrimage during which they encountered a powerful yogi and were initiated into the practice of mantra meditation. A year later their only child, a daughter, was born. Upon reaching retirement age, his teacher followed the norms of devout Hindus and entered the next stage of life. Winding up his business affairs, he made financial arrangements for the care of his wife and daughter. With his wife's blessing, he left home to seek liberation.

Knowing this much, Swami Kripalu was able to pester his teacher into finishing the story. After leaving Calcutta, he ordained as a swami and wandered for a year until he encountered the same powerful yogi a second time, who initiated him into the practice of yoga. He then retired to a hut in the Himalayas near Rishikesh, where he practiced as instructed for 17 years. Leaving Rishikesh he'd come directly to Bombay to establish this ashram. This life sketch caught my attention because it mirrored the two paths that Swami Kripalu taught, with his teacher passing from the householder path of dharma to the renunciate path of moksha later in life.

Swami Kripalu continued his probing and asked about the spiritual name his teacher was given upon becoming a swami. He was told that he could call his teacher *Pranavananda* but quickly cautioned, "Son, this 60 year-old body is not my true form. My real age in this body is only one-and-three-quarters years, but that is a mystery to be revealed to you in the future." Swami Kripalu protested this enigmatic response, but his teacher refused to answer any more questions.

The Wrestling Match: When I was with my Gurudev in Bombay, I was 19 and very active. In the morning, I would wake up early to bathe and do my exercises. Afterwards my body and mind would be filled with such joy. One day it so happened that I ended my exercise and felt like wrestling with somebody. It was a boyish feeling. If I could tussle with someone equally strong, it would feel good.

After that, I went to see my guru. He used to sit steady and still on his seat all day without moving. I would enter, bow at his feet, and my instruction would start. This morning I arrived as usual and bowed down. As soon as I looked up at his face he immediately stood up straight. Making a fist, he hit it into the opposite palm as a challenge and said, "Come on, let's fight." Because I had come with the thought of wrestling, he just knew it straight away.

My guru loved me immensely. I considered him more like a father than a teacher, and sometimes while with him I would act like a mischievous child. So I said, "You are old and if you wrestle with me I will defeat you." He retorted, "Don't tell me the outcome first; fight with me and see who wins." He was very happy and joyous, so I also became crazy with happiness. But it was not in any corner of my imagination that he would ever do this, so I said, "Do you really want to wrestle with me?" He said, "Yes, but I don't have to do anything but stand here to defeat you."

I knew wrestling and quickly attacked his body. Placing one hand over his neck and the other around his waist, I tried to entangle his legs and bring him to the ground. But he just stood there unmovable. I thought to myself, "This 60 year-old man has so much strength." I tried again, but he didn't budge an inch. I was so surprised that I thought. "How is this possible?" While I continued to push and pull with all my might, he stood there like a steel post. By the end of our wrestling match, I was perspiring all over and about to cry.

That was the first day I ever heard the word katori karan. My gurudev explained, "This is not a siddhi (power) but an ordinary yogic attainment in which one restrains the breath and fixates the mind to hold the body perfectly stiff. It can be practiced a little every day to help you remove mental disturbances and learn to control the mind."

Eight months of ashram living sped by, but the active lifestyle and ample diet that Swami Kripalu enjoyed was about to be disrupted. Pranavananda said that he would grant him yoga initiation when he'd completed a period of penance to purify his body and mind. A grueling six month dietary regimen ensued that ended with a lengthy water fast. On the last day of his fast, Swami Kripalu was initiated into yoga and taught the lotus posture and anuloma viloma pranayama (alternate nostril breathing). When the initiation ritual was complete, Swami Kripalu was instructed to live in accordance with the spiritual principles he'd been taught and use these two yogic rites to commence an intensive practice later in life. Certain that he would eventually become a swami, his guru told him, "When you have rid yourself of worldly desires, find some wise, old, cow-worshipping saint. He will give you sanyas initiation and the saffron robes."

A 41-Day Water Fast: *After eight months of training, my guru said to me: "I am going to initiate you into the ancient practice of yoga. I will give you the choicest blessing, and you shall become one of the world's incomparable yoga acharyas (teachers of yoga)." I said in astonishment, "Making me your chief student has been my great good fortune, but as for me becoming an acharya answer me one question. How can a crow become a swan?"*

My guru was undeterred by my doubting disposition and the day of my initiation was fixed. He told me that beforehand I would have to fast strictly on water for 41 days while repeating mantra. Explaining to me the purpose of the fast, he said, "In your mind are all the impurities of many births, and in your body are the impurities of one mind." If even a one-day fast was intolerable for me as a child, how would a 41-day fast be possible now? I became depressed merely upon hearing this order.

At the time, I was eating two meals and two snacks a day. On top of that, I would never turn down an opportunity for extra snacks or meals. First my guru stopped the snacks, telling me from that day on I should only eat twice a day. I pleaded, "Guruji, how will I be able to carry out this formidable task?" But he gave no comfort to my cowardice. I was utterly dissatisfied for a week, but thereafter my train gradually began to run on the right track.

After two months, Gurudev changed the routine again, instructing me, "Starting tomorrow, you should eat only once a day and that meal should be moderate." My mind was in revolt, but it mellowed when he insisted that I eat with him. After I ate the moderate portions served, Gurudev would order me to leave the table. Sometimes the sister serving us would cry in pity at my situation, but there was no trace of cruelty or oppression in his orders. They were full of a powerful and tender affection, which helped make this difficult task easier. Then I was on cow's milk alone for three months. During the first few days, I felt discomfort again, but from then on surprisingly gained strength.

Eventually, Gurudev said, "My son, starting tomorrow you should fast for 41 days and practice mantra japa." His first two words were so sweet that they had the ability to counteract the bitterness of everything that followed. Yet my mind was not prepared to believe that I could observe a 41-day continuous fast and it became a battlefield. I tried to have conviction but was very doubtful whether I could actually accomplish this task.

For the 41-day period, a small room in the house was chosen that could be locked from the outside. On the first day of the fast, Gurudev gave me mantra diksha (initiation) and with that initiation I ceased being a student and became his disciple. After instructing me in japa (mantra recitation), he took me to the room, saying, "This is where you must observe austerities for the next 40 days. There is a water pot inside. You can come to me twice a day. Each day I will lock and unlock your door and keep the keys with me." Expressing my anguish, I asked, "Guruji, must you bother to lock and unlock the door?" "Yes, I will do this myself," he said with finality. Bowing humbly at his feet, I said, "Gurudev, fasting 41 days seems too hard for me, but with your grace I will try." Placing his hand on my head, he gave me some comforting advice, "My son, the first three days will be difficult for you, but this discomfort will diminish by the fifth day. By the seventh day, you will have no difficulty."

For the remainder of that time, I came out only twice a day to briefly kneel before my guru. Solitude, fasting, silence, and the concentrated repetition of mantra were the chief features of this penance. To a 19 year-old boy like me, these disciplines seemed to be the hardest of religious ordeals. Nonetheless, my guru's advice proved true and everything was completed without mishap due to his blessing.

On the final day of my fast, I was weak but still able to walk and receive yoga initiation. When my guru repeated his blessing that I would become a yoga acharya, I contradicted him by saying, "Don't make this monkey drunk with praise. In this small pot, one cannot pour the ocean." He replied: "My son, with this initiation I have planted a mango seed. In time will it not become a mango tree?" The result being in the future, it was pointless to dispute it with him. At that time, I believed myself to be a fruitless tree. Today when I think back, I know for certain that whatever I have received in this world is because of his indescribable grace.

After the initiation, Pranavananda gathered his followers together to announce that his purpose in coming to Bombay had been fulfilled and he was abandoning the ashram. His heartbroken devotees had no option but to accept this decision. The next day Swami Kripalu and his teacher boarded a train to Mathura, where they set off on a seven-day walking pilgrimage. During the day they kept silence and visited a string of holy sites associated with the Hindu avatar (divine incarnation) Krishna. In the evening they broke silence, which enabled his teacher to explain the significance of what they'd seen. Swami Kripalu only spoke publicly about the start and end of the pilgrimage, but it appears from stories told privately to Rajarshi Muni that Pranavananda completed Swami Kripalu's education during this intimate week that included many miraculous events.

A Painful Parting.
After staying in Bombay for a year and three-quarters, my guru took leave of his pupils by saying, "Tomorrow I shall leave and only swami will accompany me." On hearing this, the entire assembly remained silent. Many wept but none expressed disappointment or debated as they were used to obeying his wishes. Coming to Bombay, my guru had brought two towels, one pair of pants, and a water pot. Leaving for Delhi by train, he had the same two towels, the same old pants, and the same pot.

During the next three days we made a walking pilgrimage to Mathura, Gokul, and Vrindavan. On the fifth day, we set out on foot to return to Delhi to complete our circuit. The distance from Mathura to Delhi is 90 miles and we traversed that distance in three days eating only a single meal offered to us without asking. I was young and before embarking to Delhi for the pilgrimage had the thought deep down in my mind that this old man who sat in meditation all day would not be able to walk very far.

As he walked on rapidly without stopping, I felt his feet were made not of flesh and blood but iron. My vanity stopped me from saying: "I'm tired," for the strength of my youth wanted to vanquish the strength of his old age.

On the third day, my arrogance collapsed and I became utterly exhausted. Sitting down under a tree, I started to cry loudly and said, "I cannot walk anymore." Wanting to bring down my pride, my guru replied, "You are conceited. If you had told me this from the beginning, I would not have walked more than 10 miles a day. Conceit is not good; be humble." Sitting next to me, he began to massage my feet and body. For how long he massaged me, I cannot say but when he finished the aching had ceased.

His next concern was my hunger: "My son, do you want to eat?" I was able to laugh at his question and retort, "In 48 hours, not a grain of food has gone into my stomach, but what good is my desire to eat without your assistance?" From ancient times, it is the disciple's task to go into town to beg on behalf of his guru. Though I had no desire that my guru should beg for me, I was in no condition to beg for myself. So here the order was reversed as my guru walked into the village to beg for his disciple.

An hour later, Guruji returned with food from a wedding party that he carefully arranged onto a thali (leaf plate). We both ate from that single plate, Guruji feeding me with the love of a mother. The food was tasty and after eating my fill I slept soundly all night. When I awoke in the morning, I found myself alone. My guru was not there; he had gone away. For two days I stayed under that tree waiting for him to return, but in the end I was disappointed. This story is now 40 years old. Despite my being his favorite student, he has never written a letter to me. As far as I know, he has never written a letter to anybody. For this reason, no one knows where he is or whether he is alive or dead.

As the story of Swami Kripalu's formative years came together in my mind, I was not blind to its Cinderella overtones. A poor and fatherless youth, frustrated by his inability to get an education, is received into the lap of luxury by an all-powerful guru figure. Recognized as his foremost student, he undergoes arduous austerities and is told the he's destined to become a great yogi. Yet the story does not appear to be told for self-aggrandizement, as even after the initiation Swami Kripalu remains convinced that he's the proverbial crow who can never become a swan. Whether this tale was fantasy, reality, or an admixture of both, Swami Kripalu returned to his hometown of Dabhoi a changed man. Gone was his despair and victimhood. In their place was positive energy and a newly sprouted sense of possibility. A student no longer, the stage was set for his adult life to begin.

Readers wanting to know more are directed to stories 1-1 to 1-4 in the appendix of teaching stories.

After living in Bombay and ending his pilgrimage in New Delhi, Swami Kripalu returned to the small town life he knew.

CHAPTER 2
Treading the Path of Dharma

Music, literature, and yoga – it is these three deep loves that have shaped my personality and given my life direction. Whenever I've felt boundless inspiration and joy, it's because I was pursuing them. Whenever I've been sidetracked from their pursuit, I have always felt excruciating pain.

My detective work to assemble the jigsaw puzzle of Swami Kripalu's early and midlife into a coherent narrative was hindered by a missing piece. There was hardly any record of what he was taught by his guru. Such a gap is noteworthy in the domain of yoga, where a teaching lineage is defined as an unbroken transmission of wisdom from master to disciple. Any diary he might have kept in the ashram was long lost, and he seldom spoke or wrote about these matters. The only thing that can be said with any certainty is that Swami Kripalu was schooled in the Indian epics and primary yogic texts. While all that remains is a punch list of principles, it appears his teacher was able to integrate them into a synergistic vision of the spiritual life that gave Swami Kripalu fresh energy and a clear sense of his path forward.

Now I would like to describe to you in short the guidance that my guru gave to me. Believe in the indwelling presence of God (Atman) and accept His non-dual nature (Brahman). Study, ponder, and digest the vision of yoga set forth in the scriptures. To the best of your ability, obey yama and niyama. Practice postures, pranayama, and meditation according to your capacity. Eat moderately and purify your speech. Practice self-discipline, self-observation, right action, and virtuous conduct. Pray, recite mantra, sing, and perform worship. Keep good company and seek out the audience of saints. These are the principles he taught me.

Judging from Swami Kripalu's actions after he returned home from Bombay, his guru must have emphasized the keystone role played by a person's *dharma* or purpose in life.* Faced with the same constellation of problems that plagued him only 15 months earlier, Swami Kripalu charted an entirely new course. Instead of conforming to societal expectations, he looked inside to discern his true calling. At this moment in his young-adult life, only one aspiration was clear to him: his love of literature. Over the next two decades, Swami Kripalu's conception of his dharma would expand to include other areas of focus, but as a 20 year-old entering adulthood he needed to choose a single starting point.

It would be years before fellow Kripalu teacher and author Stephen Cope would identify these same principles and encourage his readership to "find your dharma and do it full out," but this instruction has roots in Swami Kripalu's life story. While Cope correctly links these teachings to the *Bhagavad Gita*, they were developed in the earlier epics that Swami Kripalu recounts being taught by his guru. The *Ramayana* states, "All material gain and fulfillment are to be found in the fruit accruing from the pursuit of dharma. From dharma issues both profit and pleasure. One attains everything by dharma, which is the only true strength in this world." The *Mahabharata* expresses the same idea differently, "It is from dharma that all prosperity and enjoyment flow. Neither for the sake of pleasure, nor out of fear, nor due to greed, should one abandon the principles of dharma."

---

*Dharma is a keystone concept in yoga and a word with no English equivalent. It's impossible to provide a single definition as the term has a long history and evolved over time to reflect a nuanced understanding of what it means to follow a *path of right action*. The overarching idea is that there is a way for human beings to live that produces desirable results because it is in accord with universal law, natural forces, and *the way things actually are* or *truth*. A person following a dharmic path strives to ascertain their unique calling and accomplish their individual purpose in life. While today *dharma* is often used to describe that purpose, traditionally that was referred to by the derivative term *svadharma*, which means *self-dharma* or *one's own dharma*.

When a person consciously recognizes their most important purpose in life, their life expression must go through a powerful transformation. A seed planted in the ground must rupture before it begins to grow. You can come to know this seed purpose or dharma by noticing whenever your body and mind naturally become cheerful. At first just try to discover whatever caused this good cheer. Then make an effort to stabilize its presence in your daily life and by doing this dharma regularly remain joyous and happy. Many obstacles arise on this first branch of yoga. Do not be afraid or disappointed by them. Through the medium of yogic practices you can be victorious in any field. Householder yogis should persevere in their dharma until they attain their goals and aims. Those who excel on this path know fulfillment and are likely to become popular, prominent, and prosperous. Only as a yogi progresses on this path of sakam (with desire) yoga will their desires begin to dissipate and the second branch of nishkam (without desire) yoga present itself.

Regardless of its origin, Swami Kripalu's decision to pursue his passion for literature released a torrent of creative energy. In 1932, the year after his return to Dabhoi, he wrote a number of short stories and poems that he was able to sell to popular magazines. He also composed two plays that received critical acclaim. When a traveling theatre troupe came to town, he was able to persuade its owner to hire him as a playwright. After a successful tour, Swami Kripalu managed to land a similar position with a second repertory. Where his search for generic employment in Bombay had produced only failure, he was now meeting with success.

Sweet Jokes: *I will tell you an incident from my previous stage of life, when I was a poet, writer, and the assistant director of a drama company. Our company was touring the peninsular region of Kathiawar, which had just joined the state of Gujarat. We had a comic actor who got his start as the jester in a royal palace and then performed with two drama troupes famous throughout Gujarat. He could make the audience laugh without speaking a word – as soon as he walked onto the stage the laughter would begin. Along with being an expert humorist, his conduct showed the discretion of a gentleman and anything he said or did was always respectful. Joining him was the best actor of the drama company, who was not only handsome and highly popular but had a fine bearing. We became fast friends and whenever we met would enter a jocular mood. Being literary men, we would crack literary jokes to show the sharpness of our wit. While poking fun at one another, we strove to do so innocently and deliver our spur-of-the-moment jokes free of contempt. Along with being humorous, we were deep thinkers and capable of speaking seriously about our sorrows and what was needed to make progress in our respective fields. My days in the drama company are long passed but they helped teach me the importance of right speech, which is one's very soul in life.*

While pursuing his ambitions and interacting with his colleagues, Swami Kripalu made an active effort to cultivate what he later would call a *winning personality*. It appears his adolescent response to the stigma of his family's low status, and perhaps a degree of shame that he felt over his own lack of education, was to adopt a compensatory stance of intellectual superiority. Part of his yoga practice involved moving beyond this persona or false-self that he characterized as *conceit*.

> *Although poor as a youngster, that didn't stop my mind from becoming a big storehouse of conceit. Even at my guru's ashram, I was extremely conceited. Being his closest student, I would tell off the rich men and women. Only by observing the rules of my guru's guidance for years did my personality develop and I can say that it is possible for anyone to gain a winning personality through ordinary yogic practices. This includes speaking sweetly in front of a mirror and other exercises that teach you how to soften your eyes, heart, and thoughts. Do not consider this play acting; it is a form of learning. Actors learn their lines by repeatedly following a script, while yoga students wanting to learn nonviolence and tolerance must form new mental impressions through repeated practice. Those who do not succeed in these lessons can never be eligible for deeper yoga. The truth of this can be seen in a high saint like Swami Vivekananda, who captured the attention of your whole country through the grandeur of his personality and used it to introduce America to the yoga of India.*

While delighting in his literary work, Swami Kripalu quickly saw that being a free-lance writer and roving dramatist would not provide the steady income needed to satisfy another facet of his dharma: supporting his mother. He moved to the mid-sized city of Ahmedabad in 1935 and took a machinist job oiling equipment in a textile mill until two relatives offered him a position in a start-up music school in the suburb of Maninagar. Along with reviving his love of music, Swami Kripalu discovered that he had a real knack for teaching. The school proved popular and Swami Kripalu became one of its chief instructors. The regular income provided by his faculty position made it possible to reunite his family. He sent for his mother and brother, all of his sisters having married, and the three quickly formed a happy household.

The next five years were highly productive and a noteworthy period of Swami Kripalu's life. Above and beyond his teaching and administrative duties, he wrote more than 50 articles that were published by academic journals. It's said that he is still remembered in the field of Indian classical music for the innovative ideas he promoted in these scholarly articles. His crowning work was a three-volume dissertation that earned him the title *Master of Music*. It was also during these years that he became a virtuoso, playing the harmonium and tamboura so skillfully that he was encouraged to pursue a career as a concert musician.

As the scale and magnitude of Swami Kripalu's accomplishments in Ahmedabad took shape in my mind, I began to sense that my investigation was leading somewhere. It was easy for me as a fledgling legal aid lawyer to identify with his role at the start-up music school, but there was more to it than that. The focal point of my inquiry gradually narrowed to a single query. Everyone touted the 10-hour regimen that dominated his last three decades, but what did Swami Kripalu's yoga look like in the midst of his active work and family life? As far as I could tell, no one had ever asked that question. That's what I needed to know as a householder striving to chart the course of my own practice. I could only find a few references, but they were enough to suggest an answer.

My Past Life as a Donkey: *I will tell you a story from my life before I became a swami, when I was a musician and music teacher. I used to get up early and after finishing my morning practices would leave the house promptly at seven to teach. My older brother Krishnalal was also a musician. In fact he was one of the best harmonium players in the state of Gujarat and had given me my very first music lesson. But he was of a different nature; he woke up quite late.*

One day just as I was leaving home, my brother called to me from his bedroom. "Do you know who you were in your last incarnation?" I was surprised – where does such a question come from – and my brother knew that I was very particular about time. Although I thought to myself, "Why is he stopping me now when I could be late," I also loved my brother very much. So I paused and said, "No, I don't know, please tell me."

He said, "You were a donkey." In India, donkeys are the hardest working pack animals. They are used whenever a load needs to be carried all day long, so the word is sometimes used to refer to one who is constantly working. Although I understood his joke, I still asked, "How do you know this?" He answered, "Because you get up at four o'clock in the morning and bray Ommm. Then you leave home and all day you work, work, work. You don't return until nine at night and then go right to sleep so you can get up and do it all again."

Along with poking fun at me for being overly active, he was also complaining. To master Indian music you must continually practice and my early morning singing was disrupting his sleep. I was smiling broadly when he finished by saying, "Now you can go." In a way, my brother was right. At that time I really liked being a donkey. Despite his affectionate banter, my brother also liked that I liked being a donkey, because I was supporting the family.

When I learned that Swami Kripalu was an ambitious young man who got up early to do his practice before heading off to work, the puzzle pieces started coming together. I already knew that his mornings from childhood included a set of what he called *his religious observances* that combined prayer, devotional worship, meditation, and scripture study. I was certain this did not include yoga postures, as he only discovered the value of these years later. Reading between the lines, I felt confident that his early mornings were a time of spiritual attunement that led into his singing practice. An excerpt from a lecture on physical exercise completed the picture, revealing the core elements of his householder lifestyle.

> *I have been exercising since I was a teenager. During my adolescence, I used to go to the local athletic club. It was then that I accepted regular exercise as essential for maintaining health. For many years afterward, I practiced pushups, squats, and other calisthenics, which I found trustworthy friends because I could easily fit them into my schedule. I also used to walk several miles a day, which back then no one considered exercise, but I implicitly knew otherwise. The body plays a key role in human life. When the body is fit, the mind feels enthusiastic and we can effectively perform many actions and accomplish our aims. Exercise has always had a big place in my life, which is why I can encourage you to enjoy its benefits daily. If you want to progress in yoga, physical fitness must be coupled with overall good health and mental strength. This is why yoga combines regular exercise, healthy diet, and meditation.*

It was now clear to me that Swami Kripalu came into adulthood with an established discipline of daily practice. As a young professional, he continued to get up early to complete his routines before heading off to work. While passionately pursuing his career, he tried to eat well and squeeze in the exercise he needed to stay vigorous. All I could do was exclaim in wonderment when I realized the first half of Swami Kripalu's life was spent living a basic version of the healthy and success-oriented lifestyle he would later prescribe to householders. Even more remarkable, it was a path I was already walking. While the complete householder path that Swami Kripalu would

Krishnalal Majmundar, the brother of Swami Kripalu

teach later in life was profoundly informed by his subsequent years of hatha yoga practice and experience of samadhi, it was helpful for me to see how he had used the tools of yoga in his young adulthood.

Swami Kripalu's practice was destined to carry him far beyond the modest success he achieved in Ahmedabad as a music teacher. Looking back, it's obvious his dharma had not yet come into its full expression. The entryway into his next phase of development was a painful one, as this happy period of family stability came to a sudden and unexpected end. Twenty-eight years of age and growing in professional status, Swami Kripalu had become a desirable bachelor. Several relatives took on the task of finding him a wife, and in 1941 he was engaged to a woman he esteemed named Jyotibhen. When the normal inter-family bickering over dowry and marriage arrangements escalated into an outright quarrel, the angry families abruptly called off the wedding. This conflict was deeply upsetting to Swami Kripalu. His nephew says that it led his uncle to question the direction he was pursuing in life. I had to wonder if a measure of heartbreak was involved. All we know is that Swami Kripalu resigned his teaching post and fled to Bombay, severing all relations with his family and fiancée.

In my householder days prior to becoming a swami, I experimented with various practices. I tried different diets. To better digest my food, I used to exercise. To improve my thinking, I used to read inspiring books. I also tried to stay away from distracting social contacts. Through these experiments alone, I had divine experiences. Sometimes I became disappointed. Once in a while, I lost my enthusiasm. But always an unexpected spark of light would appear, and my mind would again become bright with inspiration. With the flame of faith restored, I would renew my efforts in the direction of progress.

Readers wanting to know more are directed to story 2-1 in the appendix of teaching stories.

CHAPTER 3

A Wandering Swami

My guru always called me "swami" but I could not accept this vocation. A swami is dependent on alms where I wanted to rely on my own industry. As a young man, I never even imagined becoming a swami but one day my heart was broken by a sudden misfortune. Illusions shattered, I renounced my home and went out seeking sanyas initiation.

Swami Kripalu never explained his impetuous flight from Ahmedabad. The record only reflects that he went to Bombay and lived there anonymously for a few months. Yet there is not a sliver of doubt in my mind about what he was doing. Swami Kripalu was looking for his guru. It's likely he returned to the vicinity of the ashram to see if anyone had news of his teacher's whereabouts. After that he probably just hung around in hopes that Pranavananda would seek him out, as he'd done years earlier on the night they met. When his guru was nowhere to be found, Swami Kripalu left the city to wander the network of footpaths that followed the meandering course of the Narmada River. His only intention was to become a swami.

From the dawn of Indian civilization, zealous men and women have abandoned conventional life to live as ascetic sages in search of spiritual truth. The tradition was millennia old when Shankara founded the Holy Order of Swamis in the eighth century as a formalized expression of this spirit of renunciation or *sanyas*. To join the order, an aspirant must be granted initiation by a duly ordained swami. Membership requires a strict set of vows that includes

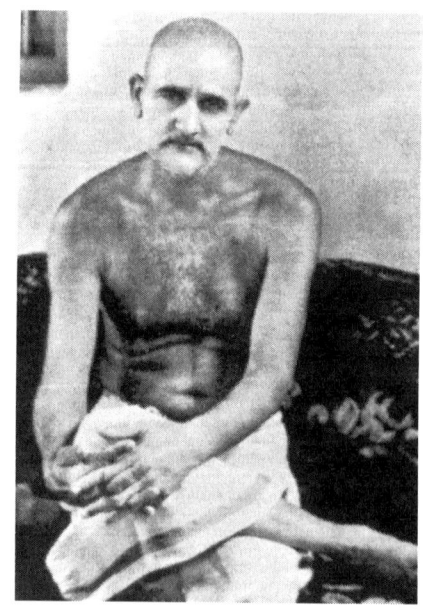

Swami Shantananda

celibacy, relying on alms, owning few material possessions, wearing saffron-colored robes, shaving the head or letting the hair grow long, dedicating time to spiritual pursuits, and foregoing any desire for comfort, name, and fame. Becoming a swami is considered a lifelong vocation in India; a return to normal life is not socially acceptable.

Swami Kripalu's wandering soon brought him to the ashram of Swami Shantananda, a Sanskrit scholar and yogi who lived on the banks of the Narmada near the village of Indore-Vasna. Impressed by Shantananda's bright countenance and straightforward manner, Swami Kripalu asked to be ordained as a swami. Shantananda declined the request but invited him to stay in the ashram for awhile, which included a large *goshala* or cowshed. After only five days, Shantananda was able to discern Swami Kripalu's spiritual readiness and agreed to initiate him into the Udasin branch of the swami order. It was Shantanada who gave him the name *Kripalvananda*, often shortened to *Kripalu*, which means *grace or compassion*.

Knowing that Swami Kripalu would live out his life without any of the scandals so often associated with guru figures, I was struck by what is recounted as happening next. After clothing him in the garb of a swami, Shantananda's expression turned grave. "Son, these ocher robes are extremely holy. Don't ever bring shame upon them. You are still a young man and it is a very real possibility that desires and passions will arise in your body and mind. It would be better to end your life than to violate the sanctity of these clothes." Inspired but also chastened, the novice Swami Kripalu took leave of the ashram and began traveling on foot from village to village, carrying only a water pot and change of clothes.

Swami Kripalu shortly after his sanyas initiation.

My First Meal as a Swami: *The saint who gave me sanyas initiation was Shantananda Maharaj, a gentle lover of solitude who lived on the Narmada practicing yogic observances. With this initiation, I vowed to be detached from everything: my relatives, home, town, everything. I left his ashram the next day to wander. I now had to beg for food and be prepared to sleep under a tree wherever my feet stopped for the day. I had never asked for alms before and was hesitant. "How can I beg for food?" I asked myself. I felt helpless.*

I walked three or four miles and came to a small town. There was a temple there and I went in, bowed to the altar, and sat in the corner of the temple. It was exactly twelve o'clock. I wasn't particularly hungry and thought to myself, "Maybe I'll go for two or three days before I ask for food. I can make it that long. But I'll certainly have to ask for alms after four or five days." As I sat in the corner of the temple, I noticed there was a second temple behind it, where a mother and son appeared to be living. I could see they did the pujas (a ritual of devotional worship) in both temples.

"Mother," I heard the boy say, "Yesterday aunty promised that she would join us for our noon meal, but she's not coming now. What are we going to do with this extra food?" "Don't worry about it," the mother said. "Go and finish your puja." The boy walked into the temple where I was sitting and he finished his puja with great devotion. Then he saw me and hurried back to his mother.

"Mother," he said. "There's a swami sitting in the temple." "My son," the mother said. "This extra food that we prepared today is for him. Go and tell him not to seek alms anywhere else." The son quickly came to me and bowed down. "Please come to our home for your noon meal," he said sweetly.

I followed the boy into the other temple. The mother was standing on its steps with a bucket of water. She washed my feet and her son wiped them with a clean cloth before taking me inside. She lit incense and asked me to sit on a wooden platform. She served my meal with love and devotion, doting on me like I was her own son. Both mother and son fanned me while I ate. I was greatly moved.

This was my first meal as a swami and I felt that God was already taking care of me. Tears rolled down my face when I left. I knew then that the Lord is the well-wisher of everyone and I would never, ever, have to worry about myself.

Swami Kripalu delighted in his new vocation and newfound freedom. Walking from place to place, he encountered solitary swamis intent on helping travelers in need. He also met swamis living together in ashrams that served as spiritual centers where villagers gathered to share meals, sing devotional songs, and hear discourses. Instead of relating as beggars and almsgivers, Swami Kripalu discovered a rich interdependence existing between the swamis and villagers. Seeing the positive role a swami could play in the life of a community, Swami Kripalu dedicated himself to living among the people and serving their practical needs.

> **Life as a Swami:** *After my sanyas initiation, I wandered from village to village along the shores of the Narmada River. At first I never spent more than a day or two in any one village and always withdrew to sleep under a tree outside its limits. Shantananda had given me two sets of clothes and some other necessary items that I carried on my shoulder. In those early days, I used to bathe in rivers and lakes. I would wash my clothes by pounding them on nearby rocks. Since I did not accept money from anyone, I was unable to buy soap. Often one of the local sisters would take the clothes I had washed and hung on a line, wash them again with soap, and return them to the line.*
>
> *As a novice swami, I was burning with the spirit of renunciation. One day while walking along it occurred to me the clothes I was wearing were adequate. Since I had renounced the world, it felt improper to cling to superfluous possessions. After reflecting on this for a while, I simply loosened my grip on the bundle I was carrying. I didn't even bother to look back to see where it fell. But this action was prompted by my inexperience.*
>
> *Soon I began to perform constructive tasks in the villages and due to their strong insistence had to stay in the homes of householders. Whenever I had to wash my one kurta (pair of pants), I would have only a loin cloth to wear around the house. So I was obliged to add another set of garments to my belongings.*

Released from his dawn-to-dusk work schedule, Swami Kripalu had more time to dedicate to his yoga practice. I found it interesting that his focus was not on any of the physical or mental disciplines equated with yoga in the West. Instead, he brought his attention to bear upon *yama* and *niyama*, the first two stages of Patanjali's eight-limbed path. *Yama* means *restraint* and specifically *five conducts to avoid*: non-violence, non-lying, non-stealing, non-indulgence, and non-attachment. *Niyama* means *observance* and *five qualities to cultivate*: purity, contentment, austerity, self-study, and surrender to the divine. Swami Kripalu observed yama and niyama as part of a larger practice that he called *character building*. While serving the villagers during the day, Swami Kripalu watched his thoughts and actions carefully. Every evening before going to bed, he used these interactions as a mirror in which he could see his character reflected back to him. Contrasting his conduct with the high ideals of yama and niyama, he strove to become a person of genuine goodwill and virtue.

> **Character Building:** *I have learned the science of character building from the scriptures, the biographies of great masters, the company of saints, and from my own experiences. Its principles are the very treasure of my life, which I freely dispense to others wanting to mend their lives. The primary principle is that bad character traits can be eradicated by strengthening good character traits. By applying this single principle, a person can formulate the best possible personality.*
>
> *It is impossible to not make mistakes in life. Difficult situations arise and knowingly or unknowingly we all take missteps. We don't realize that these mountains of mistakes are where the springs of self-knowledge can begin to flow. Whenever I behave improperly during the day and am not able to see my error, the mistake will come looking for me during my evening introspection and say, "This is where you were at fault." Whenever such a mistake appears to me so clearly, I consider it a wonderful grace, as it helps me not make the same mistake again.*
>
> *Anyone who personifies an enormous power of purposeful determination and excels in their chosen field is by necessity wedded to self-observation and virtues such as healthy eating, regular exercise, contemplative study, and the character building principles that yoga calls yama and niyama. Master these virtues and you will also be successful.*

It wasn't long before the once-ambitious Swami Kripalu felt a need to be more purposeful. While happy providing day labor to the villagers, he wanted to find a way to be of service that was more aligned with his aptitudes and interests. He remembered his love of teaching and felt drawn to deepen his understanding of the scriptural texts he'd been schooled in years earlier by his guru, but as a young swami he wasn't sure how to proceed. Returning to Shantananda's ashram, he explained all of this to his superior. Shantananda arranged for him to study with a Sanskrit master in Haridwar. Over an eight-month period, Swami Kripalu gained a working knowledge of the language and then used his knowledge to plumb the depths of the six classical schools of Indian philosophy called *shad darshana* (six viewpoints) as presented in various texts and Upanishads.

Swami Kripalu during his wandering years.

In the field of literature, I was young and could run fast. But as I grew older and became a swami, I started reading shad darshana and had to walk slowly with great thinking every step of the way. Even then I could not grasp their meaning. In Haridwar I learned that anyone wanting to understand these texts in a true sense must become familiar with their original language. Not only does each Sanskrit word have multiple meanings, but the inclusion or exclusion of a single letter within those words is highly significant. While this makes the language subtle and expressive, it also makes it difficult to discern the genuine, experienced-based meaning intended for each word by the ancient yogis. You cannot understand scriptural texts like these by reading them as a whole. For that you have to understand each word. Finding no room for my running, I started reading just one sutra (aphorism) or shloka (verse) and then becoming still right there. Only when understanding came would I go on to the next. This practice rendered me capable of reflecting with greater depth, which made me take myself and my studies more seriously.

Swami Kripalu returned to Gujarat overflowing with an inspiration that proved contagious. While staying in Sisodara for the monsoon season, the villagers wanted him to teach them Sanskrit so they too could read the ancient texts. Impressed by their thirst for knowledge, he selected a set of well-known verses for them to learn and chant. Drawing on his background in theater and music, Swami Kripalu proved a captivating instructor. Over the four-month rainy season, his first group of 60 pupils developed into a small school of highly-motivated students. Word spread and Swami Kripalu was asked to establish similar schools in villages all along the Narmada River.

Swami Kripalu on Teaching: *For many years, and even today, I have been a teacher. I love that work and feel that my life has developed by being in that position. In India, a true teacher is called an acharya. Only a person with a great love for their subject, who progresses along the path of learning through their own practice and thus becomes able to teach others through their own life experience can become an acharya. An acharya remains a perpetual student, always eager to learn and grow. An acharya has to be continuously aware of the state of mind of his students. Knowing that a person cannot concentrate on a task they don't like, an acharya develops the art of capturing the interests of students with different temperaments and learning styles. An acharya is like a farmer who is always planting seeds that will eventually sprout and grow in the field of their student's lives. I myself am still in seed form. I haven't become a true teacher yet, but don't be discouraged by this. We can all become acharyas, but it happens in stages, one step at a time.*

Although the schools were a great success, Swami Kripalu was keenly aware of the barrier posed by the scholarly Sanskrit language. Instead of disparate verses, he wanted to teach his students a complete text in their native tongue, which he felt would enable them to grasp the spiritual principles at the depth required to apply them in their lives. Swami Kripalu chose the *Bhagavad Gita*, which condenses the six viewpoints and all the principles of yoga into a relatively short text that's easy to study because of its compelling storyline drawn from the *Mahabharata* (Great India), a cultural epic well-known to the villagers. Secluding himself in Rishikesh, he undertook the ambitious project of translating the Gita's eighteen chapters into simple Gujarati verses suitable for chanting. Swami Kripalu completed this task in six months and called his translation *Gitagunjan*.

> *You must have heard of the Bhagavad Gita written by sage Vyasa. Vyasa used the story of the Mahabharat to write about yoga in an enchanting way that layers all its wisdom into a single text. The Gita is a dialogue between our all-knowing soul and the embodied self when it becomes a spiritual seeker. All the secrets of yoga are embedded in the Gita, and every stage of yoga is depicted in its eighteen chapters, not just in words but also in action and images.*
>
> *A person can go to a river and get a cupful, pot-full, or barrel-full of water. In the same way, the Gita can help a householder yogi fulfill their desire for health, prosperity, and happiness while also helping an advanced yogi achieve liberation. This is why I can say the Gita has an answer for every problem. You will receive from it whatever you are ready to hear and understand.*
>
> *No matter your aim in life, the Gita is a reliable guide. Beginning students should know that hiding behind every word of the Gita are passageways into deeper truth. Only a person practicing yoga can proceed into these secret chambers. I am telling you this based on my own experience, which is why I hope that your study of this special scripture starts soon.*

Gitagunjan was an immediate hit. Under Swami Kripalu's tutelage, hundreds of men and women were able to memorize it start to finish through the discipline of repetitive chanting. More importantly, the familiarity they gained with the text left them hungry to know more and asking Swami Kripalu to explain its symbolic meaning and practical significance. For the next three years, Swami Kripalu traveled up and down the Narmada River teaching Sanskrit classes at five in the morning. At five in the evening, he would play the harmonium and sing before lecturing on the Gita. All the village shopkeepers would close their stores early, creating a holiday atmosphere that enabled everyone to attend.

Swami Kripalu's lively discourses combined scholarly insight with entertaining anecdotes. Participants recount how his robust body, ringing voice, and magnetic personality endeared him to audiences wherever he went. During these years, he inspired many people to embark upon the spiritual path. Taking on the mantle of a spiritual teacher, he initiated students into the practice of mantra meditation and strove to provide all his followers with ongoing guidance.

Swami Kripalu delivering a discourse.

A Rising Orator: *About six years after becoming a swami, villages started to invite me to give discourses on the Bhagavad Gita, and I would travel there on foot. Back then I had not yet begun yoga sadhana. I was totally satisfied with my daily routine, which included study, chanting, ordinary meditation, and reciting various hymns in praise of the Lord. Outside of seclusion, I was able to give more of my time to the people.*

Whenever I went to a village to speak for the first time, it was my practice to stay for one month taking only milk. This made my body very alert and my mind one pointed. Sitting in the lecturer's seat, I was in command of all my faculties and able to express myself fully. Over the course of the month, the entire town would become spellbound by my lectures and give me so much love that I would forget I was fasting.

After the villagers had taken me into their hearts, 25 to 50 men and women could be found sitting at my residential place at any time of day or night. Some of them were lawyers and other officials. Considering me a rising orator, they wanted to know the secret of my success. Hearing that I was only taking milk, the lawyers told me, "If I go to court with a full belly, my presentation will be poor and I'll come back a loser." The judges said, "If I've eaten too much before taking the bench, I can't discern the meaning of the lawyer's arguments and find myself yawning." These people already knew that proper diet plays a vital role in the ability to perform their duties well. All these years later, it's hard to remember that I was once a famous lecturer, who could speak extemporaneously on any subject at any time.

A portrait in blessing pose taken of Swami Kripalu for distribution during his years as an orator.

As his reputation spread, people started traveling from near and far to hear Swami Kripalu lecture. His popularity grew into fame, and invitations to speak began arriving from all over Gujarat. Eventually his fame pinnacled into celebrity status. Just the opportunity to catch a glimpse of him was enough to bring out a crowd. Showered with gifts, Swami Kripalu kept nothing for himself. He continued to live simply and insisted that everything given to him be used to uplift the lives of the villagers. This trustworthiness led wealthy people to make large donations, which he used to establish community centers, health clinics, libraries, and vocational schools throughout the state of Gujarat. No longer able to meet personally with all his students, he began to write practical booklets to guide them along the spiritual path.

More than eloquence or good works, it was Swami Kripalu's genuine love for people that set him apart. The Narmada River villagers found in him a man who understood their challenges and honored their struggles, who cared enough to tell them stories that made them laugh and cry, who sang to them, and respected their intelligence by educating them. To them he was a role model who ardently aspired to the highest but was not arrogant, and who inspired everyone to be more and do better. Held dear by the villagers, esteemed by people of influence, and eventually beloved throughout all of Gujarat, Swami Kripalu was recognized as one of India's great humanitarian saints.

******

Piecing this story together, I was inspired to see how Swami Kripalu had fused his passion for literature, his musical talent, his love of teaching, and his commitment to yoga into a single expression that he offered to the world and that in return brought him great success. But I was also troubled by a significant loose end. What became of Swami Kripalu's mother and brother after his abrupt departure from their close household in Ahmedabad? It wasn't long before I found two pertinent anecdotes.

My Mother Becomes My Disciple: Unbeknownst to me, a village in which I was speaking extended a special invitation to my mother, who stayed there happily while attending my lectures. Before returning home, mother humbly expressed a desire to me. "Swamiji, I am old now and cannot follow you. If you come to Dabhoi just one night a year, I will feel content." After my renunciation, mother called me "Swamiji" just like everyone else. Hearing her request, I affectionately gave my consent.

A year later, I was on my way to Rajpipla and nearing Dabhoi when I suddenly remembered my promise. It was almost lunch time when I arrived and found my mother performing her daily worship. She was overjoyed to see me but continued what she was doing. Ten minutes later, I was sitting cross-legged on a chair when she approached me carrying a ceremonial tray. Sitting down in front of me, I could not determine her intentions. Then in a sweet voice like that of a young girl she said, "Extend your feet." Surprised, I asked, "Extend my feet? Why?"

"I am going to wash your feet for today I want mantra initiation from you. I want you as my guru. I have great faith in you, for you have never deceived me. My husband was a devotee of the Lord, and both my sons are renunciates. Now, like a solitary tree standing in the desert, I am alone in this world. Swamiji, I am illiterate and foolish, but I have faith that you will take me to the other shore. Please give me guidance so that I can pass the rest of my life in devotion to God and die in peace."

During my youth, my mother spoke very little. She would mostly listen, since her husband and sons had dominant temperaments. Also, my mother had always tolerated pain well and rarely cried. But she was crying profusely now, her throat so choked with emotion that she could no longer speak. Each word pierced right through my heart, for I had never heard her talk so soulfully. My very ordinary mother suddenly appeared great to me. For the first time in my life, I was proud that she was my mother. My eyes overflowed with tears, and I got up from my chair and embraced her.

Bowing down at her feet, I exclaimed, "Mother, how wonderfully you have spoken. Yet you should not talk this way because you are my guru. It is you who has inspired me. You are the boat that takes everyone to the opposite shore. A boat does not require another boat, so you do not need me as your guru."

My words did not influence her at all. As usual, she announced her decision firmly. "Give me mantra initiation, just as you have initiated the others." I sat back down on the chair. Although her tray lacked adequate supplies for the ceremony, she had complete faith. After she lovingly washed my feet, I gave her mantra initiation and the pertinent guidance. She reverently offered me one and a quarter rupees as homage to her guru and then fed me the foods I like most. Whenever I remember this event, I drown in the depths of my mother's greatness.

The record beyond this single anecdote is scant but suggests that Swami Kripalu's mother was supported by members of her extended family. While poor, she was able to live out her life in peace. Equally little is known about his older brother, who became a free-form religious devotee and itinerant musician who performed under the name *Pagal Maharaj*.* The following anecdote describes the end of their alienation.

Brotherly Reunion: *A few years had passed after I renounced my home and became a sanyasi. My elder brother only knew that I had journeyed far away. One day while out walking he was approached by an acquaintance who told him, "Your younger brother has become a swami." He stood rooted to the spot, pondering what seemed like valid information. It took only a few minutes for him to make a decision. He'd been on his way home but changed his plans. From that moment on, he let his hair grow long. Thus, he also renounced home and began traveling the path of saints.*

---

*Pagal Maharaj means the *crazy or moonstruck king*, probably a reference to the heartfelt religious devotion expressed in his music.

Five or six years later he located me in a small village. We hugged each other and broke into loud crying. After we released each other, he prostrated himself before me because I was a saffron-clad swami and he was a white-garbed celibate. Onlookers were touched by this scene and removed themselves so we could talk in private.

For a few moments he sat silent with downcast eyes. Then he spoke, "Once I confided to you that it was my strong desire to become a sanyasi and you persuaded me to remain at home. Then all of a sudden you leave your family and take sanyas yourself. Didn't you deceive me?" In our youth my elder brother had wanted to renounce but I had argued against it. Back then I never thought that I would one day become a swami. Upon hearing that he felt deceived, all I could do was straightforwardly tell him what had happened. Afterward he was satisfied by my honest statement, and we hugged each other and began crying anew. We parted in unity, having shared our family life and now sharing the holy life as well.

Although Swami Kripalu's interactions with his mother and brother after Ahmedabad were infrequent, neither remained emotionally estranged from their beloved and increasingly illustrious son and younger brother.

Readers wanting to know more are directed to stories 3-1 to 3-2 in the appendix of teaching stories.

CHAPTER 4

Pranotthana

I gave discourses on the Bhagavad Gita for many years. Everywhere I was considered an expert but in truth my knowledge was elementary. Only after pranotthana (prana awakening) did I see how the Gita not only guides those seeking fulfillment but also leads one to the highest liberation.

My curiosity about Swami Kripalu's life was self-sustaining because it kept sparking new lines of inquiry. Aware of his frustrated dream for an education in childhood and the ambition stoked in his formative years, it made sense that he was driven to achieve a high degree of success in midlife as a teacher and orator. Yet knowing that he would spend his last three decades as a reclusive monk, I began to wonder: "What led Swami Kripalu to relinquish the status he obviously enjoyed as a celebrated public figure?" Sticking with my studies, I soon got my answer.

It was Swami Kripalu's custom to spend a few weeks each year on retreat in the Himalayan foothills. Traveling to Rishikesh in the winter of 1949, he found an abandoned hut on the outskirts of town and settled into a daily routine. After a predawn bath in the Ganges, he spent his mornings in prayer and meditation. His midday meal was supplied by a local institution that served free food to swamis and other *sadhus* (holy men). In the afternoon he studied scripture then took an evening walk before going to bed. Engaged in this routine, he had an experience that heralded a pivotal shift in his life.

A Mystical Encounter: *Some years after becoming a swami, I was staying in the Himalayan mountain area at the pious place of Rishikesh. One evening I walked to the top of a small hillock to gather twigs from a Babul tree. These twigs are used as tooth brushes in India. As I started cutting a branch, I saw an individual walking down from the mountain. It was cold and my body was covered with lots of woolen clothes. He had a little cloth wrapped around his waist, but the rest of his body was bare to the elements. There are many yogis and sadhus who move in that land, so I did not pay any attention to it.*

While cutting the twigs, I was startled to hear the yogi address me from behind: "Swami." At once I recognized the voice of my guru, who always called me by that name. Yet my uneasiness did not subside. While the voice was familiar, the difference in appearance was the same as the difference between earth and sky. My guru was 60 years old, but the luminous saint standing before me resembled a youth of 18 years.

Making out my predicament, he gave me a broad smile as if to introduce himself. "Swami, don't you recognize me?" Looking at him I noticed his bright eyes, which were twinkling with mischief. Well aware of my teacher's extraordinary powers, I became convinced that he was my guru. When I was a boy, he had lots of love for me. Whenever I was disappointed in some way, he used to take me to his chest and hug me. Forgetting to bow down, I clasped him firmly. He held me, stroking my head lovingly while I wept. Remembering myself, I bowed down at his feet. There being no seat for me to offer him, he sat upon a stone.

Once years before he had told me that his 60-year old body was not his true form but that someday I would see it. Back then I had not understood, so I asked now, "Gurudev, is this your true form?" He replied, "Yes, this is the body that has been purified by the fire of yoga." I continued asking, "Gurudev, what is your name in this body and how many years old is it?" All he would say is, "My son, you will have to find that out."

The body of a purified yogi is like electricity. There is such power in that body that it can take any form and even enter into a dead body. Just being in its presence changes the current of your mind. Reunited with my guru, I was overcome with ecstasy. We conversed freely and when he motioned that it was time for him to go I lowered my head and cried out that he should not forsake me again. Looking up, he had already disappeared into the gathering darkness.

It is commonplace for aspirants in meditation to have a vision of a cherished sage or saint from times passed, but these are emotional experiences conjured up by their sincere devotional feelings. Visions

> *like this may be meaningful, but they are entirely different from being in the physical presence of the deathless body of a great yogi.*

This is the full extent of Swami Kripalu's firsthand account of the revelatory conversation that took place between him and his transfigured guru on that Rishikesh hillock. It's necessary to draw upon additional disclosures made to his close student, Rajarshi Muni, to piece together this mind-bending tale. This fuller version of the story explains that Pranavananda was not actually *Swami Kripalu's guru* but rather *a disciple of his guru*. After 17 years of practice in Rishikesh, Pranavananda had progressed far in his practice but died a natural death before "completing the cycle of yoga." Just moments after his last breath, his guru entered and revived Pranavananda's 60 year-old body. Using that body, he was able to establish the Bombay ashram and train Swami Kripalu without attracting undue attention. This is why his guru had told Swami Kripalu in the ashram that he could call him Pranavananda, but his true age in that body was only one-and-three-quarter years.

Sitting on the stone in Rishikesh, his teacher finished the story by saying that the day after their post-ashram pilgrimage ended he had discarded Pranavananda's corpse outside of Delhi. While all this sounds absurd to us as Western readers, Indian lore is replete with tales of yoga adepts entering other bodies. It's an ability mentioned in many texts and a recurrent theme in the tradition as a whole.*

Despite his Indian upbringing, Swami Kripalu was a modern man. Back in his hut huddling for warmth, he didn't know what to make of this encounter and openly questioned whether it was fantasy or reality. Yet it's clear that he took it seriously because he began looking at his own life and practice differently. Prior to this encounter, he considered his teacher a fatherly old man, albeit one with miraculous powers. He believed these powers had been obtained by practicing a combination of religious piety, penance, and virtuous action that had perfected his moral character. As Patanjali teaches in the *Yoga Sutra*, when a yogi becomes established in non-violence all hostility ceases in his presence. Established in truthfulness, all his utterances come true. Firm in the vow of non-stealing, great wealth comes to him of its own accord.**

Through coupling his character-building practice with fasting, celibacy, and moral vows like these, Swami Kripalu had been doing his best to follow in his guru's footsteps, which as a disciple he felt duty bound to do.

---

*The *Yoga Sutra*, *Pashupat Sutra*, and *Siddha Siddhanta Paddhati* all list the ability to enter another's body as a known power of a yoga adept. See verses 3:39; I.20-29; and 5.32-37.

** See sutras II:35-37 and then II:43.

Once I was impressed by my teacher's siddhis (powers) and exclaimed, "Gurudev, you are a great perfect master!" When he burst into laughter, I was astonished and asked, "Why are you laughing? Are you not a perfect master?" He clarified, "According to the scriptures, I have not attained the attributes of a perfect master. Only when a disciple of a guru becomes a siddha yogi, and then a disciple of that disciple becomes a siddha yogi, can one be called a perfect master. So only after you become a siddha, and a disciple of yours becomes a siddha, might it be said that I am such a master." Upon hearing his words it was me who was laughing: "This can become truth only by your grace."

A siddha yogi does not possess the feeling of superiority and sees equality in everybody. Anyone considering himself great and others lesser is ignorant. That is why the scriptures say that a guru bestows grace on a disciple without any expectation of reward. He knows the duty of a lit candle is simply to pass on the light and enable others to do the same. Yet it is only natural for the second candle to think "this is my guru" and have a sense of gratitude. Feeling indebted, he tries to wipe out his debt only to find that it can't be done even by lighting innumerable other candles.

If we consider the first candle to be the guru, we must acknowledge that it was also lit by some other candle. So guru and disciple are both indebted to carry on the lineage. This is why it can be said that a guru may have a million disciples but if not one among them has attained the highest then they all are of no consequence. Only a disciple who rises in society and then attains to the highest stages of yoga through practicing the sadhana given to him by his guru is a true disciple and fit to become a guru himself. No sadhaka (practicing yogi) can understand this. Only after becoming a siddha (accomplished yogi) will he feel the responsibility.

After initiating him, his guru had prophesized that Swami Kripalu would become one of the world's foremost teachers of yoga. Since then he had attained fame and exercised influence to a degree he'd never thought possible. But after seeing his guru's resplendent form, it no longer seemed that outer accomplishment and societal recognition was what his teacher had meant. His guru had said that *his body had been purified by the fire of yoga.* Swami Kripalu knew the word *tapas* is usually translated as *austerity* or *penance* but originally meant *to heat until it glows.* I wondered if this older definition was a reference to the fire of yoga. If so, there might be a different way to interpret a later verse of the Yoga Sutra that says, *Established in tapas, impurities of the body and senses are destroyed and all occult powers gained.*

When his retreat ended, Swami Kripalu knew there must be some next step for him to take. But he felt more than ever like the proverbial crow trying to become a swan. Unsure what to do, he returned to Gujarat and resumed his life as an itinerant lecturer.

That summer Swami Kripalu was in Rajpipla presiding over its annual Guru Purnima festival. He was sleeping on the veranda of the home of a villager named Bhagwandas Valia. After completing his evening introspection, he felt fault-ridden and far less than the worthy disciple his guru deserved. Climbing into a cot for the night, his eyes were drawn to a distant star that was so bright it caused him to wonder why he'd never noticed it before. Gazing into the darkened sky, the star's rays seemed to be streaming toward him. In a moment of surprise, the same radiant yogi he'd seen in Rishikesh appeared before him in a vision of light and said, *The time is ripe for you to practice yoga.* The luminous vision faded from sight before the stunned Swami Kripalu could jump up or utter a word in response. Unable to sleep, he tried to make sense of this experience as well as his earlier encounter. While a single event could be dismissed, he took the second as confirmation that something objective and important was happening. His next step was now obvious. It was time for him to commence his intensive practice, just as his guru had told him years earlier.

Swami Kripalu practicing sitting meditation prior to his experience of *pranotthana* or *prana awakening*.

Swami Kripalu went to Halol the next day, where he had founded a charitable institution that had a suitable space for him to practice. As instructed years earlier, he began with a meditative breathing exercise commonly known as *alternate nostril breathing*. The regular practice of what the yoga tradition calls *anuloma viloma pranayama* heightened the sensitivity of his body, prompting him to simplify his diet. After three months of systematic practice and spare eating, Swami Kripalu experienced the awakening of the life force of the body that yoga calls *prana*.

My First Prana Experience: *At the age of nineteen, I had the good fortune of being initiated into yoga by my divine guru. The only asana he taught me was lotus pose, saying: "This is the seed of all postures; you will accomplish countless other postures through it." The only pranayama he taught me was anuloma viloma, saying "This pranayama is the key to yoga; by properly practicing it you will know all yogas and tantras." Although I could not grasp the secret behind these statements, I listened very carefully to his instructions.*

I began my practice at 38 years of age in the tiny village of Halol, India. I did pranayama in three one-hour sittings: morning, afternoon and evening. Over time I increased these sittings to one-and-one-half hours. Since there were many mosquitoes, I practiced on a bed covered by mosquito netting. One day I slid into a strange sleep and could not remember anything until waking an hour later. I found my body in a position new to me, still sitting in lotus but with my chin stretched forward and touching the floor. I was perplexed why this had happened and imagined it occurred because I was physically tired. However, I was really not a bit tired, so how could that be the reason?

Thinking it might be because I was practicing on a bed, the next day I became very serious and decided: "Let the mosquitoes bite! I will not do pranayama

Swami Kripalu in Umalla, on the steps of one of the many charitable organizations he inspired or founded.

> *under that mosquito net anymore." Placing a mat on the floor, I began practicing and continued for a period of time. All of a sudden, I stood up and my body began performing various postures, movements, and dances. I was overjoyed and mystified by these experiences.*
>
> *After that incident, new experiences manifested every day and the variety of yogic techniques occurring in my meditation amazed me. Up to that point in my life, I had not read any hatha yoga texts, nor did I even know the names of the poses. I sent away for several books. As I read the descriptions of various postures and pranayamas, my joy was boundless. They precisely matched my own experience.*

Yoga teaches that the power of prana is alive in all of us, beating our hearts, digesting our food, and carrying out all the tasks essential to health through the intelligence of the autonomic nervous system. Techniques such as deep and rhythmic breathing rouse this vital energy to higher than normal levels of activity. Through his intensive practice of pranayama, Swami Kripalu had experienced *pranotthana*, the release or awakening of pranic energy. After activating his energy with a few rounds of alternate nostril breathing, Swami Kripalu became able to relax into meditation and watch his body spontaneously perform all the techniques of hatha and eventually raja yoga. Only later would he learn that this was the esoteric core of the ancient *Pashupat* yoga tradition into which he'd been initiated by his guru, whose enigmatic instructions had provided him the key to unlock its secrets when the time was right.*

Swami Kripalu was mystified how these powerful and often intricate techniques could emerge directly from the bodymind without the need to learn anything externally. Engaged in this dynamic and rapidly-evolving practice, he became convinced that yoga had not been devised by humans. It was instilled in us by nature, a seed lying dormant but ready to sprout when the

---

*Swami Kripalu's pranayama practice was not entirely out of step with other hatha yoga schools. The *Dattatreya Yoga Shastra* states: "The wise yogi should spread out a seat covered with fine cloth, assuming the lotus position. Then he should block the right nostril with the thumb of the right hand and gradually inhale through the left nostril as deeply as he can. Then he should perform breath retention. Next he should exhale through the left nostril gently, not forcefully. He should inhale again through the right nostril and after holding for as long as he can gently exhale through the left nostril. Sitting down in the morning, midday, evening, and again at midnight, he should perform 20 breath retentions in this manner. If he practices tirelessly in this fashion four times a day for three months, purification of the channels results. When the channels are purified, perceptible signs appear in the body of the yogi. (Section 54 et seq.)" Despite the close correspondence of his practice and these instructions, all indications are that Swami Kripalu was relying solely on the verbal instructions of his guru, as he only became aware of this and other hatha yoga texts later.

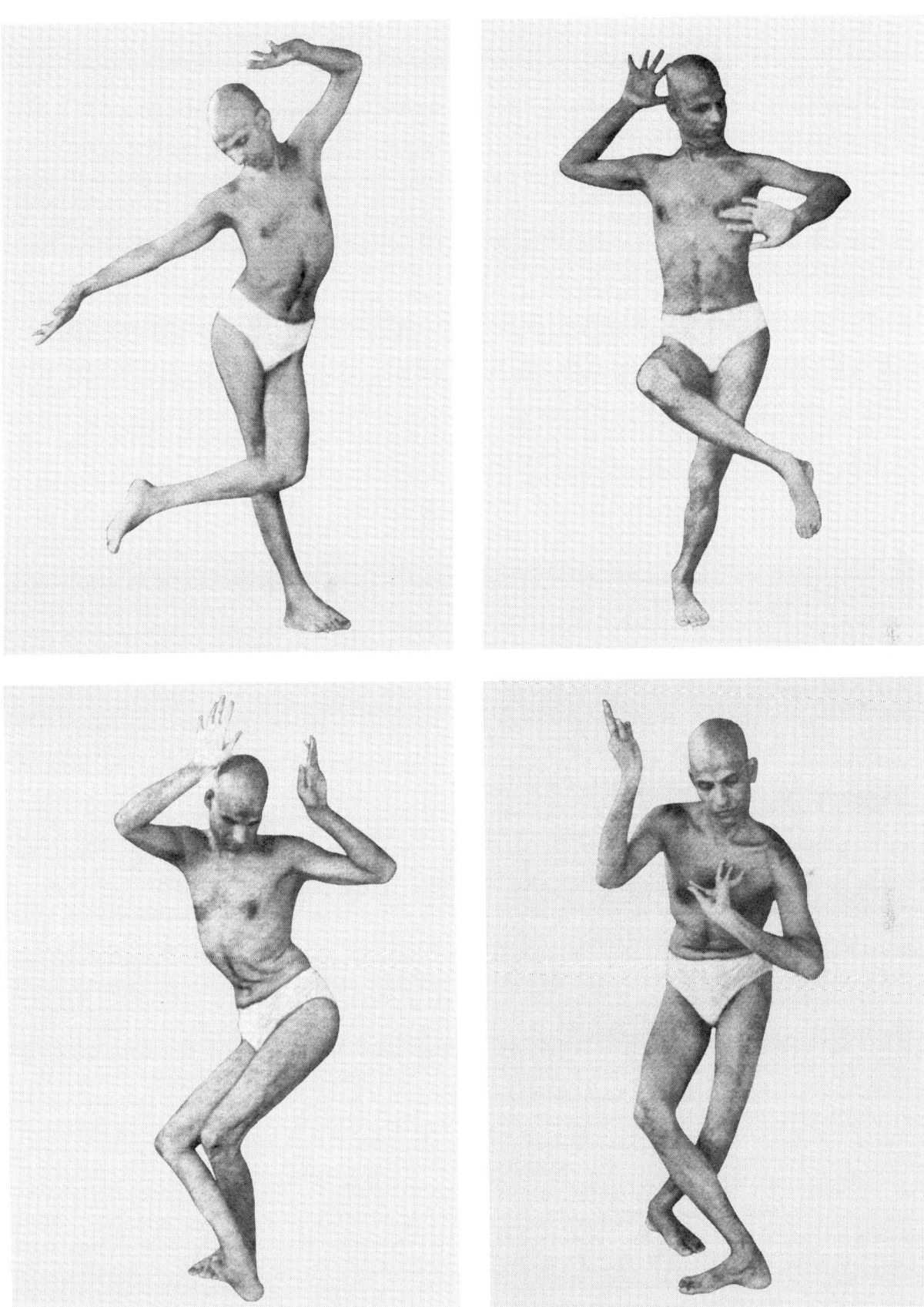

After pranotthana, Swami Kripalu's meditation practice shifted to an active form of yogic contemplation that included a wide range of dance-like movements as illustrated in his book *Asana and Mudra*.

conditions were right to unfold our higher potentials. Over the ages, the methods arising from this *sahaja (natural) yoga** had been systematized into many sects and schools, but its genesis and genius stemmed from its organic roots. He felt exuberant at having finally found the means through which a crow could become a swan and more importantly a way for him to engage in the same disciplines that must have transformed his teacher.

> **Natural Yoga Sadhana:** *In ancient times, the pranic energy in the body of a deserving disciple would be released by guru's grace and yoga would start automatically. From that point on, nothing remained to be taught. All the yogic processes would manifest spontaneously in the disciple's body and mind without the need to learn any technique from anyone. The practice of yoga would itself lead to the knowledge of yoga. All the manifestations that occur in the body and mind of such a yogi are the result of pranotthana, the release of pranic energy. With pranotthana, the body becomes like a machine and begins to perform asana, pranayama, meditation, and other kriyas (purifying actions) automatically.*

Swami Kripalu's practice swiftly expanded to include a stunning array of postures. Next came various *kriyas* or *purifying actions* that accelerate the body's cleansing and healing processes, further freeing up the flow of energy. Those were followed by *anahat nada* (unstruck sound), the spontaneous chanting of sounds that activate different nerve plexuses and brain centers. After these dynamic actions occurred in his practice, Swami Kripalu would fall into introverted states of *pratyahara* or *sensory withdrawal* deeper than anything he'd experienced in his years of sitting meditation. The effects of Swami Kripalu's practice were apparent for all to see. His body grew slender, strong, and extraordinarily flexible. His whole being radiated energy. Every village wanted Swami Kripalu to establish his ashram there, but he did not want to bind himself to any single place. Halol, Rajpipla, Asoj, Mota Fofalia, Oligam, Malav, Kanjetha, and Vejalpur are just some of the villages in which he practiced.

---

*The Indian tradition uses many names for the type of yoga that Swami Kripalu was initiated into by his teacher. One of them is *sahaja yoga*, which means *natural* or *spontaneous* yoga. Once prana is awakened in this approach, all willful techniques are abandoned and practice becomes a process of surrendering ever more deeply to the power and intelligence of this energy. Another traditional Indian name is kundalini yoga, however that term is used by numerous yoga schools in the West to describe other approaches that continue to employ willful techniques such as vigorous postures and pranayama to volitionally stimulate this energy. Although Swami Kripalu was clearly practicing a form of kundalini yoga, that term is not used in this book to prevent confusion. Instead, the terms *sahaja yoga* and *natural yoga* are used interchangeably.

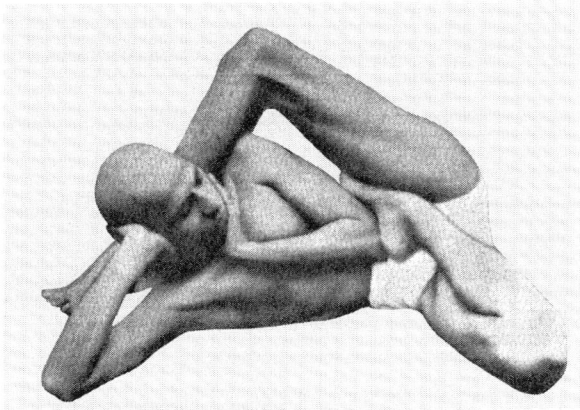
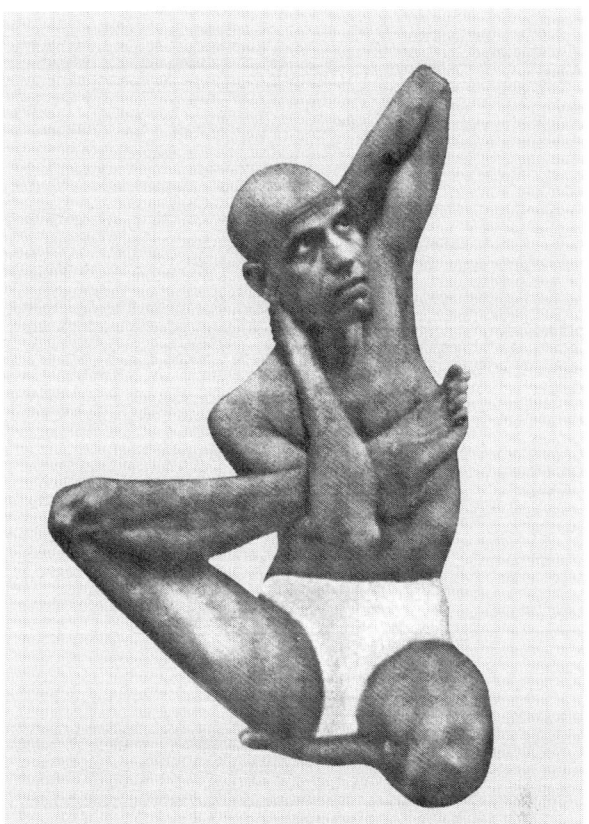

While in meditation, Swami Kripalu's body spontaneously moved into a wide-variety of yoga postures as illustrated in his book *Asana and Mudra*.

One day in meditation I experienced itching in a tendon underneath my tongue. The itching became so severe that I began to rub my fingernail on it. Since my nail had grown long, blood began flowing but I remained absorbed in my practice. After the conclusion of my meditation, I asked for a mirror and saw that the tendon beneath my tongue had been cut. I was mystified by this development. From then on the friction, movement, and milking of the tongue occurred every day. I had never heard of khechari (moving through the sky or space) mudra (energy seal). My guru had never mentioned or given me guidance about it, so I could not understand why these actions were occurring. Only later would I learn that this was the inception of the queen of all the energy seals, with whose help nirvakalpa (non-fluctuating) samadhi can be accomplished.

> **A Divine Madness:** *I've always seen the villagers as my own family and strived to live a life similar to theirs. Yet the sadhana that I do is very unusual. When I was living in Vejalpur, I used to roar like a lion, cry loudly, laugh heartily, sing, dance, clap and bang my hands and feet hard on the ground. This routine would start at three in the morning and continue until ten at night. The headmaster of the English school lived in the next house and the poor man was greatly troubled by me. He frequently muttered, "This is not yoga; this is madness," and eventually changed his residence. Other neighbors were also tormented by me, and I could well understand the state of their minds. It was a madness, but a divine madness.*

Spellbound by the power and intelligence of prana, Swami Kripalu expected to move through all the stages of yoga in a matter of months. He wasn't entirely deluded in this belief, as he quickly began moving in and out of a spectrum of ecstatic states that included the lower forms of samadhi. But he yearned for a *supreme samadhi*, a stable state of transcendental being that did not come and go. He aspired to become what the *Bhagavad Gita* calls *a yogi of steady wisdom* (*sthita-prajnya*). That proved elusive and to achieve it he gave himself entirely to his practice, often meditating around the clock.

When the healing and revitalizing energy of prana is freed to do its work, it eventually awakens the evolutionary energy that yoga calls *kundalini shakti* (serpent power) and describes as lying dormant at the base of the spine. As this even more potent force started to stir in him, Swami Kripalu began to perform *khumbaka, bandhas,* and *mudras*. *Khumbaka* is holding the breath either in or out for prolonged periods, which excites the nervous system and activates this primal energy. *Bhandas* are *locks*, which

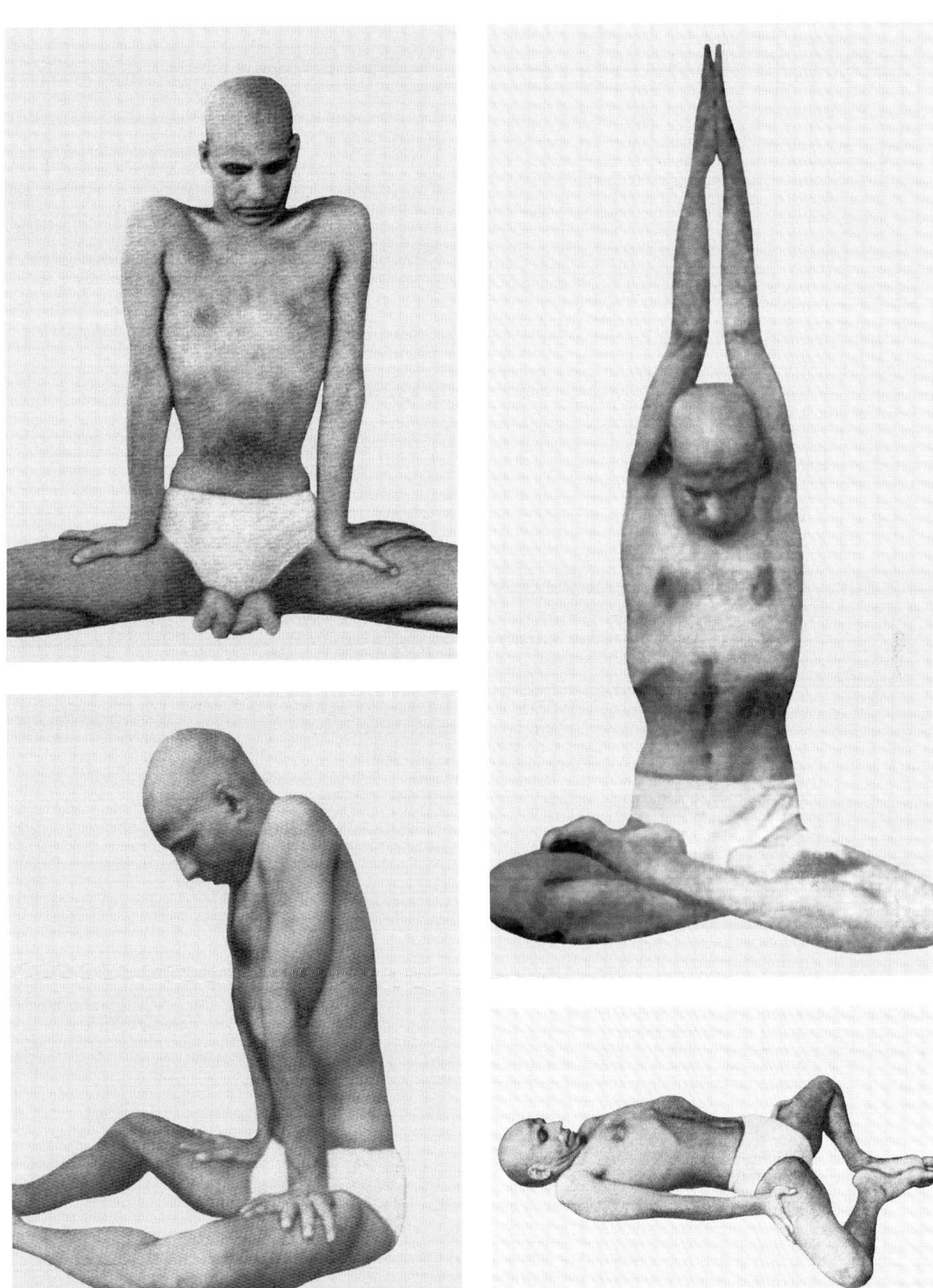

Swami Kripalu practicing *bandha* (the locks) as illustrated in his book *Asana and Mudra*.

contain the energy in the pelvis and trunk, enabling it to build to high levels. *Mudras* are *energy seals*, advanced postures and subtle gestures that cause the energy to coalesce at different bodily points, enabling it to untie knots of constriction (*marman* and *granthis*). As the kundalini energy begins to rise up and be felt in different areas of the body, it creates profound states of inner absorption in which awareness of the outer world can fall entirely away.

One day in 1954 while engaged in this practice, Swami Kripalu wandered away from his temporary residence in Rajpipla, lost to the world in a rapturous state. He ended up naked in the neighboring village of Kanjetha, where some devotees took him to a temple on the banks of the Narmada. Afraid he might wander off again, they decided to spend the night with him in a protective vigil. A few hours had passed when Swami Kripalu, who'd been sitting quietly in meditation wrapped in a blanket, suddenly stood up and without any warning dove into the river.

The Narmada is one of India's largest rivers and it was well into monsoon season. The waters were surging with strong currents and Swami Kripalu was instantly carried away. Vanishing into the dark of a moonless night, the villagers who witnessed the event felt certain his life was lost. When a few started to weep one exclaimed, "We are not helping him by crying. Let's form a search party and proceed along the riverbank toward Shinor. With dawn approaching, there is some hope we may find him." As the story is told, the whole band began running along the riverbank, their lanterns darting through the night like fireflies.

Swami Kripalu during the early days of his kundalini awakening.

Meanwhile Swami Kripalu was being swept downstream, tossed about by a raging current and frequently pulled under water. For some time he struggled with all his might to stay afloat and keep from drowning. Having eaten and slept little for days, exhaustion began to overtake him. His hands and feet grew numb. Certain he was facing death, Swami Kripalu cried out in desperation to his guru, *I am drowning, please save me!* Miraculously this plea brought an immediate response, a voice from the darkness that Swami Kripalu could somehow hear over the roar of the river: *Swami, stop swimming*. Convinced his mind was failing, he kept right on struggling, but he heard the message repeated a second time, *Swami, stop swimming, surrender*.

Recognizing his guru's voice, Swami Kripalu experienced a moment of relief. Gathering his courage, he relinquished any effort to stay above the surface. As soon as he relinquished control, his body assumed fish pose and began breathing in a way that swelled his abdomen with air. Now buoyant, he floated atop the raging torrent. When the river broadened, he drifted with the slowing current, reveling in a state of bliss and chanting a mantra that spontaneously came to him.* It was morning when he approached Shinor and was found by the search party, unable to believe their eyes when they saw him alive and unscathed. Swami Kripalu took this harrowing experience as a direct message from his guru that it was safe to surrender to the flood of energy coursing through his system.

> **Prana and Kundalini.** *The release of prana is not the awakening of kundalini, but it does help awaken this evolutionary power. In fact there is no other way to awaken the kundalini except through the release of prana. Teachers of the modern age conflate these two, but from the point of view of the ancient yogic scriptures prana and kundalini are different. While the release of prana is a praiseworthy step in yoga, it cannot penetrate the chakras (energy centers) and granthis (knots), nor can it purify the mind and body fully. All these tasks are carried out later by the kundalini after its awakening. While many yogis claim they know kundalini, most only know exercises that excite the prana.*
>
> *There is a story in India about a famous scientist who was stuck on a problem. He studied and studied but could not find the answer. One day while taking a shower the answer came to him unexpectedly and he ran outside naked shouting, "I found it! I found it!" A yogi who searches and searches for God and awakens kundalini does the same thing. In my early days, I would jump into the waters of the Narmada and plaster my body with mud. Sometimes I roamed through the villages without clothes because I did not feel that I had a body. Back then I didn't know that it was easy for the nerves to become overworked, making a yogi God-intoxicated.*

---

*This became a mantra that Swami Kripalu repeated for the rest of his life: *Om Namah Shivaya Gurave, Satchitananda Murtaye, Namastasmai, Namastasmai, Namastasmai, Namo Namah* or *Oh Lord Shiva, I bow to you in the form of the guru, embodiment of being, consciousness, and bliss, to Thee I bow, to Thee I bow, to Thee I bow, respectfully.*

It was events like this that led Swami Kripalu to scour the yogic texts to understand the transformative fire and process raging within him. He found over 40 different schools and sects that referred to this yoga by different names and was amazed to discover many of his experiences clearly depicted in their writings. For example verse 2.70 of the *Hatha Yoga Pradipika* contains this description of *plavani* (floater) *pranayama*: "By completely filling the stomach with air that has been moved internally, the yogi can easily float like a lotus leaf even in deep water." Compiling these references and contrasting them with his own experience, Swami Kripalu began to discern a panoramic view of yoga.

He saw that some texts had a broad perspective, dividing the process into sequential stages to form a helpful map. Others had a narrow lens, focusing in on a single phase to provide critical guidance. Many were esoteric, veiling their messages in symbols or stories that only an adept practitioner could decode.* He also saw how many of the techniques he was doing spontaneously had been adapted by modern yoga schools to be done volitionally and stimulate the flow of life force, uplift health, catalyze psychological growth, and facilitate the practice of sitting meditation. Seeing the value of these disciplines to help aspirants acquire physical and spiritual fitness, he recognized that what he called the *willful practice* of postures and pranayama was an important preliminary step for students wanting to ready themselves to embark on the path of surrender and sahaja yoga.

---

*The sages used a variety of means to keep their secret teachings from falling into the hands of the uninitiated. The most common was to embed the teachings in a symbolic story that has multiple levels of meaning. Some texts purposely omit key details that must be supplied by a teacher to unlock its teachings. Others use metaphors whose message is difficult to discern. Over the centuries much of this hidden meaning has been lost, which is why Swami Kripalu's ability to interpret these esoteric texts was so highly valued. The traditional guidance is that 12 years of willful practice should be done before commencing surrender yoga, but Swami Kripalu placed no such restriction on his students, feeling this a very individual matter. For the great majority of householders seeking success and Self-realization, volitional yoga done with an attitude of surrender is their primary practice. Sahaja yoga for moksha is appropriate for relatively few.

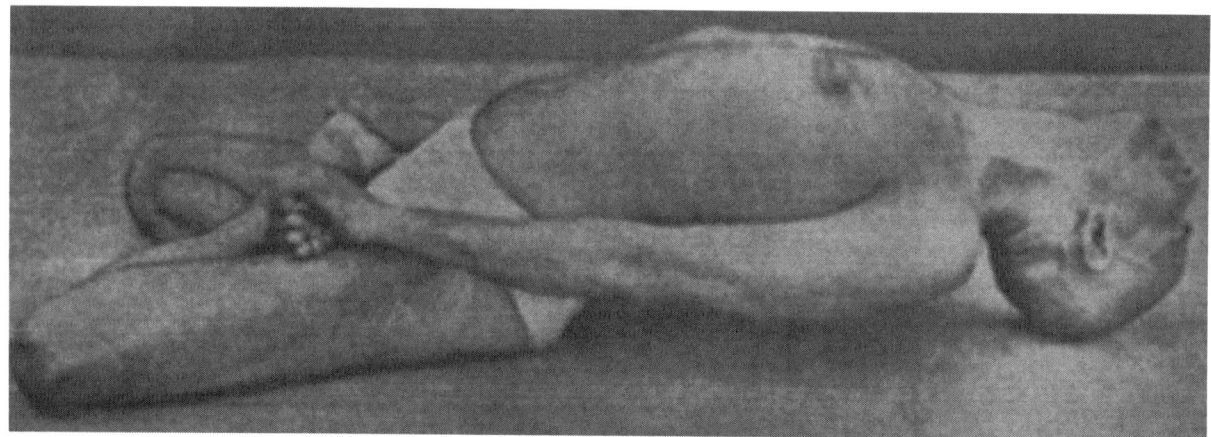

Swami Kripalu in *matsyasana*, the *fish posture* in which plavani pranayama is practiced, in a photograph taken near the time of his Narmada river experience.

Swami Kripalu came to believe that over the millennia the Indian sages had collectively brought forth a complete revelation and comprehensive vision of the spiritual path. He intuitively sensed that it was possible to integrate all of yoga's authoritative texts into a grand synthesis that could unite its diverse sects and rival schools. Living in seclusion he struggled to bring forth this synthesis, not only to support his own practice but as a form of service to the world.

> *India is the land of yoga's origin, where its practice has been carried out individually and collectively for thousands of years. Experienced yogis have always pondered their practice and offered critical evaluations of its results, so there is an ocean of yogic literature that is very deep and also spreads far and wide. Without a boat in the form of a teacher, it is easy to drown in it. After embarking on my practice, I had the desire to go through that literature and was extremely surprised to find my experiences tallying with those of the ancient yogis, whose guidance is valuable not because it is old but because it contains the essence of truth.*
>
> *An experienced yogi does not consider one type of yoga best and the rest inferior. He understands that there are many different approaches based on the nature and goals of the practitioner. Broadly speaking, this literature explains how a person should live from birth to death, with different texts answering different questions. What are the duties of a student? What are the duties of a householder? How can we maintain our health? How should we treat our family? What is our responsibility to society? How should we envision and relate to the universe? How can we act to meet with success? Seen deeply, this literature explains how one who advances to the final stages of yoga can gain spiritual liberation through the kriyas of prana and kundalini awakening.*
>
> *Even the most minute details of this great path of life have been explained in such a way that you can follow it no matter your nationality or religion. I believe this heritage is for the entire world. All humankind has an equal right to it, but to expound its beauty and magnitude is beyond my capacity. It must be experienced, and I have only come to understand it gradually by practicing it myself. It is currently my hope to assemble all the ancient teachings into a single text that I am tentatively calling the Ancient Yoga Book. It would be printed in Hindi and English so it can be useful to serious yogis everywhere.*

After years of study and lecturing, Swami Kripalu was intimately familiar with every verse of the *Bhagavad Gita*. Informed by his practice, he was amazed to discover a previously unseen layer of advanced yoga instruction encoded in his beloved text.

> *I once asked my guru, "Which yoga is best and how can it be achieved?" He replied, "The best yoga is surrender yoga." While listening intently, I was young and failed to understand his meaning. Unaware of this, I spoke confidently on the subject of surrender for many years. Only recently have I come to a stage where I can read the books of great masters and take truth from them.*
>
> *When prana becomes powerful, various kriyas and other activities are generated in the body. To permit these activities to occur without trying to stop them is called Ishvara Pranidhana or surrender to God in the Yoga Sutra. In the Bhagavad Gita, the release of prana and surrender yoga is indicated but only indirectly: "The Lord dwells in the hearts of all beings, Arjuna, and by his maya (illusion) causes all beings to revolve as though mounted on a machine. Seek refuge in him alone, and by his grace you will gain supreme peace and the eternal abode." Similarly in the Srimad Bhagavatam, Lord Krishna says to his disciple Uddhava: "When a devotee completely surrenders to me, I manifest in their atman (soul)." After this, Lord Krishna describes the condition of such a devotee while in meditation: "He is my true devotee whose body is filled with energy, whose eyes spill over with tears, and who laughs loudly, dances, and sings freely without becoming shy."*
>
> *Such a yogi enters his meditation room and surrenders himself totally to this energy, welcoming all of its manifestations. Whatever happens, he just lets it happen. This type of self-surrender is difficult to understand without experience, but we have all ridden on a train. The locomotive is a machine and has no wish to go anywhere. The engineer takes it wherever it needs to go and all the cars follow along the train tracks. In the same way, when a surrender yogi turns control over to the prana energy the Lord becomes his engineer and leads his meditation forward. He firmly believes that all the actions occurring in the vehicle of his mind and body are being performed at the initiative of the Lord.*
>
> *The Gita teaches that we should offer whatever actions we perform to God, and that actions done in this spirit of devotional surrender bring mental peace. This basic form of surrender yoga is clearly stated because it can be practiced by all. The deeper form of surrender yoga is not easy to see because it is meant only for advanced yogis.*

Perhaps the most salient guidance that Swami Kripalu gleaned from his studies was a warning on the danger of excessive practice. Seeing the error of his ways reflected in the written record of earlier sages, he adopted a daily schedule that allowed for ample practice but also recognized his need for regular meals, adequate sleep, and engaging intellectual pursuits. After making this change, Swami Kripalu ceased being a source of concern to the villagers. Now aware that he was only passing through the precarious early stages of kundalini awakening, Swami Kripalu abandoned any idea that he could scale the ladder of yoga in a matter of months. Humbled but resolute, he vowed to devote himself exclusively to his practice until he had reached its highest rung, which he still believed would occur over the next few years.

A yogi whose life energy is activated becomes extremely happy. Interesting experiences of different kinds continually occur. In their delight, more and more time is spent in meditation. Longing to accomplish samadhi, some yogis abandon sleep, eat minute quantities of food, and meditate incessantly. Such a yogi can become insane, succumb to diseases, or even die. This is why the scriptures prescribe a 10-hour limit on meditation with any extra time spent in study or service.

Last year I imagined that I would have entered nirbija samadhi by now. Even though I enter samadhi often, it is not mature and I descend back into the realm of mental fluctuation. While last year's expectations might be delayed, my love for meditation continues to grow, my desires are disappearing, and I am progressing day by day. With the grace of God, I will reach to the final stage where there is no possibility of regression.

******

Ensconced in my own routine of getting up early to have an uninterrupted block of time to practice before heading off to work, it was hard to see 10 hours a day as any kind of limit. At first the whole notion only served to rekindle my renunciate fantasies. However I had to sit up and take notice when I began to find bits and pieces of a parallel teaching for householders, which I was able to compile into a whole message that showed Swami Kripalu was sensitive to the predicament of busy yogis like me.

The Problem of a Householder: *A renunciate yogi usually resides in a solitary place and it's understood that his main activity is spiritual practice. While he may undergo mental disturbances due to internal causes, these disturbances can be remedied by changes to his schedule or environment and do not last long. However the problem of a householder who wants to grow spiritually is acute. Most of their time is taken with work, and they are always tired from the press of outside obligations.*

Moreover, family worries often intrude upon their mental peace. While a quiet place to practice is preferable, their surroundings at home are likely to be noisy, as few can afford an isolated room for meditation.

Despite these obstacles, a sincere householder knows that a yogi who cannot observe regularity in practice does not progress. In such a situation, how can one manage? Such a yogi should work out a convenient schedule that allows for fifteen minutes of daily practice. This much at least is essential to keep up one's positive spirit. Beyond that, a householder yogi also promises to observe a time limit. Practice can gradually be lengthened according to one's energy and circumstances up to a maximum of two hours. This time may be divided into two or more sessions to suit one's convenience.

This is the yoga that can be done while living in family and society. Through its practice, a householder's health, mental peace, and enthusiasm is protected, enabling them to grow spiritually while also attaining success. If a householder lacks good judgment and exceeds this time limit, they are likely to lose interest in their societal duties. The scriptures warn that such a yogi will not attain either worldly success or spiritual liberation.

Despite my initial resistance, I gained a lot from this inquiry. It suggested there was an amount of practice that was neither too little nor too much – a sweet spot. It taught me the intensity of my yoga practice was not fixed. It could be gradually increased as my system grew stronger. Most importantly, it introduced me to a radical notion. The purpose of my householder practice was not so much enabling me to access non-ordinary states of consciousness as helping me be more centered and effective in my life. While a householder like me practicing two hours a day was in no danger of becoming delusional, I learned by experience that exceeding this limit poses a different risk. Too much time on the mat could leave me withdrawn, self-absorbed, and unable to engage effectively with the outside world. A final piece explaining the role of retreats, like Swami Kripalu's annual trip to Rishikesh, completed the picture.

You must create the right surroundings for your practice to progress. First learn to make your residence a suitable place, as then you won't have to go anywhere to do your daily practice. But experiencing the truths described in the yogic scriptures requires a peace of mind hard to create in ordinary life. Just by going to a yoga ashram or other sanctuary for a time, many difficulties are removed. You can live simply in a natural setting with others going in a similar direction. Focusing on your practice, you can have in-depth experiences. While these experiences are preliminary, they are inspirational and form seed impressions that get planted deeply in the mind. If you nurture this newly acquired knowledge, you will be able to bring it alive in your everyday life.

The river doesn't come to your home. You have to go get the water. This is why I encourage you to leave your customary residence every now and then to enter a different surrounding where you can receive new light, new inspiration, and new practices. This is how you can quickly progress on your spiritual path and reach the state in which you don't have to go anywhere special to do your practice.

It was only by making peace with the realities of my householder life that I was able to return to the later chapters of Swami Kripalu's life story and learn from them. *When the student is ready the guru appears* is a well-known yogic adage. As Swami Kripalu's self-actualization process came to fruition, it seemed to me that his guru had literally appeared to him in Rishikesh and Rajpipla to open a doorway into a whole new dimension of practice. Seeing how he'd walked through that door without hesitation, I wondered how far this second leg of the yogic journey could take him.

Readers wanting to know more are directed to stories 4-1 to 4-2 in the appendix of teaching stories.

CHAPTER 5

Twelve Years of Silence

Silence is a great penance and through its proper practice even the impossible is made possible. Some people ridicule this method by saying, "What use is locking up the mouth when the mind is the real culprit and cause of trouble?" While this may be correct, such people have never observed a vow of silence.

Even by Indian renunciate standards, the daily schedule adopted by Swami Kripalu was rigorous. Most yogis undertaking disciplines on this scale rely upon the support of an ashram, but Swami Kripalu chose to continue his custom of traveling from village to village. Having frequented many ashrams, he did not want to get mired in everything entailed in directing a spiritual community. So he remained a solitary yogi intent on his practice who periodically moved from place to place, which had the benefit of spreading the burden of housing and feeding him across his many supporters.

A Day in the Life of Swami Kripalu: This is the schedule Swami Kripalu maintained from 1950 to 1981, which reserved 11 hours for practice to ensure that 10 would always be completed.

3:00-3:30 AM	Rise and shower
3:30-6:30 AM	Sahaja Yoga Meditation
6:30-7:15 AM	Meet with visitors
7:15-8:30 AM	Writing and study
8:30-10:00 AM	Sahaja Yoga Meditation
10:00-10:30 AM	Mealtime
10:30-12:00 Noon	Writing and study
12:00-2:00 PM	Sahaja Yoga Meditation
2:00-4:30 PM	Writing and study
4:30-9:00 PM	Sahaja Yoga Meditation
9:00-3:00 AM	Sleep

During the time allotted for meditation, Swami Kripalu would play the harmonium, chant, and surrender to the manifestations of his awakened energy or shakti. These automatic actions (kriyas) continued even in his sleep. During the time allotted for writing and study, Swami Kripalu wrote books and letters. Any unusual work, meetings, or travel was also done then. If a special celebration or public appearance required Swami Kripalu to deviate from this routine, he would stay up later to complete his 10 hours of practice.

Five years of clocklike practice had passed when Swami Kripalu received an invitation to speak in the tiny village of Kayavarohan. Over that time he had stepped away from his role as a public figure to embrace the life of a reclusive yogi. Intent on his practice, he avoided disruptions of all kinds and routinely refused such requests. Yet Swami Kripalu accepted this invitation and what happened next astounded him to an extent that surpassed all the miracles, visitations, and visions he'd experienced in the past.

The Enclosure of Lord Lakulish

In 1955, I received a call from a village elder inviting me to speak at Kayavarohan during their holy week. While Kayavarohan is only ten miles from my native Dabhoi, I had never seen it. As a seeker of salvation, solitude is dear to me and I had long lost interest in delivering lectures. At the time this request was made, I was not going anywhere for even a one-day lecture. But somehow I said "yes" and afterwards regretted giving my consent in an off-guard moment.

Only one disciple of mine lived there and arrangements were made for me to stay at her family's residence. On the appointed day, I arrived in the evening to deliver my lecture. The next morning after meditation, some of the residents called on me and said, "Swamiji, this Kayavarohan is an ancient pilgrimage site. Should you kindly agree, we will conduct you through its sacred ruins and relate its illustrious history." Their sincerity touched me and I expressed my assent by saying, "We will start in the afternoon after my mid-day meditation."

They returned promptly on time to commence my tour. As we entered a holy spot, one of my companions announced the presiding deity. As we came out, someone else narrated its history. If anything was missed, a third would speak up to complete the telling. As my eyes observed all the subtle images of the site and my ears attended to their knowledgeable narration, I fell into concentration.

Three hours passed this way and the sun was setting when we came to the last spot. One of my companions said, "Our tour is coming to an end. Your lodging place is only 500 steps from here. This is the enclosure of Lord Lakulish." Entering the rustic shed, my eyes instantly fell on a beautiful statue and my heart started beating fast. Tears filled my eyes, my throat choked, and I could not speak. Feeling faint, I had to hold the wall for support. I was so surprised that there was no end to my surprise. If you want to know what came over me, please listen carefully.

The statue was a perfect image of the luminous saint who appeared to me in Rishikesh and again in Rajpipla. The same dwarfish body, the same outline of face, the same eyes; I could not be mistaken. From the history I'd heard from my companions, I knew this was an ancient site and that historians dated Lakulish as living 1500 years ago. According to the lore of the Puranas, Lakulish was a contemporary of Krishna who lived 5,000 years ago. Whether he was born 1500 or 5,000 years ago, how could he have appeared to me in recent times? I could not reconcile this contradiction.

The visible transformation of my mental state dumbfounded my companions. As they escorted me to my lodging place, no one uttered a single word. There I bathed before entering my evening meditation. As soon as I took my seat, a great spark of meditation took place. For a long time, I had been striving to master a specific stage of yoga but could not succeed. I attained to that stage suddenly and my mind danced with joy. When my normal period of meditation was over, I did not feel like getting up. Yet I had to abide by the scriptural time limits. With great difficulty, I got up from my seat and lay down in bed.

I tried to sleep but my mind would not come out of meditation. The history I had been told appeared in front of my eyes, and I felt that I was seeing a true happening. My state of consciousness was such that it painted the entire story in front of me. I saw the morning sun rising over the horizon. In its light, I could see a beautiful city of innumerable Shiva temples. In that land there had not been just one yogi, but many great yogis who did their penance there. Darkness fell and the city gradually faded from sight. The night of darkness lasted quite some time. Then the sun rose again. In its light, I saw the same city but magnificent with Lord Lakulish in it. Although both cities were located at the same place, they appeared different because of a long passage of time.

Some invisible power was inspiring these visions and from it I heard these words: "Son, the first city you saw was Medhavati and the second was Kayavarohan. You are our choice to reestablish this mahatirtha (great pilgrimage site)." Following these words, I had the darshan (sight and presence) of Rishi Vishvamitra and Lord Lakulish. Tears of joy filled my eyes as I humbly bowed before them and said, "This pilgrimage site has been forgotten for many years. I'm a swami without an ashram or possessions and have been moving from village to village. In order to reestablish this shrine it will take hundreds of thousands or millions of rupees. I myself cannot do this work, but if you are giving me your blessing then I'm willing to start." Back came the reply, "You have only to act as an instrument of Divine will. The task will take care of itself." This blessing received, my mind was overcome with a feeling of ecstatic joy and in a few moments I was fast asleep.

Looking into Indian history, Swami Kripalu learned that Lakulish* was a known figure who lived during the second century. He is credited with reviving the Pashupats, one of the earliest schools of yoga. Little is known about Lakulish's life except for legends depicting his miraculous birth and death. More is known about the Pashupats, a staunchly ascetic sect of monotheists who believed that a singular source and spiritual force underlies the cosmos and indwells our being. This unitary force remains hidden to most people, who are hypnotized by the constant flow of sensations, thoughts, and desires passing through the bodymind. This allows the animalistic drives (*pashu*) of the body and egocentric conditioning of the mind to dominate their psyches. To remedy this state of spiritual blindness, the Pashupats developed a variety of yogic techniques to enable practitioners to awaken this force, master (*pati*) their instinctual nature, and realize their true identity. A yoga adept on this path was called *pashupata* or *master of the animal self*. Lakulish was more than a yoga master to the Pashupats. He was the 28th incarnation of Lord Shiva, who had taken birth as Lakulish to reinvigorate its ancient line of teachings.

Swami Kripalu's research lent credence to the idea that Kayavarohan was not founded by Lakulish. Indian lore credits that to Vishvamitra, a celebrated *tapasvin* (practitioner of austerities) who predated Lakulish by over 10 centuries. Vishvamitra is recognized as one of the seven great rishis whose collective wisdom established what we know as Hinduism. The story of this significant figure in Swami Kripalu's yoga lineage is told in the appendix of teaching stories. Scholars believe that Vishvamitra lived circa 1500 B.C.E. or earlier, when he presumably founded the site, built its original shrine, installed the first *jyotir lingam* (*radiant sign of Shiva*), and propagated an early form of mantra yoga. It remained a remote pilgrimage center until it was inhabited by Lakulish and grew into a flourishing city renowned for its prosperity, high arts, and spiritual culture. Indian lore recognized twelve *mahatirthas* or great shrines especially holy to the followers of Shiva, each of which contained a jyotir lingam representing a different aspect of Shiva. Swami Kripalu was certain that Kayavarohan was the first of these auspicious shrines, which oversaw the other 12, before it was ransacked and forgotten.

---

*This book uses the Hindi spelling. In Sanskrit it is Lakulisha.

The distinctive black statue of Lakulish seen by Swami Kripalu was found by a farmer plowing his field in 1866. It was brought it to the village and installed in a meager temple, where it remained for almost a century. This statue differs from all others found at Kayavarohan, which were cut from common stone and display the ravages of time. Legend says it is made of meteorite, an impervious material, but it's uncertain if this claim has been verified.

I have studied this shrine from the point of view of yoga and also turned the pages of history books. Its grandeur cannot be described in words. The number of such shrines remaining in India today can be counted on the fingers of one hand. It was from these places that the Vedic religion developed and spread its pure culture throughout the country. They retain and preserve the Holy Essence of that glorious age.

It was from here the great sage Vishvamitra perceived and made famous the Gayatri mantra, the recitation of which illumines the mind with wisdom (medha). At that time, it was called Medhavati, which means "place of purified intellect." The installation of the first jyotir lingam was done at the hands of Vishvamitra because of his devotion to Lord Shiva. The rishis Arti and Bhrigu also performed their penance here. Only later was Lakulish born and he lived at this holy site. It then became known as Kayavarohan and was given that name for a specific reason. Kayavarohan means "Shiva descended into a body." This is the divine body (divya deha) of my beloved Gurudev that passed through the flame of yoga. At Kayavarohan, Lakulish trained his most intellectually astute disciples into acharyas (accomplished teachers) and then entrusted them to administer all the other shrines, each embellished by a lustrous idol made from the substance of a fallen star (meteoric stone).

Lakulish enjoys the same respect in India as the torch-bearers of other religions. Everywhere he was revered as a perfect knower of yoga. When Lakulish was present in Kayavarohan, powerful kings came from all over to receive his counsel and blessings. Lakulish established Kayavarohan as the center of the Pashupat sect and it was from here that he spread yoga throughout the whole of India.

My guru was a siddha yogi, and so was Lakulish. Lakulish established the Pashupats and was a proponent of monotheism. My guru initiated me into the Pashupat sect and its one-God theory as well. There is no difference whatsoever between the physical form of the Lakulish statue and my guru as he appeared to me on that hillock in Rishikesh, and there are innumerable other reasons testifying to their sameness. As such, I do not believe them to be different.

With Lakulish as their preceptor, the Pashupats grew rapidly in size and influence. A network of Shiva temples radiated outward from Kayavarohan to cover all of India by 600 C.E. when the movement began to fade. Until recently historians linked the decline of the Pashupats with the conquests of Muslim invaders, who looted their temples and forced followers to either convert or be killed. New research suggests the Pashupats did not disappear entirely but merged into the yoga school of Matsyendra and Goraksha, the sages who drew upon their techniques to develop hatha yoga and its repertoire of postures and breathing exercises so closely identified with yoga today.

Swami Kripalu accepted his experience at Kayavarohan as a sacred call to rebuild the shrine and revitalize its long-lost yoga tradition. Life had positioned him perfectly to play this role. He was the only known initiate in its otherwise extinct yoga sect. The local residents trusted him implicitly and the respect he'd earned throughout Gujarat lent legitimacy to the project. His celebrity status was needed to attract outside interest and resources. He even found an immediate partner in a local businessman, Hirabhai Patel. Only one thing stood between Swami Kripalu and the spiritual directive he'd received: his solemn vow to stabilize his samadhi before returning to life in society.

> *The morning after I received the inspiration from Rishi Vishvamitra and Lord Lakulish to restore Kayavarohan, a firm resolve took root in my mind to build an imposing temple and establish a yoga university. My companions from the day before called upon me at seven o'clock and I immediately asked them, "Who is the most respected person in this area?" "Hirabhai Patel who owns the cotton gin," was their reply. I suggested they send for him. Two persons got up and within fifteen minutes Hirabhai was taking his seat.*
>
> *Although I was totally unknown to Hirabhai, I gave voice to my innermost thoughts. "Yesterday these friends took me around the local temples and I was mightily thrilled with the statue of Lord Lakulish. If the village residents agree to place it at my disposal, I will build a magnificent temple on the outskirts of town to house the statue." He replied choked with emotion, respectfully, yet as though quite intimate to me. "Swamiji, you have spoken my heart's desire. To revive this shrine is my life-long ambition."*
>
> *Clarifying my position, I said, "At present, I am practicing yoga and will not be able to commence this activity until I attain a certain stage of meditation." Hirabhai paled, "Can you kindly indicate how many years this yogic attainment will take?" I replied, "It all depends on God's will; it is difficult to fix even an approximate time limit." Appearing crestfallen, he asked, "Shall I live until then?" Hirabhai was advanced in years and this question made me pause and think. But having firmly resolved to not take any work actively in my hands until completing my samadhi, I returned to seclusion.*

Twelve Years of Sadhana in Silence

Swami Kripalu did not speak publicly about his experience in Kayavarohan but word got out nonetheless. With his name back in circulation, his privacy and custom of moving from village to village became harder to sustain. Feeling pulled to finish his practice and commence work on the temple, Swami Kripalu grew less tolerant of the interruptions to his schedule required by his periodic shifts in locations. In January 1958, Malav hosted a festival celebrating Swami Kripalu's 45th birthday. Afterwards he settled there in a small ashram built by a devoted cadre of villagers eager to care for him. The arrangement worked well for all concerned, and the stability it provided inspired Swami Kripalu to take a 12-year vow of silence, the purpose of which was to enable him to complete his sadhana. With the support of all his followers, he engaged in the most intensive practice of his life, using a chalkboard to communicate and seldom leaving his meditation room.

In 1958 there was a big celebration for my birthday and later that year I went into silence. Afterwards people would see me writing on a slate and say, "Kripalu, you do not talk but you write. It is all the same and talking is more convenient. Your time would be saved and we would be better satisfied."

These people are correct that this silence of mine is not of the highest caliber. When I went to Kayavarohan for the first time, God pushed me into a stream of activity. Believing God has willed me to work for the rebirth of this holy place, I resort to writing to keep in contact with the world. However such people would be incorrect to conclude that this ordinary silence has not protected me well. A yogi observing silence writes only when necessary. As a result he is only asked important questions. Most of his conversations are over in five minutes; his longest interview does not last for more than 10 minutes.

Observing a vow of silence is not possible unless one also studies holy books, engages in prayer, eats moderately and fasts when called for, maintains celibacy, and exercises. Even then the tongue may cease to move while the mind remains active and keeps right on ticking. So meditation must be practiced for the mind to become still and for real silence to be born. This inner silence only comes in the pure consciousness of samadhi, which is not easily obtained. Only by taking refuge in all these disciplines can the true goal of a vow of silence be achieved.

Most people cannot remain silent all day but they can learn to curb their tongue. Practicing mauna (silence) or mitdarshan (speaking only when necessary) one morning a week, on holy days, or while [on retreat] at an ashram can be a means to learning how to check our speech. But the most auspicious moment for anyone to take a vow of silence is when a disturbance arises in the mind. We all know that if we are upset and react quickly to criticism with defensiveness the result is never good. Nor is it skillful for us to reprimand others without forethought. It is much better to be reticent and think the matter over calmly first. Otherwise the swords of attack and retaliation injure everyone concerned. When our mind is in a disturbed state, we cannot listen carefully to others or give good counsel. So it makes sense to be hesitant to speak when our mind is upset, but just remaining verbally silent is not enough. Our actions may proclaim our displeasure loud and clear. An angry husband or wife can say nothing but disturb everyone by banging about the house.

As pebbles tossed into a lake produce ripples, a speaker's words produce impressions in the mind of a listener. A person speaking with affection from a calm mind will create similar feelings in the mind of a listener. A person speaking bitter words born of a disturbed mind will cause reciprocal feelings to arise in the listener. This is how speech has the power to make an enemy of a friend, or a friend of an enemy. Truly the spoken word is the most important factor in determining an individual's relationship with the rest of the world.

A wise person's words may be few but are worth more than diamonds, rubies and pearls. However we talk and talk, which shows that we do not value our words. Until we cease considering our own speech to be trifling and choose our words consciously, others will not value what we have to say. We are not alone in this, as all those around us also talk too much, so that together we feel the whole world is full of nothing but upsets and disturbances. This is why it's said that silence is more useful to a worldly man than a detached swami. Thankfully there is one time in which everyone practices silence. After we fall asleep, there is no more speaking. While this silence provides a respite, it doesn't help us learn to control our speech in the waking state.

If we genuinely want to cease being garrulous and quarrelsome, the practice of silence can help us dispose of old vices and advance to new virtues. The peaceful mind that results will not pollute the atmosphere with untruth but spread the perfume of sweet speech, radiate the light of truth, and act to bring others profound happiness. It takes all the strength and ingenuity of a giant to control the elf of the tongue. Yet a person who succeeds in rooting out bitter speech and wicked actions can win the world and reach God.

Operating from the home base of an ashram enabled Swami Kripalu to enter another highly productive period of his life. Despite a complete lack of construction experience, he conveyed an organizing vision for the temple that architects were able to translate into a striking design that galvanized the local community and generated broad support for Kayavarohan's renewal. He also continued the disciplined text study and scholarly writing that had already produced the first of his three major works: *Asana and Mudra* (1953), an encyclopedic textbook of yoga intended for all students from beginner to advanced that is almost 800 pages in length and illustrated by 227 photographs of Swami Kripalu doing the practices being taught. Next would come *Science of Meditation* (1977), a 200-page treatise on the eight stages of practice set out in the *Yoga Sutra* and his first book translated into English for a Western audience. The last to be published was *Revealing the Secret* (1981), a thoughtful, thorough, and highly-personal 150-page commentary on the *Hatha Yoga Pradipika* for practitioners wanting to travel the path of sahaja yoga.*

Swami Kripalu also made a significant shift in his role as a teacher during this period, personally mentoring an eclectic group of dedicated students who'd coalesced around him. Joining three apprentice Indian swamis and the married Yogi Desai were an Indian woman initiated as a yoga sadhika (female practitioner) who would eventually become a swami, an American spiritual teacher from California, an English woman living in Canada, and a Frenchman of African descent.** Sizing up this diverse cast of characters, it seemed apparent that they were selected to play a role in a yoga movement reaching beyond the geographic and cultural confines of India.

In the shelter of his silence and structured schedule, the pace of Swami Kripalu's movement through the stages of sahaja yoga accelerated. After the kundalini awakens in the lowest centers as sexual energy, it begins to ascend toward the highest centers in the head. Along the way, it concentrates in different regions to purify and strengthen the system. Wherever it coalesces, the body naturally assumes a supportive posture or *mudra* (energy seal). A profound state of inner absorption ensues, allowing the energy to build, break through to a new level of freedom, and continue its ascent. The *Hatha Yoga Pradipika* lists 10 *maha mudras* (great energy seals) and corresponding bodily locations where this process is known to occur. As Swami Kripalu's practice progressed through all these major and many lesser mudras, he was able to explain their efficacy using a blend of yogic and contemporary terms.

---

*It is difficult to tell when the actual research and writing work that produced these later books was done, as there were significant lapses between manuscript writing, translation, and publication.

**His close students at this time included Swami Rajarshi Muni, Swami Vinit Muni, Swami Ashutosh Muni, Yogi Amrit Desai, Aashaben Parikh of Rajpipla who later received sanyas initiation by Rajarshi Muni and was given the name Yogini Maiya, Charles Berner or Yogeshwar Muni, Elizabeth Briscoe or Ma Om Shanti, and Lauture Massac or Shubhadarshan. The inclusion of two women was noteworthy given prevailing gender norms.

The endocrine glands control all the organs of the body through their secretions. If the function of these glands is weak, one's health suffers. If their function is medium, one enjoys the disease-free state. If their function is robust, an individual reaches their maximum development. Asana (postures) performed with pranayama nourishes all these glands with an increased blood supply. As the weakness of the endocrine glands vanishes, physical and mental health appears.

One can also perform asana with bandha (locks), kumbhaka (breath retention), and kriyas (purifying actions). These techniques further stimulate the glands to produce secretions that make a yogi lustrous. Through the correct practice of the locks, the practice of various mudras (energy seals) begins. Mudras are the developed forms of asanas; they act like pumps to make the downward flowing life energy upgoing. Under their influence, the yogi's mind becomes pure, his physical body becomes celestial, and liberating knowledge can descend. Even the march of time ceases to have any power over him, which is why the author of the Yoga Kundali Upanishad says that mudra brings about the destruction of old age and death.

While there are countless mudras, the ancient teachers have given predominance to only 10 and a true yogi will realize them through proper sadhana. We don't suspect that a superhuman can emerge from an ordinary person through these practices. However practicing this yoga is not an ordinary task – it is an extraordinary task – and many years of valiant effort and endurance are required to progress through its stages. Even then its attainment is always based on grace, so any credit should be given to God.

It was during this prolonged period of secluded practice and study that Swami Kripalu actualized the potential glimpsed by his boyhood teacher and became a powerful yoga adept. It's impossible to specify the date of his *Self-realization*, a stage that contemporary teachers often equate with full enlightenment. In characteristic fashion, he didn't make much of this attainment, considering it one of many milestones on the much-longer path of moksha. Yet it's clear in countless ways from his talks and writings that Swami Kripalu did pass over this recognized threshold.

As direct knowledge dawns, all doubts vanish. This is the achievement of Self-realization, the stage in which a clear and doubtless view of the final goal is attained. In truth, the real practice of yoga (yoga aimed at union) can only begin after Self-realization. Lord Krishna calls a Self-realized yogi "one who is Self-possessed" and explains in the Gita why this beyond-mind state must be attained to control the senses and overcome bodily identification. Maharishi Patanjali says that with Self-realization all

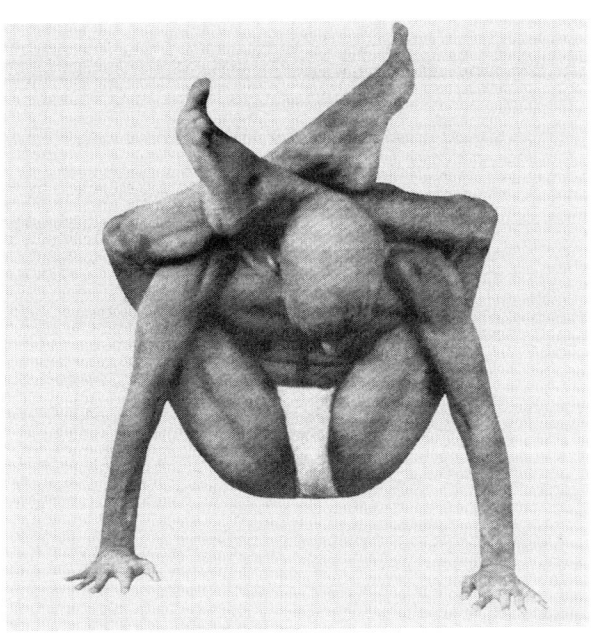

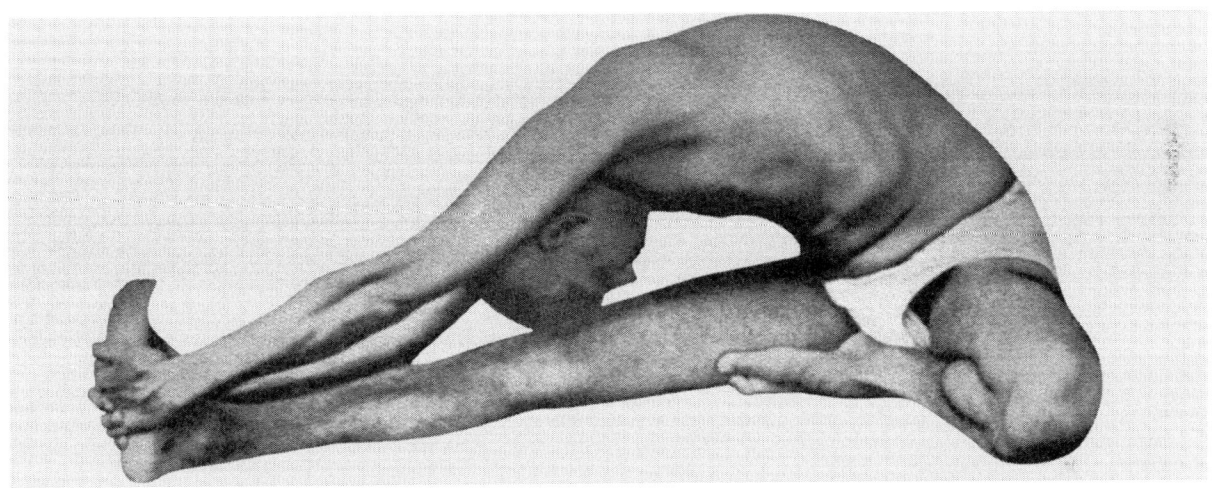
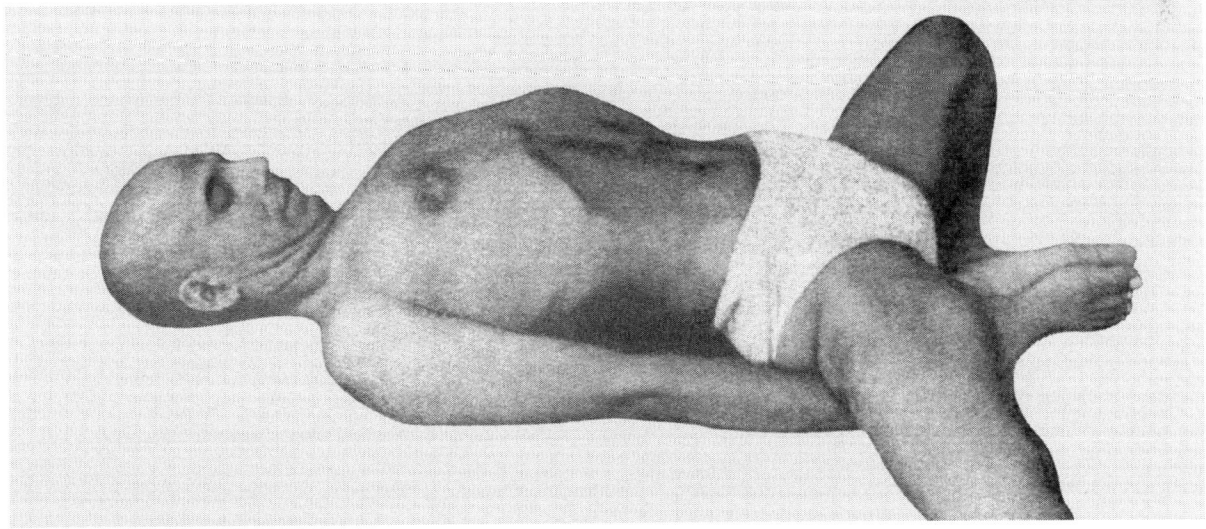

Swami Kripalu practicing bodily mudras as illustrated in *Asana and Mudra*.

obstacles are removed, faith is enhanced, and worldly enjoyments no longer distract. It is only after crossing to this stage that a yogi's inner journey will not be cut short by various obstacles.

The word "realization" in the above stanza signifies a purity of spirit that arises when the screen of illusion covering the intellect has been removed. Such a yogi is distinct from ordinary aspirants because the attention is now fixed on yoga (union) and not avoiding pain or seeking pleasure. But that yogi is not endowed with the highest knowledge, supreme detachment, the eight major powers, and a body purified by the fire of yoga. The ancient sages say that the labor of one who does not reach to these levels is "without fruit" because it has yielded neither liberation nor the divine body. Of course such a yogi does gain health, nobility, respect, wealth, and other worldly accomplishments. But only one who continues to the divine body is a complete yogi.

As the home of a renowned yogi, the village of Malav prospered during those years with the construction of a health clinic and major improvements to its schools, town hall, and water system. While the villagers attributed all these and other boons to his reputed yogic *siddhis* (powers), Swami Kripalu steadfastly denied having any unusual capacities. He attributed everything to the grace of God and the faith of the individuals involved. In various talks and writings, Swami Kripalu explained the relationship of yoga and such powers.

Swami Kripalu at the Malav ashram.

On Yogic Powers or Siddhis: *Many powers can be acquired through the practice of yoga. The common man is only interested if yogis can fly in the air or walk upon water. In his fascination with these siddhis, he forgets that young birds start to fly only a short time after they're hatched and newborn ducklings easily walk on water. If you are enthralled by miracles, please ponder whether it is wise to use years of your precious lifetime to gain the power of flying. What important purpose would be resolved? Yet I must admit that at times I myself have become preoccupied thinking about the enigma of miracles. So having invited your question, I will try to answer it in detail and with an open heart.*

The first powers that come to a yogi are bodily health and mental strength reflected in positive qualities such as determination, logical thinking, good memory, creativity, and decisiveness. These are not siddhis but the reflection of well-functioning faculties. They should be engaged to virtuously fulfill one's aims and cherished desires in life.

The practice of sahaja yoga is meant for moksha only but it is also a path to siddhi. When a yogi practices mantra, asana, pranayama, or meditation properly, prana will awaken and rise up. By any of these methods pranotthana can happen, but this awakening of pranic energy does not direct a yogi toward just one path. It impels him in the direction of multiple yogic paths.

It can be said that a genuine seeker of liberation follows a straight path to their goal, but a yogi after pranotthana experiences numerous distractions and does not find it easy to walk this narrow footpath. Swaying from side to side, he is tempted by these distractions to diverge onto one of the other paths, which appear wide and inviting. The end of these other paths is the various siddhis.

Most yogis are desirous of these powers on some level, and sooner or later they get tired and take recourse in one of these paths. These yogis are very much yogis, but their great mistake is to allow themselves to be seduced away from their pursuit of liberation. After stepping off the path of moksha, the siddhis which have so far remained distant come close. This is a stage that almost every yogi goes through. If such a yogi begins to exhibit their miraculous powers, he will be surrounded by people and become famous but find himself unable to complete his sadhana.

When such a yogi gets a siddhi, he becomes extremely happy. For example, he may be able to hear or transmit thoughts from a person whether close or far, or see objects and people thousands of miles away. While the bodily intoxication of liquor goes away in a day or two, the ego-intoxication of a yogi who receives even one siddhi is almost limitless. Pride swells his mind and he feels as if he can establish his supremacy over the entire universe. If he grows attached to fame, he may tell lies, spread false propaganda, or engage in all sorts of drama to sustain his recognition. This kind of man can act in ways that do great harm and destroy the positive reputation of yoga built by all the great masters of the past.

The difference in a genuine seeker of liberation is that he is able to resist these distractions by remembering that the greatest siddhi of yoga is not material powers but the supreme peace at the level of the soul (atman shanti) and highest spiritual knowledge (Brahman-vidya) that comes from realizing one's unity with God. A yogi who sticks to this path must continue his practice of asana, pranayama, and meditation for many years after pranotthana. To describe all the problems I have faced would discourage you, but I can give you one example. Years ago when I gave public lectures, I used to be able to express myself in eloquent words and poetic sentences that combined into a powerful expression. That was my art of speaking, but it was also a siddhi, and one that I was able to let God take away to keep me out of mischief.

The scriptures teach that a yogi who perseveres in his sadhana until no worldly or spiritual desires remain in his heart attains to all the siddhis in the end. But this sadhana is entirely different from the practice of yoga for miraculous powers. Such a yogi does not display any siddhis that come his way but surrenders them back to God with the result being that he remains dispossessed of any powers. Not a single siddhi is attained by him until the highest samadhi is achieved. Only this perfected yogi may be rightly called a siddha yogi, whose powers can be discretely put to use to benefit humanity and contribute towards the welfare of the world.

My teacher was such a yogi. Miraculous events emanated from him like a lamp radiates light and a flower spreads its fragrance. And yet whatever he was doing was happening spontaneously and never like he was performing a miracle. Because he was in touch with the subtle levels underlying reality, these things happened naturally in the same way the sun rises and sets. The fact of his siddhis became visible and experiential for people like me, but he was not exercising any powers intentionally. They got exposed without his intention.

Miracles can also be performed by saints, but these are not rightly considered siddhis. A saint is a representative of God, who is the reservoir of all miracles. By building up attachment to God, a saint creates a pipe or conduit, which is why miracles often flow out the spigot of a true saint. But saints don't see these as powers; they just love and want to help people. This is the nature of every saint, who opens his heart to bless the person but knows any miracles come from the grace of God.

I advise all my students – do not go after siddhis – as those who are after powers are already lost on their journey. Being a yogi is not becoming a snake charmer. Use the techniques of yoga for improving your health, increasing your well-being, and deepening your love of others and God. Give more importance to purity and humility than powers or miracles. Remember that the only true siddhi is atman darshan, the realization of the soul.

******

Even after unraveling the ins and outs of his guru's appearances and different guises, I still didn't know what to make of this chapter of Swami Kripalu's life. Its plot line was markedly mythic. All the details fit together so perfectly. Was his discovery of the Lakulish statue truly a divine occurrence that connected all the disparate dots of his earlier life? Scrutinizing the record, my faith in Swami Kripalu's honesty remained intact, but I also had to entertain the possibility that his zealous practice made him prone to hallucinatory visions.

As a student practicing in Swami Kripalu's lineage, the story had other implications. Although he didn't shout it from the rooftops, its message was clear. His boyhood guru was actually the perpetually youthful Lakulish, who was none other than Lord Shiva, the immortal progenitor of yoga. I felt certain that something earth shaking had happened to Swami Kripalu in Kayavarohan. Otherwise he would never have jeopardized the seclusion he so cherished by taking on the momentous task of rebuilding the temple. That was enough to start me wondering, "How was this reclusive yogi, who had been out of circulation for two full decades, going to rise to the occasion?"

The scriptures of yoga say, "God residing in the temple of one's body is the guru of all gurus and the real world teacher. All other temples and gurus are mere agents or representatives." However great yogis of the past have given much importance to these representatives and even declared that a true guru is equivalent to God. In my spiritual preparation, I regarded my guru as my spiritual father. Engaged in my practice, I regarded him as a great yogi and guide. After my experience in Kayavarohan, I see no difference between my guru and God.

Readers wanting to know more are directed to stories 5-1 to 5-2 in the appendix of teaching stories.

CHAPTER 6

Rebuilding the Temple

Today, after twelve years, I am giving up silence. Before my silence, while lecturing on the Gita, I would occasionally relate episodes from the inspiring life of the swami who gave me sanyas initiation. About the guru who showed me the way to yoga when I was but nineteen years old, I said nothing. So today, in order to purify my soul, I've decided to talk about Sri Pranavanandaji Maharaj, the second of these great men who have determined my life.

On January 4th, 1971, the 57 year-old Swami Kripalu used his annual birthday celebration to officially reenter public life. 25,000 people came from near and far to hear his much-heralded *Coming Out of Silence Speech*. For the first time, he told the story of meeting his boyhood guru, residing in his ashram for a year-and-a-quarter, seeing his radiant form in Rishikesh, and discovering his true identity at Kayavarohan. Speaking openly about the vision that motivated him to restore the Kayavarohan shrine was a masterful way to publicize the construction project that was underway and in need of support. But what really caught my attention were his closing words. After graciously thanking the villagers of Malav, he directly addressed my question of how this temple was going to be built. His answer was simple: God was going to do the work.

Now (before ending) I wish to say something about the village of Malav, which during my stay of twelve years has looked after me with love. The day before this festival, I mentioned that I was going to talk about my silence, relate some events of Pranavanandaji's life, and speak about the service done by the village. Immediately the village elders said: "There is no need to speak of us; do not waste time talking about our service." These are the sentiments of pure souls. Truly the love, service, and dedication of this village can never be forgotten. When I told them that after today I am going to live in Kayavarohan they were very sad. Although I tried to console them by saying that God had willed me to attend to its shrine and so I have to go, I too felt very sad at the thought of leaving.

This work at Kayavarohan is not mine; it is God's. I am merely performing his service. If God has not willed me to start the rebirth of this holy place, then I have just been suffering from illusions and the consequences will be disappointing. However, full of faith and believing it to be God's will, I am carrying out this task of rebuilding the temple. If any question of failure arises, I shall not let anyone else be blamed. I shall stand alone before the assembly and admit: "Those who have supported me are innocent; I alone am guilty and have misled them." But having unshakable faith in God, I know this will never come to pass. Instead, the work will turn out even more beautiful than is presently expected. In no corner of my soul is there any fear that this great and holy shrine will not be revived. God alone is going to do this work, yet when it is complete the garland of flowers will erroneously be given to me.

Today I have spoken after twelve years of silence. I had doubts in my mind as to whether I would be able to speak for an hour and a half, but I have and with the deepest feeling. Even though my speechmaking has been hampered by my lack of practice, you have all listened to me in loving silence, and I thank you for that from the depths of my heart. Now, with this blessing, I shall end my speech. May you all be happy. May you all be healthy. May no one ever be unhappy.

Ground had been broken for the temple four years earlier, but from the start the project was plagued by delays, funding shortages, and work stoppages. In a stroke of genius, the temple administrators announced a completion date that coincided with Swami Kripalu's 60th birthday. Everyone participating in the Coming Out of Silence festivities heard the proclamation: "Come what may, the statue of Lord Lakulish will be installed in the spring of 1974." Considering the herculean amount of work that remained to be done, it's clear they opted to take a calculated risk, betting that everyone's love for Swami Kripalu would create an immovable deadline and end the pattern of postponements.

Swami Kripalu accepted that he needed to play a leading role in the push to finish the project. He moved to Kayavarohan and settled into the upper floor of a house adjacent to the noisy construction site. While continuing to practice 10 hours a day, he became the public face and thought-leader of the restoration effort. Instead of adopting a narrow perspective linking the shrine at Kayavarohan to the revival of a single sect, he advocated for the vital role played by temples and spiritual centers in society as a whole.

The importance of temples, prayer halls (mosques), and spiritual centers has been accepted by all religions from ancient times. It was these temples that served as the fountainhead from which dharma (religious ethics) and civilization spread all over the world. Whatever humanity exists in society today is due to the temples and holy saints who established them. In modern times, there are many different institutions that serve humanity with more being created every day. Temples are the birthplace of all of them.

In India our temples, saints, holy scriptures, classical music, and dance are the very soul of our civilization. In saying this I include those Jains, Buddhists, and Moslems living here for they are also Bharatiya (Indian) and have adopted and contributed to our civilization in their own way. We can see the value of this civilization by looking outward to foreign countries where many Indian temples are being built as places where non-Indians can put on our traditional dress to sing and dance while praying to God, with others leaving their homes to come here and study yoga.

At this time when the Indian civilization is being put on a high pedestal for having universal value, we should honor it here. If you want to live a noble life, if you wish to see future generations flourish, you should make the protection of our spiritual culture the highest object of your life. But its preservation cannot be achieved by the construction of majestic buildings alone. That will only be possible when we all make the effort to become true followers of the ancient rishis and sages. These saints saw temples as not just places of religious inspiration but centers of service where ever watchful well-wishers contemplated the welfare and needs of the people and acted to address their grievances. May God give us the grace to become true Bharatiyas.

The project gained momentum with the appointment of the noted Baroda industrialist, Nanubhai Amin, to the role of chairman. Sadly Hirabhai Patel died before the temple was finished, but his fervently-uttered deathbed wish that "construction continue uninterrupted until its completion" added to the urgency. The bold pronouncement of the administrators proved prophetic. On May 3, 1974, the temple was inaugurated with a throng in attendance to witness the installation of the Lakulish statue overseen by his holiness the Shankaracharya of Dwarka. Swami Kripalu said in his public address, *On this auspicious occasion, my heart goes out to the soul of Hirabhai Patel. I feel his absence today with an insufferable pang of agony. Wherever he might be, I convey this holy message: Dear brother, the temple has been built. The statue has been installed. Your sons and the elites of the shrine have cooperated in the fulfillment of your last wish. Your spiritual ambition has been realized. May your soul be at peace.* The inauguration was followed the next day by a slightly-belated but grand sixtieth birthday celebration.

Rebuilding the Temple

Three shots of the Kayavarohan Temple; Swami Kripalu preparing to address inauguration attendees; with the Shankaracharya of Dwarka, whose presence signified his acceptance of Kayavarohan as a 13th mahatirtha.

Reflections on Temple Construction: *I founded the Kayavarohan Shrine Association in 1965 and laid before its Board an ambitious plan. Hirabhai advanced the institution 60,000 rupees and later extended that to 100,000 rupees, but when board members learned the total cost of the project was a full 50,000,000 rupees many felt faint. This caused Hirabhai to confide to me in solitude, "Swami, people do not believe in shrines or mahatmas. They believe in miracles. You are a yogi. Even a single miracle will attract innumerable people and generate faith in them." I laughed aloud, "Hirabhai, there is one drawback to your proposal; it has no foundation. If I was in possession of yogic siddhis, I would not have set up this association. I would have banked only on miracles."*

Two years passed before the association could be registered to do business. Local residents gifted land to the institution and construction began, but innumerable difficulties cropped up to slow our progress. Floods, drought, famine, political instability, conflicts between community leaders – all these followed one after another. The project lumbered forward like a bullock cart until the appointment of Sri Nanubhai to the Executive Committee. With everyone working according to his directions, it quickly became a high speed motor car.

One day in solitude, Sri Nanubhai expressed his innermost thoughts to me, "Guruji, let Rajarshi Muni and I act as your hands and feet." After that Sri Nanubhai and Sant (saint) Rajarshi started working together enthusiastically. They gave detailed thought to the best manner in which to conduct the remaining work and then every aspect of the celebrations to follow. Clearly God who is all-merciful had sent me the right disciples at the critical time.

19 years had elapsed since my divine dream when it came time to install the statue in a special ceremony that went on continuously for four days. A multitude of 25,000 people participated, but then a most unusual event happened. Unbeknownst to us, another sacred site nearby celebrates a festival once every 18 years that is attended by 100,000 people. All these people found out about this new temple through a pamphlet, and the entire festival made a side trip to Kayavarohan. So in just a few days it became known to 125,000 people. From there, its fame has spread everywhere.

Given all the difficulties that had arisen to block its progress, I had to admire that Swami Kripalu not only initiated the temple project but persevered through years of difficulty to its completion. I felt at the time that there was a practical lesson in this for me. Although my goals were modest in comparison, I needed a daily dose of determination to overcome my own challenges. But the real value of this episode in Swami Kripalu's life only became apparent years later.

It was 1997 and Kripalu Center was struggling to emerge from the guru scandal that had torpedoed its ashram community in October, 1994. The majority of residents had left and the mood of those that remained was dark. An idea had been hatched to reorganize the institution into a program and retreat center, but the work required to implement it was staggering. An outside CEO had been hired to do the job, but she crashed and burned as competing staff factions paralyzed efforts to move forward. In the process, cash reserves had dwindled to the point where the professional advice was to file bankruptcy. When the Board asked me to return as President, Danna and I felt called to join the renewal effort, but I had little leadership experience and failure seemed inevitable. As Swami Kripalu demonstrated with the temple, when life drops an impossible task into your lap, there is always the possibility that somehow, if you step forward in service, God will do it.

A Second Level of Significance

Swami Kripalu gave several speeches associated with the temple's installation that piqued my curiosity. Reading them carefully, I was not at all surprised to find his view of the Kayavarohan temple transcending the typical notion of a religious house of worship. But his vision extended far beyond his progressive ideas on cultural renewal. In Swami Kripalu's eyes, this temple was a sacred space that enshrined the "secrets of yoga" and was thus able to silently impart a potent type of spiritual education.

A true temple is not a show piece of architecture; it is the place where the complex mysteries of yoga are depicted in the best possible manner. When reading a piece of drama, an ordinary impression is formed in the mind. When the same drama is acted out on stage by skilled artists, the impact on the mind and heart is extraordinary. This is entirely in accord with the science of psychology, which teaches us that different sentiments are aroused when we come in contact with various individuals, ideas, objects, and atmospheres. This ability of our surroundings to incite positive or negative sentiments becomes quite evident if we closely observe our experience.

The images of God appearing in a temple provide an education about the universe surrounding us that has qualities and forms. They are incomparable works of art, endowed with devotional feelings, prepared on the basis of the scriptures, and marked with mysterious symbols of yogic problems and their solutions. Worshipping these images causes pure sentiments to arise in the mind, where they can remain steady for a long time. This with-form meditation is most useful from a psychological

During the installation ceremony, the Lakulish statue was lowered through the temple roof to reflect the yogic teaching that higher spiritual forces can descend into physical form.

point of view, as it engenders peace, love, and heartfelt qualities such as humility, simplicity, self-control, tolerance, and non-violence. How an inanimate idol of stone can bring about a love for all animate beings is a profound mystery. But this is something well-known to saints, for whom meditation on God without form then becomes easy.

The reason that yogis carve statues and build temples is to preserve this secret symbolism of yoga. The pictorial alphabet they use conveys the immortal experiences of yoga and provides future aspirants the solutions they need to persevere in their practice. All the yogic secrets are embedded into the architecture and contents of the Kayavarohan temple. The Lakulish idol is not just a statue of dazzling beauty. It is a textbook of yoga, but in order to read it you must become a yogic worshipper and progress in your practice.

The Taj Mahal is an ideal work of art, but it was not sculpted in the language of samadhi. While everyone can receive inspiration from its beauty, it has no secret streams from the esoteric river of knowledge to convey. But when a yogi in a particular stage of practice comes into the Kayavarohan temple it is an open book. The symbolism is unveiled and these secrets can be understood very clearly. Seeing all the images and then looking at the main statue, tears will roll from that yogi's eyes.

Hearing that there were yogic secrets to decipher, it was impossible for me not to scrutinize everything at my disposal in a quest to bring them alive in my practice. One of the curious features of the Lakulish statue is that it shows a yogi in meditation who sports an obvious erection. This juxtaposition of sexual energy and spirituality is an important teaching. Anyone embarking on the spiritual path with a measure of ardor is likely to find that their interest in sex and outer pursuits temporarily subsides as they turn away from more conventional forms of gratification. But if they stick with their practice, they may enter a second phase where their sexual energy and other appetites markedly increase.

Saints of all religions have been anguished by this development, which often causes them to castigate themselves for a lack of mental purity. Others have gone further to punish their carnal bodies, sometimes quite severely, in an attempt to make their sexual thoughts and feelings stop. Still others express the energy by acting out in ways that harm individuals and generate scandals that denigrate the tradition. The Lakulish statue shows that this is not the yogic way. The primal energy must be allowed to awaken, revitalize the body, and ascend to the heart, head, and higher centers. Swami Kripalu was clear that this teaching applies to both householders and renunciates.

In both householder and renunciate yoga, it is necessary to awaken the evolutionary power. Without this, it is not possible to develop spiritually. Householders awaken this power in its partial and tolerable form. This is the way for them to progress in yoga while living in society. What makes renunciate yoga unique is that it awakens the evolutionary power in its complete, uncontrollable and terrifying form. The awakened energy is then allowed to surge powerfully through the system and the mind becomes unsteady. Because of this, self-control can be lost at any time, and disease and hallucinations are always standing nearby. Traveling on this path, I have come close to death five times and can say that renunciate yoga is only beneficial for individuals who have given up all desires and are willing to live in seclusion and practice only yoga for the rest of their lives.

A householder activating primal energy in its manageable form through healthy lifestyle and regular yoga practice uses the well-known techniques of asana, pranayama, and meditation to channel it into higher forms of expression. Alongside their yoga, householders were expected to practice moderation in their sexual activity (brahmacharya) to ensure they had ample energy to succeed in life and fuel their spiritual growth. The only yogic secret a householder like this needs to know is that encountering strong sexual energy is a sign that their practice is working. Skillful efforts should continue to channel it into healthy outlets as the bodymind is gradually purified.*

A celibate renunciate who awakens this energy in its furious form needs to take recourse in a second set of techniques to avoid problems and allow it to ascend and rapidly purify the system in pursuit of liberation. This is the defining difference between these two paths, and it is these renunciate techniques that are the subject of the yogic secrets. The difficulty of managing this "intolerable energy" is what explains the cloistered lifestyle of Swami Kripalu, with one meal a day brought to his house, no food kept in the kitchen, and limited people contact. Absent these safeguards and techniques, the awakened energy will find an outlet in overeating, sexual partners, or the pursuit of mental obsessions including money and power.

Some readers may be like me: a lover of yoga who dreams of doing the deeper practices. Enthusiastic yogis like us have a tendency to grossly underestimate the problems that can be caused by a premature unleashing of sexual energy, which can leave one feeling driven day and night by an overpowering compulsive force. Swami Kripalu minced no words in making this point.

> *When an aspirant's kundalini power has been aroused, strong sensuality awakens and his whole body is set alight and burns with desire. Facing a raging onslaught of sexual desire, he cannot find a way out of this predicament and becomes very afraid. As this passion blazes up, he encounters the fire of yoga in his own body and thinks, "Have I succumbed to some fever – why is there so much heat?" As days pass in this way the fire of this force keeps on increasing. The soles of his feet burn with heat, like iron objects put in a fire, and he feels the blood, flesh, and other constituent elements of his body melting. The ancient sages used the term "burning austerity" in their scriptures deliberately. It means to purify the body and mind by smelting. This is why Patanjali and others call yogis "the burners of impurity" and only an aspirant who encounters this fire of yoga will understand. If he succumbs to sensuality and desire, he will meet with a severe downfall. Unless proper help is available, he will be harassed by the sexual energy and forced to give up his sadhana to regain mental control. Only if he acquires the knowledge of special yogic techniques through the grace of God, guru, or scripture can he continue to tread the yogic path. If he does so, spontaneous mudra practice will begin and he will become aware of the various glands and energy centers existing in his body and experience the slow process of their blooming and flowering. Nirvikalpa (without fluctuation) samadhi cannot be achieved without passing through this fire.*

---

*There are without doubt many areas of knowledge, subtle distinctions, and spiritual doorways that a householder yogi must learn or pass through to advance to Self-realization. However none of these must be kept secret. They can generally be addressed directly in teachings and texts. It is because certain renunciate practices can distract, mislead, and cause harm that they are kept secret.

Given his personal experience, it was easy for Swami Kripalu to explain how the mudras when empowered by awakened-energy can uplevel physical and mental health – see Chapter 5. But confronted by the inconvenient truth of his his guru's true age and identity, he struggled to understand how they could possibly render a human being so long-lived as to be called immortal. I was fascinated to find a transcript memorializing his response to this question when asked directly.

A student once asked me, "Please explain the basis of the divine body in scientific terms." This truth was brought to light by the great seers and sages of the past, who approached the most difficult problems of life in a systematic fashion. So the best answer to this question can be found in the scriptures these masters left behind including the Yoga Sutra, Pashupat Sutra, Yoga Bija, Yoga Chudamani Upanishad, Shandilya Upanishad, Shvetashvatar Upanishad, Yoga Kundali Upanishad, Maha Upanishad, Hatha Yoga Pradipika, Goraksha Paddhati, and Gheranda Samhita. But most aspirants cannot study all these scriptures, so I will tell you the basic principles on the basis of my experience.

Birth, childhood, adulthood, old age, and death are the stages of bodily life. This cycle goes on and its stages seem like unavoidable bonds, a fixed order of things that cannot be opposed. The scriptures agree that anyone, even an ardent yogi, who has death will have birth because in this there is no choice. But the greatest of yogis discovered a way to interrupt this cycle by preventing death. That is why their texts declare that the mudras (energy seals) allow a yogi to drink the soma – the nectar of immortality – which brings about the destruction of disease, old age, and death. But scientifically how could this be so?

Those who think that the divine body is attained by drinking the juice of some plant or alchemical formula do not know the science of yoga. Yes, these yogis do drink a nectar, but the juice they drink is not to be found in the external world. The divine body is brought into being when the outward flowing glands of an adult once again become inward flowing like in childhood, a reversal process engendered by the energy seals.

Until boys and girls enter puberty, their sexual fluids are not discharged and lost. They are absorbed into the blood and this fuels their vigorous health, bodily maturation, and mental flowering. When they become adolescents, the sexual drive asserts itself and one day or another their lower door opens and never shuts again. With their energies flowing down and out, they become travelers on the path of aging and death.

There is a world of difference between a siddha yogi or yogini and a prepubescent boy or girl, but the secret source of their bodily health is the same. By bringing the mind to one-pointed concentration in the center of the eyebrows, a yogi can close the downward passageway so their sexual fluids begin to once again mix with the blood.

Just as full excitation of the genitals occurs in the earlier mudras to increase the production of these fluids, full excitation of the tongue occurs in khechari mudra. First the tubule vessel bundle is cut asunder. Next comes the moving and milking of the tongue. When the tongue is stable in the uvula and the gaze remains established in the center of the eyebrows, the yogi receives the splendid opportunity to drink the nectar of immortality (the secretion of the pineal and pituitary glands that the tip of the tongue is stimulating). At first he becomes free from ailments, but his body continues to undergo changes and his old age is gradually taken away. In the beginning, he may look middle aged and later like a young man and in the end a youth. This is the special characteristic of the divine body: the old body fades away and a new, young body is obtained without death. This is why the author of the Hatha Yoga Upanishad says that the yogi, being freed from old age, becomes a youth of sixteen years.

The seers and sages who made these discoveries were neither infatuated with the body nor afraid of old age and death. They were seeking to reach the highest consciousness. Old age and death were obstacles in the way, so they overcame them and became urdhvareta yogis, which means one who has completely overcome lust so all their sexual fluids and energy are rising upward to be transmuted into light. The divine body is the outward sign of this inner accomplishment.

My beloved Gurudev shone with this light; there was such power in his eyes because he was urdhvareta. The history of India attests that every 500 to 1000 years a great seer or sage like Kapila, Patanjali, Yajnavalkya, Vasishtha, or Jnaneshvara reaches to this divine-body stage and lives among the people, with society bearing witness to their perpetual youth. My aim is to become urdhvareta like my guru, so I follow the teachings of these great masters. On this path only an individual who has achieved the divine body is considered a complete yogi. All other outstanding people are to be regarded as sadhaks (practitioners). An urdhvareta yogi possesses a power of intelligence and abilities that are unimaginable. This is why such great persons, adored by the world, are considered to be incarnations of God.

In several speeches, Swami Kripalu repeated an inspiring statement that he never went on to explain: *In Kayavarohan, I beheld the supreme truth of the ages and through its inspiration alone became eager to serve it.* Only after all my study and sleuthing did I gain an idea of what he was perhaps trying to communicate. It was in Kayavarohan that Swami Kripalu saw firsthand that an individual practicing sahaja yoga in its renunciate form – through ardent efforts, yogic wisdom, and Divine Grace – could overcome death and attain to a state that was god-like. Having seen this ultimate goal or *telos* of yoga, which reflects the power of the evolutionary drive instilled by nature in each of us, Swami Kripalu immediately felt a responsibility to preserve this astounding truth discovered by the ancient Indian sages for future generations through the art and architecture of the temple.

Being a simple student, it was impossible for me to evaluate the validity of this belief. Instead of getting lost in an intellectual debate, I chose to shelve my doubts and disbelief, affirm that the yoga practices I was doing were providing me many tangible benefits, and ask the obvious next question. Why did Swami Kripalu leave Kayavarohan and come to America?

Readers wanting to know more are directed to story 6-1 in the appendix of teaching stories.

CHAPTER 7

Coming to America

From a distance, I was able to imagine that America was a place where yoga and the ideals of ancient India could take rebirth. Today, I see it personally.

With the Kayavarohan temple built and festivities over, Swami Kripalu resumed his silence in the form of *mitdarshan* (the practice of speaking only when necessary) and made frequent use of his chalkboard. He was eager to return to his quiet life of study and practice, but living next to the temple complex made that impossible, as its visitors and volunteer staff generated a constant stream of activity. It was now five years since he'd left Malav where his privacy had been respected and his willingness to reside in a public place was reaching its limit. He let the temple administrators know that a solution needed to be found.

Two more years passed before a house could be built on the outskirts of the temple grounds, which he moved into in 1976. While the noise lessened, he was still regarded as the temple's spiritual head and expected to make daily appearances. He was also regularly called upon to weigh in on important decisions and resolve leadership disputes. Another year passed in this manner and Swami Kripalu began to talk about finding a hut in Rishikesh where he would be left alone to complete his sadhana. When that idea was opposed, he asked his top student to take his place in Kayavarohan while he moved back to his tiny Malav ashram. This provided some relief, but the proximity of the two towns made it easy for the administrators to keep him involved in temple business. It seemed that no one was taking his need for solitude seriously.

Swami Kripalu had numerous students living in the West and he'd repeatedly turned down invitations to visit their yoga centers in Europe and North America. When Yogi Desai and Charles Berner (Yogeshwar Muni) extended yet another invite in early 1977, they must have conveyed the notion that leaving India was the only way to resume his one-pointed practice, as the 64 year-old Swami Kripalu stunned everyone by immediately announcing a four month trip to America. He had never before been out of India.

Despite the protests of his Indian followers, Swami Kripalu remained firm in his decision. He would leave for America in three months. Sendoffs were organized in Kayavarohan and Bombay, where he stayed for a week with the family of Ramanbhai Patel in the coastal suburb of Borivali. When the time came, Swami Kripalu boarded a jet scheduled to land at New York City's Kennedy airport on May 20, 1977. After a lengthy flight, he arrived shortly after midnight and wrote a chalkboard greeting to several dozen students gathered in a special reception area reserved to welcome him.

My travel to America was a trick of fate. I'd been longing for seclusion and thinking of going to the Himalayas permanently. Several of my disciples were running ashrams in different countries. They had often invited me to visit but I'd always declined because of the disruption it would cause my sadhana. This time things happened in such a way that I consented. They simply asked me very kindly, and I said, "Okay, I am coming," and the trip was arranged quite suddenly. This is how the destination of my pilgrimage of seclusion was accidentally changed to America.

Swami Kripalu addresses his JFK welcoming party.

> *I am extremely pleased to meet you. At present, I am in such a critical stage of yoga sadhana that I cannot travel even two furlongs. Yet under such circumstances, I have arrived after traveling thousands of miles in a plane. I attribute that to the miracle of your love. Only saints can do miracles and if that is true you are all saints. Now I pray that your love can do another miracle in helping me reach my highest goal. I am the well-wisher of your country, which is thirsty for spiritual knowledge. On this special occasion, my heart is overflowing with good wishes that you and your country may similarly attain to that which you most aspire. My heartfelt blessing to you all.*

Swami Kripalu left the metropolitan airport on a late night drive to the rural retreat center of Yogi Desai in Summit Station, Pennsylvania, which already bore his name. It was 4:00 AM when the car carrying Swami Kripalu turned onto a winding gravel driveway that led to the Kripalu Yoga Retreat and was met by several hundred more welcomers. Setting his chalkboard aside, he motioned for a microphone. Clearing his throat, he surprised everyone by delivering his first talk in the West.

> *You'll have to excuse me as brother tongue is a bit rusty. I haven't spoken for a long time and it's like trying to start an old engine. I passed the last several hours from New York to here with great difficulty. My whole being was being drawn into meditation, so much that I had to almost fight it. When a yogi enters samadhi, the mind becomes no mind, and this should not be allowed to happen publicly.*
>
> *There was no possibility of my coming here and yet I have come. Upon becoming a swami, I surrendered my life completely to God. It must be God's will that I am here. Some force has brought me here. I attribute that to the magnet of your love.*
>
> *The spiritual heritage of India is glorious. It is called Sanatana Dharma, the way of eternal truth, a spiritual path that is sublime and forever alive. Its outer form, the one you are practicing now, is worthwhile but preliminary. You can easily shave your head, wear Indian clothes, or take a Sanskrit name, but it is not so easy to digest the true principles of yoga and express them at the level of living. Still it is good you have begun to travel this path, and you will be able to experience its beauty and profundity more and more. If you can digest even a few of the principles I teach, my coming here will be worthwhile.*
>
> *When the people of India look at the glory of their past, its spiritual brightness and depth, they are ashamed at their country's current state. The ancient rishis who gave birth to that heritage lived on a high plane that is almost beyond description. Only a few people in India are still trying to live that way. From a distance, I was able to imagine that America was a place where the ideals of yoga and*

ancient India could take rebirth, but today I see it personally.

I have not come to propagate Indian religion or even spread yoga and meditation. I have simply come to meet you. I am still in seed form myself. I haven't yet become a tree that can give shade to others. Only a perfect master who has reached the final heights of yoga can give its knowledge to the world in a pure form. I have faith that I will finish my sadhana here and that your love will be a great help to me. After leaving you, I will take a bath and go into my meditation room and pray to God, "For a day and a half, I have not been able to be with you." Then I'll enter into meditation and start my sadhana.

I am very much pleased by everything I see. Consider me your spiritual grandfather. May all of us march together in a great procession to the gates of heaven and all the way to the feet of the Lord. That is my blessing. Since this is the day of my coming, I have spoken verbally in order to add to your joy. Later on, I will speak only on special occasions. My special blessing to you all.

Swami Kripalu in the upper right speaking to a group at the Summit Station Yoga Retreat soon after his arrival in the States.

Even after coming here (to America), it was my intention to keep my silence. But seeing you and feeling that you are my children desirous of practicing yoga, I decided that if I speak a little and teach you personally by my own speech it is better. This way whatever I tell you is coming directly from my experience. So after 17 years of silence, I'm going to speak for two or three months, and then observe silence again.

Over the next three months, Swami Kripalu visited yoga centers in New Jersey, California, and Montreal, Canada. Moved by the sincerity of the students he encountered, he set aside his silence and spoke twice a day, delivering over a hundred talks interspersed with a wealth of teaching stories. He also played the harmonium and sang *bhajans* (devotional songs) that he'd written at important junctures of his life, after which he would explain the meaning of the lyrics.

The three magical months of talking, teaching, and storytelling that followed Swami Kripalu's arrival in America soon came to an end. On September 11, 1977, he announced that he was re-entering seclusion and moved into a small, two-story cottage near the top of a steep hill overlooking the Sumneytown yoga ashram to pursue his sadhana with undivided attention. The cottage had been designed and built by volunteers in 1973 and christened *Muktidham*, the *abode of liberation*, with a dream that Swami Kripalu would someday come from India to practice there. Yogi Desai's wife, Mataji, personally cooked his daily meal and coordinated a small crew of ashram residents who kept the house clean, brought fresh flowers for his altar, and performed necessary maintenance tasks.

Swami Kripalu found life in America to his liking. He loved Muktidham, which had a downstairs room where he could study, write, and receive visitors, and an upstairs room where he practiced during the day and slept on the floor at night. He reveled in the sense of solitude fostered by its elevated location and wooded surroundings. He lived alone with no telephone, radio, television, or food. His only contact with people occurred at 7:00 AM when close students could visit and at 10:00 AM when his daily meal was delivered. He communicated via a slate chalkboard and also wrote letters to India describing himself as *very cheerful*. Finally, he was in a place where he could do his practice undisturbed.

In Sumneytown where I live, it is extremely beautiful. Although such natural beauty is common in America, the setting would delight the heart and eyes of anyone. My house is totally secluded in a thick forest with many tall trees. A small garden around the house adds even more beauty. It is completely tranquil; sometimes deer walk by.

This is a proper place for yoga and I like it very much. I want to do nothing but yoga sadhana and have no interest in any other activities. Since America is a foreign country, I have to obtain permission from the government again and again if I want to stay. If this were not the case, I would pretend this is Uttarkashi, a small town on the banks of the Ganges River 8000 feet high in the Himalayas, and stay here permanently.

Before coming to America, Swami Kripalu had read a Gujarati version of the Bible to learn about the religious background of the people he would meet. He was taken by the New Testament and considered Jesus a great yogi whose penance had perfected his moral character and brought him miraculous powers, and whose ascension raised profound questions about our potential for spiritual salvation and eternal life. After settling into Muktidham, he began writing *The Passion of Christ*, a heartfelt retelling of the crucifixion story, and regularly referenced Jesus in his talks.

Christmas Discourse: *I am very glad to be present among you on this day of Sri Christ's birth. Great masters may be born in an unknown place, but their life does not pass in darkness. Sri Christ is one of the great light bearers of the world. Yesterday I received a book that had a picture of holy Christ hanging on the cross with nails in his hands and feet. I was so overwhelmed by his agony that I had to close the book. The picture created a profound change in me, and I was carried into the past two thousand years ago, and the life of Christ came alive for me.*

Swami Kripalu as he appeared shortly after his arrival in 1977.

Sri Christ gave great importance to purity and self-control because one cannot enter the kingdom of heaven without pure thoughts and actions. Many individuals, when finding lots of impure qualities in themselves, become disappointed. They feel that this great army of evil qualities cannot be destroyed in spite of millions of efforts. But here it is necessary to keep in mind one principle. When one seed of goodness gets planted, a whole garland of virtues comes to us.

Today on this auspicious celebration of Christ's birth, let us plant one seed of virtue. Although there are many virtues, love is the highest among them. Wherever there is love, there is God. Wherever there is love there is happiness, peace, and bliss. This is known as Vaikuntha or heaven. Ordinarily we believe that those who are breathing are alive and those who do not breathe are dead. But this belief is not completely true. Only if love exists within a man is he alive in a true sense.

Those who plant the seed of love in their heart will have to nourish it with the water of patience. Whenever you are able to practice patience with your family members and loved ones, know that true religion is entering into your life. Love has a divine power. When the grand tree of love grows in the heart of a person, his language, eyes, and actions are miraculously transformed. As a result, individuals who come in contact with him also receive the seeds of love. Thus, love brings happiness to oneself as well as to others.

Our close ones are thirsty for love. If we do not offer them the cup of love, the reservoir of our heart will become a poisoned reservoir. Today on the auspicious day of Christ's birth celebration, break through the barriers that prevent the reservoir of your love from flowing. Allow the torrent of love to flow towards your loved ones freely, and let them dive into it. This is my message to you. Sri Christ loved prayer very much and considered it the highest means of devotion. Let us meditate silently together for a few minutes before ending.

For the next four years, Swami Kripalu sustained his intensive 10 hours-per-day practice schedule. He only spoke twice a year, once at his January birthday celebration and again on *Guru Purnima*, the traditional Indian July festival of the full moon that honors spiritual teachers. On these occasions he delivered a formal discourse, speaking in Gujarati from a written script with the help of an English translator. He also appeared weekly on Sunday afternoons to enable people to be with him, keeping silence but often writing a message on his slate. He remained prolific, writing four substantive tracts on different aspects of yoga, two devotional songs, and continuing work on his commentary to the Hatha Yoga Pradipika. With Swami Kripalu in residence, both the Sumneytown ashram and Summit Station yoga retreat buzzed with activity. At a time when

The Muktidham abode of Swami Kripalu; before his altar; relaxing in his study; at his sitting desk.

yoga was largely unknown, hundreds of Americans and Canadians embarked upon its path of self-development by virtue of his inspiration and written guidance.

During his first year in America, Swami Kripalu received a steady stream of pleas from his Indian followers to end his visit. *Most Merciful Gurudev, You have been the creative force behind Kayavarohan. It is solely due to your inspiration that the temple was built, and it is only through your presence in India that its dynamic progress can be maintained. We therefore, most humbly, pray that you be kind enough to return to us as soon as possible.* Swami Kripalu replied, *It was only by divine inspiration that I took up the task of serving the holy place of Kayavarohan. I made it my home in spite of the distractions to my sadhana, which is dear to me. Eventually, so many disruptions arose that I was constrained to leave. I have never thought, even in my dreams, that Kayavarohan was my work. If it is God's will that I remain instrumental in serving that holy place, then I shall surely be back.*

Swami Kripalu writing a message on his chalkboard.

Despite the disappointment of his Indian students and the uncertainty involved in renewing his visa, Swami Kripalu extended his stay from four months to four-and-a-quarter years.

While in America, Swami Kripalu's yoga practice continued to evolve with his expression growing ever more subtle. The postures, kriyas, and bodily mudras that characterized his earlier practice grew less prominent and were replaced by *dhyana mudras*, flowing hand movements and gestures often accompanied by spontaneous chanting. While rhythmic and entrancing to watch, these movement flows are best seen as an outward reflection of meditation, as their purpose was to transport him into an active and embodied samadhi.

Swami Kripalu doing *dhyana mudras* (meditation gestures).

> **Swami Kripalu Reflects on his Yoga Sadhana:** *Today is my 66th birthday, and I have been a swami for 37 years. My nature has totally changed since entering the final stages of yoga. In the past, I deferred to the likes and dislikes of my disciples. Now, even if I try, I cannot act that way. I'm an old yogi wanting only liberation. All my disciples must now lock their desires in a box and throw away the key. That would be true devotion to their guru.*
>
> *It's difficult to know how far my sadhana has come. I can only say that it proceeds tirelessly on its pilgrimage and continues to progress. I don't know when it will reach its destination, because sometimes it appears to be close and at other times far away. A complete yogi is free of mind. The scriptures say that as long as an aspirant yearns for liberation, he's an incomplete yogi. Only when he forgets even this desire does he become a true yogi. Since I still eagerly await liberation, I must be in a stage prior to this statement.*

Swami Kripalu came to America a robust man in excellent health. In early 1978, he started losing weight, which he took as a positive sign. Ardent yogis often commenced their practice with a period of fasting in which the body becomes thin or even emaciated. In his commentary on the Hatha Yoga Pradipika verse 2.78, he called this the *first lean*. Once established in a regular practice, the yogi would regain a natural weight. But in the end stages of practice, he taught that the fire of yoga (*yogagni*) blazed up to completely purify the yogi and produce the radiant body displayed by his guru. He called the emaciation produced during this end stage of yoga the *second lean*.* As Swami Kripalu lost weight, his body began to generate intense internal heat, which tracked with this description. No one knew what to expect, as there was no record of a modern yogi passing through this process.

> *For the past year, I have been in a stage where prana and apana (the upward and downward flowing energies) have united and rush into the head with the speed of a tornado. My mind is attempting to merge with the inner light, which various texts describe as the way that the beyond-mind state arises. Because of the enormous power of these energies, the mind becomes extremely shaken. With these energies working in my brain, my head remains as hot as a boiler. This continues night and day, whether I'm asleep or awake. It is difficult for me to eat and when I do eat to taste what I have eaten. As a result of these difficulties, a yogi can suddenly start behaving like a child or a crazy person. Sometimes I don't understand if my feet are wearing my shoes, or my shoes are wearing my feet! I could never have imagined, even in my dreams, that it would be this difficult to become a sthitaprajnya (a yogi who has stabilized a state of samadhi). Don't worry about me at all. Being under the constant protection of my Gurudev and the Almighty, I am absolutely at peace.*

---

*All the photographs from *Asana and Mudra* featured herein were taken of Swami Kripalu during the late stages of his first lean. The photos on the prior page were taken in his second lean.

During 1979 and 1980, the ashram community watched their spiritual grandfather bear the rigors of this emaciation. Swami Kripalu remained in good spirits, even when strange burns appeared on his hands and feet, towels soaked in ice water had to be placed on his head to enable him to tolerate the heat, and it became difficult at times for him to walk. Everyone took solace in the happy disposition he displayed, his confident assurances that his practice was headed in the right direction, and the brightness of his eyes. It was a skeletal Swami Kripalu who began his January 1981 birthday celebration by saying, *To start off the festivities, I am in the mood to crack some jokes.* After a string of one-liners, he delivered an insightful discourse on personality and character that made it clear there was absolutely nothing wrong with his mind.

This is the point in his life story when I entered the picture, meeting Swami Kripalu during one of his Sunday afternoon appearances in May of 1981. While pencil thin, he didn't occur to me as ill. Much to the contrary, he seemed the most vital person I'd ever met. Looking back it makes sense to me that no one suspected that his time in America, let alone his life, was coming to an end. Yet it was only two months later on Guru Purnima when he gave his final public discourse in America on what he described as his favorite topic: love.

At times I feel hesitant to speak because I cannot express myself in your language. Is there any language that is not exclusively yours or mine? Yes, it's the language of love. The language of love is the language of the heart and feelings. While the language of words

Excerpt from January 1981 Discourse: Human behavior is so intricate that even wise men with sharp intellects are led astray when trying to analyze it. On the path of yoga, a broad understanding of psychological principles is put forth to help a person not only understand right action but put it into action. According to this view, character traits are the etchings carved into the mind by one's repeated thoughts and actions. Knowing this, personality is easy to understand. It's the sum total of our character traits. Character traits are the pieces that when put together make up the whole of our personality. Yoga teaches us how to remove the character traits that bring harm by strengthening those that incline us in the direction of right action and growth. We can easily straighten out the tail of a dog, but the moment we let go it snaps back into its original shape. So too with our personality, which is why the character building process inevitably requires patience, enthusiasm, and perseverance.

Touching his hot head; laughing off his symptoms; lecturing masterfully; near the end of his time in America.

is elaborate, it doesn't always convey our true or intended feelings. The wordless language of love is directly conveyed and always received with crystal clarity.

Some time ago, a person raised his hand in a lecture and asked me a question. "You're telling us that each person is searching for religion. I agree that we are all searching for something, but I don't think its religion." This reflects the problem with words. Let's not use religion then, or Sanatana Dharma, or even yoga. Now tell me, aren't we all searching for love, happiness, peace, and bliss? Whenever we lose contact with these, our bodies slump in grief or boredom. But when we find them, all our searching stops and the restlessness in our mind ceases. Real religion always manifests as love, happiness, peace, and bliss.

There is a famous verse in the scriptures of India: "Truly, the wise proclaim that love is the only path. Love is the only God, and love is the only scripture." Impress this verse upon your memory and chant it constantly if you want to realize your dreams of growth. Many of you have flowerpots in your homes. Don't you also wish to plant and nurture the seedling of love in the flowerpot of your heart? The fragrance of a flower can perfume a house, but love's fragrance can perfume the entire world.

The path of love is very ancient. When I was born, I received the initiation of love. Now, with the same love, I initiate everyone else. Countless times, I have dipped into the world's highest scriptures and received only love from them. In love there are no barriers of language, no costumes, no egos, and no distinctions of any kind. Lord Love is everything to me. Love is my only path. I am in fact a pilgrim on the path of love.

Soon after this discourse, Swami Kripalu's hands and feet began to swell. Several physicians were brought to examine him. Despite the urging of his closest students, Swami Kripalu chose not to pursue any form of medical diagnosis or treatment, saying that a yogi who cannot face death will never reach the feet of the Lord. When it became apparent his condition was serious, Swami Kripalu decided to return to India. On September 27, 1981, his American followers gathered to say goodbye. While his attitude remained positive, those attending were overcome by sadness at the thought that he was leaving them. His last message was written on his slate.

Parting Words. *I came here to America solely to meet you and imagined I would only stay for a few months. But today four and a quarter years have passed away. During my stay, I've had the good fortune of bathing in the lake of your love and drinking its waters daily. These four and a quarter years have passed by like four and a quarter days. I have experienced great happiness with your service. I consider the love of every one of you as the love of the Lord Himself. For me, it has been a divine gift.*

Today, our sweet dream has come to an end. At the last Guru Purnima celebration, I said that I would be going into complete seclusion. That decision was necessary for my sadhana. Now I beg your permission to say farewell. I belong to the Lord, and I sincerely pray that I will always belong to Him.

Beloved children, do not give up virtuous conduct and self-discipline even in the face of death. Keep unflinching faith in the holy lotus feet of the Lord and continue to practice mantra recitation, bhajans, chanting, meditation, pranayama, postures, observing holy vows, fasting, moderation in diet, the study of scriptures, and other disciplines. I extend my blessings to everyone. Your loving grandfather.

Two days later, Swami Kripalu walked out the front door of Muktidham for the last time and turned to face the building. With graceful dignity, he brought his hands together in prayer position to offer his respect to his American home. Then he lay face down on the ground and stretched his arms overhead in a gesture of deep reverence for the four years of shelter and solitude it had provided him. He said goodbye to his residence with the same love we might show in bidding farewell to a beloved friend. A few minutes later, he was in a car and on his way to the airport. Oblivious to this unfolding drama, I was not yet through my third week of law school.

The gathering called for Swami Kripalu to say goodbye to ashram residents; Swami Kripalu shortly before he left America.

Readers wanting to know more are directed to story 7-1 in the appendix of teaching stories.

CHAPTER 8

Return to India

"Lord, I am yours." This prayer is my sadhana. I have lived with this prayer and earnestly wish to die with it on my lips.

Swami Kripalu flew to Bombay on September 29, 1981, where he once again stayed in the Borivali home of Ramanbhai Patel. Reports back to the states were positive as he was able to resume his normal schedule. But word of his return began to spread and by mid-December it was apparent that he would need to leave the city to escape the numbers of people wanting to see him.

Swami Kripalu went to Ahmedabad on December 25, where a private bungalow had been rented to serve as his residence. He tried to restart his routine but his condition quickly worsened over the next three days to the point that he could only lie on a floor mat covered with blankets. Although his whereabouts had to be kept secret, Swami Kripalu was surrounded by those dearest to him. Alert and coherent, he maintained his sweet disposition and allayed everyone's concern by saying this was just part of his sadhana.

On the evening of December 28th, Swami Kripalu uncharacteristically did not want to retire at his regular time. Two close disciples stayed by his side as he talked intimately about his life, yoga, and God. Conversing late into the night, his mind remained sharp and clear until sleep finally came.

Swami Kripalu Reflects on his Life: *After my sanyas initiation, I started traveling the shores of the Narmada River. As a novice swami, I slept outside or stayed in temples, and the villagers would invite me into their homes to share meals. I would arrive at the appointed time and sit with them on an ordinary floor mat. When nothing was laid down, I sat on the ground. To me the love of my hosts was of primary importance. The quality of the mat was secondary.*

As my name and fame spread, society began to respect me. Ordinary mats disappeared and were replaced by comfortable rugs, backrests, and chairs. Usually I traveled on foot, but people started making arrangements for me to ride. Then my hosts began to provide me with private residences and even beds with silken-sheets. A swami is expected to move within different levels of society and live in accordance with the way that each class lives. Some of these luxuries I liked and some I didn't. I was simply cooperating with other people's wishes and doing what was normal and convenient for them. Yet my mind was constantly stuck with one pain. I was gradually becoming distant from those simple and devoted villagers who had provided for me when I was young and unknown.

To make matters worse, in my early years as a swami I was able to give more of my time to the people because my secluded activities were minimal. But then I started yoga sadhana and anyone wanting to see me had to make an appointment ahead of time. Even then they would hardly get 5 or 10 minutes with me. Many people disliked this arrangement and came to the conclusion that I had become uncaring and a lover of luxury. With all my heart, I can only say that I am the same person now that I was all those years ago. There has not been any change in my love or personality.

When Swami Kripalu woke at five the next morning, he was too weak to get up by himself. After being helped into a sitting position, he asked to be left alone so he could meditate. At one-thirty, he again requested help getting up so he could sit for meditation, but sharp pains prevented this and he had to be laid back down upon a pillow to rest. At six in the evening, he began rapid breathing and then all breath ceased. Those with him reported that his face took on the look of one in deep meditation, and then shifted into a blissful expression. A lengthy period followed in which it was unclear whether Swami Kripalu was dead or in samadhi, as he had left instructions that it was possible for him to enter a death-like state and remain there for hours or even days. With his body perfectly still, his face remained serene. A Brahman priest was summoned to perform the equivalent of last rites, after which the continuous chanting of mantra was started.

Doctors were called to assess his condition. Two came swiftly and neither could detect any vital signs. Both declared him dead but also noted that Swami Kripalu's body remained curiously life-like and supple. A third doctor arrived later that night, followed by another in the morning. All four were of the opinion that Swami Kripalu had expired but none could explain the absence of rigor mortis. Everyone waited for some definitive sign that his soul had passed on. By eleven o'clock the next night, swelling in the abdomen made it clear that Swami Kripalu had died December 29, 1981, at the age of 68. Word went out to all his followers. Blocks of ice were placed on trays to keep the room cool, and the mantra chanting was sustained until the following evening by a steady stream of disciples and devotees coming to pay their respects to their beloved teacher.

When I look back on my life, nowhere can I find evidence of unusual foresight or brilliance. To the contrary, I have acted foolishly not just once but innumerable times. Only by grace has the stage I have reached been attained. Only this grace seems the ultimate truth to me.

Swami Kripalu's departure from this life was treated as the *mahasamadhi* or conscious departure from the body of a great saint and announced on All India Radio. His corpse was laid on a bed of flowers and driven from Ahmedabad to the Kayavarohan temple. It is not considered proper to bring a cadaver inside a temple, so his body was brought to its front steps for a final audience with his beloved guru. Then it was taken to his former residence on the temple grounds, where people came to pay their respects. From there the funeral procession continued to his former ashram in Malav, where he laid in state to receive the villagers who'd cared for him for years before. A large pit grave had been dug on a site directly across the street from the ashram, donated for that purpose by one of his favorite families. Despite the short notice, there were thousands in attendance. Heaped with flowers, he was buried the afternoon of December 31st only 40 hours after his death. The curious flexibility of his spine and joints remained, enabling his body to be easily interred in the manner appropriate to a saint, upright and seated.

Absent any embalming, burials must take place quickly in India, and it's the custom to memorialize the passing of a loved one on the 16th day after death. For Swami Kripalu, this was January 13th which happened to be his 69th birthday. As the day dawned, Malav was overrun by a fleet of cars, carts, vans, and busses carrying people from throughout the region for a final ceremony. A standing throng surrounded a tiny domed temple built by the villagers directly over the grave and made entirely of marigolds. Inside, a simple altar bore a small photograph of Swami Kripalu encircled by a garland of flowers. After the proper public rituals, an assembly of swamis, saints, and dignitaries entered a much-larger tent adjacent to the gravesite to give his eulogy. Its dirt floor

Two shots of the marigold temple; people gathered for the burial and memorial service; dignitaries sitting upfront with Yogi Desai speaking.

was covered with Indian cloth and patterned rugs. The speakers sat on a raised dais on either side of a large photograph of Swami Kripalu circled by another garland of flowers.

Surrounding the tent were people belonging to all levels of society. Rustic farmers stood elbow to elbow with village shopkeepers, local artisans, professional people, and wealthy urban merchants. Everywhere were grandmothers, grandfathers, parents, and countless children. All had come to pay their last respects to a man they truly loved. After the ceremonies were complete, the tent and makeshift temple emptied as the dignitaries made their way across the street to the ashram. The crowd followed in their footsteps and a small army of servers appeared carrying oversized kettles of steaming food. Everyone present was served an Indian feast of puris, dhal, rice, and sweets. Swami Kripalu loved and lived his life in accord with the Vedic maxim *Vasudeva Khatumbhakam*, which means *the whole world is one family*. In a fitting tribute, old and young, rich and poor, low caste and high caste, householders and renunciates, all sat down on the ground to eat from leaf plates in an uncommon act of unity.

In India there are inspiring phrases written on the trolleys and buses. While getting on and off or watching them drive by, you will read some line that conveys the essence of the culture and teachings. This is just like your advertising, only it is used to promote spiritual values.

******

After immersing myself in his life story, it felt imperative to know as much as I could about its ending. I was grateful for two accounts that made this possible. The first was from a married couple, Eric Baldwin (Umesh) and Nor Baldwin (Vasanti), who'd grown close to Swami Kripalu while living in the Pennsylvania ashram. As an ashram photographer, Umesh had developed a personal relationship with Swami Kripalu while taking pictures of him, including many of those appearing in this book. While traveling in India, they heard about his return through a seemingly chance encounter on the streets of Ahmedabad with one of his swami caretakers and were able to visit and speak with Swami Kripalu the day before his death. They stayed on to participate in all the events associated with his burial and memorial service.

Yogi Desai and Sandra Healy (Krishnapriya) also attended the memorial service. Afterward, Krishnapriya wrote movingly of her experience. While en route to Malav in a van of non-English-speaking Indians, she was unable to participate in their conversation. Gazing out the window, she began to notice that many of the buildings facing the road featured a picture of Swami Kripalu along with a short quotation written in Gujarati script. These were not new paintings but years old, a form of public messaging that she likened to billboards. Arriving at the gravesite, she was dumbstruck by the size of the crowd assembled, which she described as equivalent to that of a rock concert or major sporting event. Her conclusion was that it was almost impossible for Americans to grasp the scale of Swami Kripalu's popularity in his home country.

In the 1980s a *mandir* or shrine was erected on the gravesite where Swami Kripalu's memory remains alive today.

Reflecting on his death, I saw how Swami Kripalu had progressed through all four stages of the traditional yogic lifecycle called the *ashramas*.* I'd read about these in college – student, householder, retiree, renunciate – where they'd struck me as interesting but a little simplistic. Seeing them mirrored in Swami Kripalu's life made me realize their value. In each stage, a person has a clear individual focus and societal role to play. The task of a student is to honor their parents and respect their teachers to obtain the best possible start in life. Although Swami Kripalu's schooling was cut short after the death of his father, he was able to successfully complete this stage through a combination of his own tenacity and the help of his guru.

The role of a householder is to pursue their calling in life by developing their talents in early adulthood to support their family and expressing them masterfully in their prime years to maximize their contribution to society. While Swami Kripalu didn't marry and raise children – the conventional householder duties – he did pass through this stage as a music teacher supporting his mother and brother. More significantly, the process of self-actualization underlying this stage carried into his initial years as a swami when he served as a Sanskrit teacher, rose to fame as an orator, did many good works, and cultivated the virtuous disposition that made people consider him a true saint. Happily engaged in these pursuits, Swami Kripalu achieved outward success and enjoyed a genuine sense of fulfillment.

---

*The four stages of life were *brahmacharya* (celibate student); *grihastha* (literally house-holder); *vanaprastha* (forest-dweller but often translated as hermit or retiree); and *sanyas* (renounced). A member of the Brahmin caste was expected to progress through all four stages. Swami Kripalu recognized that in modern India the ashramas had ceased to be a practical teaching, yet he occasionally referenced them because he felt they espoused yogic values that lent spiritual significance to every stage of life.

In ancient India, four ashramas or stages of life were prescribed. A child remained a student until age 25. At 25 they married and entered the householder stage to engage in an active family and community life. At age 50, they and their spouse began to retire, dividing their time between spiritual practice and tending to their family and community with an eye on molding the next generation. At age 75, they entered the final stage of complete detachment. Often the husband would leave home to live amongst the forest-dwelling sages. Today it should not be said to anyone young or old that they must give up their family to follow a guru or engage in the spiritual life. But this system was an important element of the Vedic civilization, as it helped a person travel the path of character building and spiritual growth for their entire life.

The role of a retiree is to step back from the demands of midlife over the course of their 50s and 60s to mentor the next generation, gradually passing on worldly responsibilities to focus on spiritual pursuits. Swami Kripalu's entrance into this stage was dramatic and marked by the advent of his intensive sadhana. While withdrawing suddenly from his work as an orator, he wrote books to pass on knowledge, trained a cadre of close students, and undertook the Kayavarohan temple project that was the capstone of his public life. It was also during this stage that Swami Kripalu became a yoga adept. Knowing firsthand the rigors of intensive practice, Swami Kripalu advised his renunciate students to step away from their worldly responsibilities in their late thirties, as great vitality was required to practice sahaja yoga.

The final stage of the lifecycle was *sanyas*. Entering it, a person's only duty was to strive for yoga's ultimate goal of *moskha* or liberation. By freeing himself from the constraints of his celebrity status in India, Swami Kripalu was able to fully embody this stage during his last four years in America. Swami Kripalu was a believer in reincarnation and combined the ashramas with that doctrine to create a multi-lifetime view of the spiritual path.

> *Very few souls are able to complete the path of yoga in one lifetime. In some birth, their liking for the spiritual path grows strong and they become a genuine seeker. After this, they walk the path of krama mukti – liberation by successive births. Only after becoming an extraordinary seeker can they walk the path of sadyo mukti – liberation in this present lifetime – upon which the ocean of existence is crossed in a single leap. However all travelers on the path of yoga should not bother about the results of their practice. Moksha is dependent on grace and not one's efforts. What is obtained through effort is known as the fruit of action. Grace is mere grace, and not the result or fruit of any action. Indeed it is by God's grace and for our own protection that most of us are diverted onto the successive path.*

I am not aware of any public statements made by Swami Kripalu that suggest he attained moksha, but he never touted his accomplishments. Yogi Desai recollects an experience that suggests this could be an open question: *During his time in America, Bapuji (Swami Kripalu) would share with me the different experiences he was going through in his sadhana. One day he wrote on his slate: "Amrit, today the name you have given to my home here, Muktidham, has truly been fulfilled." I understood at that moment that he had reached the final state of complete liberation.* It's also important to acknowledge that the yoga tradition recognizes two distinct avenues to liberation. In his life, Swami Kripalu aspired to become a *jivan mukti*, which means *one who is liberated while still in the body*. But that did not preclude him – or any yogi – from becoming a *videha mukti*: one who *gains liberation in the process of casting off the body.*

Regardless of whether or not he reached its ultimate goal or final expression, Swami Kripalu's life showed me that yoga is not a discipline of renouncing outer pursuits in favor of spiritual enlightenment. It's a pathway to success in each stage of life that reliably carries a faithful practitioner to fulfillment and Self-realization. Bringing this insight back into my studies, I was surprised to find this view implicit in Swami Kripalu's teachings. Somehow my renunciate bias had led me to overlook what now seemed obvious. I had to laugh at myself, knowing that Swami Kripalu was absolutely correct when he penned those opening lines of *Science of Meditation* that had pushed my buttons the night after I'd met him. The task of a novice yogi is to establish a platform of health, purposeful action, good character, and outer accomplishment. It is only by mounting this platform that the later stages of yoga come into reach.

Ending my review of Swami Kripalu's life, I had to admit to being no closer to knowing if the more fantastical elements of his story were true. Yet there was no doubt that his life had taken him on a remarkable journey, one that carried him from obscurity to public renown in India, and eventually brought him to America. Along the way he had profoundly influenced countless people, including myself, and for that I daily remain grateful.

Yoga is a vehicle to carry us forward that teaches us how to enjoy our journey through life. First it shows us how to attend to the health of body and mind, as these tools must be made to work effectively to undertake the journey. Then it brings forth all our positive capacities, the essence of which have been with us from childhood, to ensure our success. To complete the journey, many spiritual qualities are also necessary. If we try to obtain all these at once, we invariably fail, so yoga brings them into being one by one. This is why I can say that a yogi intent on making this journey will succeed in their worldly life and progress spiritually too.

Readers wanting to know more are directed to stories 8-1 to 8-2 in the appendix of teaching stories.

Epilogue

Four decades after Swami Kripalu's death, I encourage every discerning reader to complete the journey of this book by asking an important question, "What about his life story really matters?" If its value lies solely in the nostalgic feelings of a dwindling group that he touched in person, perhaps it's a tale best read and then forgotten. But for me, as someone interested in practicing yoga to bring forth my full potential, his story remains alive; replete with powerful lessons and archetypes that continue to enliven my life.

The rags to riches nature of Swami Kripalu's earlier life should not be minimized. As individuals, we all need to discover our unique talents, develop them to high levels, and endeavor to find success. Self-actualization is a complex task, and almost everyone wakes up to find themselves with a whole host of challenges to face and overcome. Swami Kripalu navigated these challenges by listening to his inner calling, which led him to a form of self-expression and livelihood that he loved and others valued. Success did not come quickly; along with time it took disciplined effort, but doing this personal work was an essential part of his yogic unfolding. By actualizing his ambitions, Swami Kripalu built character and gained a maturity that prepared the way for what came next. In this respect his life story reflects the psychology of Carl Jung when he said, "The first half of life is devoted to forming a healthy ego, the second half to going inward and letting go of it."

The power of Swami Kripalu's energetic awakening in midlife was extremely rare and the swiftness with which he scaled the ladder of yoga extraordinary. Gifted yogis like Swami Kripalu act out the stages of the transformative process in a way that brings them into high relief. While our life journeys will likely be less dramatic, we will pass through a lot of the same territory. My experience is that many facets of Swami Kripalu's later life offer universal lessons useful to anyone seeking inner development and Self-realization. Instead of rendering his teachings irrelevant, the depth of Swami Kripalu's practice enabled him to offer principles that prove reliable and long-lasting. Where many teachers have given me something in particular of value, Swami Kripalu's teachings proved a steady beacon keeping me on course and moving toward the zenith of spiritual development.

Meeting Swami Kripalu was like having a character step right out of the pages of the Upanishads. On some basic level he was different, with all the planets of his personality orbiting around the sun of his quest for liberation. That is the timeless solar system he inhabited. Yet he was also a modern man, grounded in a scientific world view, intent on rediscovering the perennial wisdom through rigorous practice and study, and only then restating it in contemporary terms. My experience is that his ability to act as an intermediary between today's yogis and the sages of old did not end with his death. For me his words remain potent, imbued with heartfelt purity, and continually able to open doorways into realms and realities that I don't know exist.

Swami Kripalu told a story that he never explained called *The Lord's One Wish*. After studying his life, you may understand why I see it as biographical.

Once two saints were standing in heaven. The young saint had just arrived and was new to his surroundings. Looking around he noticed that there was a large highway next to where they were standing. "Brother," the old saint said, "Watch this highway for awhile with me."

Soon a large procession passed by in front of them, with one man walking in front and leading thousands of followers.

"Who is that supreme leader?" the young saint asked. "His name is Sadguru Shantiji," the old saint said. "He was a true teacher on earth. Look how many people he has brought home to the Lord."

A man or woman with an elevated mind does not harbor a plethora of little resolutions. Rather, a single, monumental resolve inspires, binds together, and governs all his myriad decisions for action. Such all-encompassing resolve defines and characterizes his vision of life. For such an exalted soul, every aspect of his manifest personality gravitates around his unifying resolve. As a result, his life exemplifies his vision as much as his vision shapes and defines his life. While dismal events can deflate the willpower of even a sturdy soul, a steady flow of inner inspiration spurs an inspired soul to continued action and prevents them from falling prey to lassitude. This phenomenon of innate inspiration is indeed the gift of Divine Grace. It becomes manifest as undaunted faith, tenacity, self-reliance, and decisiveness of purpose. When a man or woman can remain assiduously firm in their avowed purpose, even in the face of dire circumstance, such steadfastness alone will lead them to the pinnacle of success.

The long procession passed and soon another began. It was a bit smaller, but still quite large. Another great master was leading this procession. "Who's that?" the young saint asked. "His name is Sadguru Anandaji," the old saint said. "He too was a true teacher on earth. Look how many people he has brought home to the Lord."

Seven such processions passed by, each led by a great master. Finally, a last procession came into sight. There were only two people, walking arm-in-arm and conversing, which caused the young saint to ask, "Why are there only two people in this procession? And who is the poor saint with only one follower?"

"That's the Lord," the old saint said. "See how He keeps his new son close? Someday that son will return here with a large following. The Lord is not interested in walking at the head of a procession. His only wish is that we prosper and grow spiritually to the point where others are inspired to follow us home.

While unstated, I believe that Swami Kripalu was the "new son" in this story. For reasons he never understood, God favored him by coming to teach him personally. Being the recipient of such grace, it was his responsibility to inspire others to set out on the path of right living. Once embarked, his duty was to guide them to an authentic spiritual awakening so they could join him in crossing the threshold into heaven. That's exactly what his teachings have done for me. After helping harmonize my work and married life, his yoga instruction carried me to the unity at the heart of all things, and then taught me how to return there regularly. The result is that in the midst of an active and fulfilling life, I've also grown spiritually. While I had to do the work, it was Swami Kripalu who bestowed that boon, and I wish the same for you.

As Swami Kripalu neared the end of his life, he felt that he was in uncharted territory and those surrounding him had a sense that anything could happen next. While he did not achieve some glorious end on earth, he did streak through the sky of his life shedding a lot of light. In India, the Kayavarohan temple remains a vital religious and cultural center. In America, Kripalu Center for Yoga & Health continues to serve as a national hub of the yoga movement. His legacy of teachings are now online and available worldwide. Yet I think his greatest contribution is also the simplest. Inspirational figures matter; exemplars matter; and people who walk their talk matter. Viewed from that perspective, Swami Kripalu's life story continues to be relevant to all of us who aspire to grow, serve, and awaken to life's magnificence.

It is only fitting to end this book the way Swami Kripalu always ended his public talks – with a blessing. These are his words:

May everyone here be happy.

May everyone here be healthy.

May everyone here be prosperous.

May no one be the least little bit unhappy at all.

My auspicious blessing to you.

Appendix of Teachings Stories

I have loved stories since childhood and made it a habit to reflect upon them like a careful scientist to see what elements make them attractive. I've seen that we are all hungry for inspiration, but our minds need proof and demonstration. So what these stories do is give us examples of other saints and yogis who got results, so we can see how their life worked. The history of this Pashupat tradition just bombards us with story after story so our faith becomes firm.

Swami Kripalu was a masterful storyteller who could hold an audience spellbound as he retold religious myths, poked fun at human nature with humorous yarns, or shared incidents from his life. John Mundahl's book, *From the Heart of the Lotus: The Teaching Stories of Swami Kripalu* artfully presents 102 of his tales. Rather than offer a sampling of Swami Kripalu's wide repertoire, this appendix highlights 15 stories directly related to his life. Along with two personal anecdotes, it includes the seminal legends of the yoga tradition into which he was initiated, and a few teaching stories whose message is especially pertinent. Here are the titles, numbered to correspond to the text chapter they augment, and the page number where the story can be found.

1-1: The Resurrection of a Millionaire's Son	141
1-2: Bankimbabu Meets His Guru	143
1-3: The Dreadful Fast Day of Bhima Ekadashi	148
1-4: Names are Many, Truth is One	152
2-1: A Meal at the Muslim Hotel	155
3-1: Lord Buddha Demonstrates the Dharmic Life	157
3-2: Come with Me to the Home of the Lord	158
4-1: Eklavya, Student of Archery	160
4-2: The Crow and the Swan	165
5-1: Legend of Vishvamitra's Tapas	167
5-2: Legend of Lord Lakulish	175
6-1: The Businessman's Silence	180
7-1: Two Great Swamis Come to America	182
8-1: The Death of Lord Buddha	185
8-2: The Old Man Chooses a Dentist	189

Each story is briefly introduced, told in Swami Kripalu's words, and followed by commentary. Readers wanting to continue their studies after finishing this appendix would be well served by starting with John Mundhal's *A Sunrise of Joy: The Lost Darshans of Swami Kripalu*.

1-1: The Resurrection of a Millionaire's Son

This legend introduces Swami Kripalu's teacher and wastes no time in describing his miraculous powers. The full version of it appears in *Infinite Grace: The Story of My Spiritual Lineage* by Swami Rajarshi Muni. While never told publicly by Swami Kripalu, this dramatic tale does mesh with statements he made about his teacher walking into Bombay carrying only a water pot, quickly acquiring the use of a mansion, remaining nameless to his disciples, and foretelling the arrival of the young man destined to become his foremost student.

******

Laxmichand Seth was a virtuous and wealthy man from the Indian state of Rajasthan. He lived in Bombay, where he had a flourishing business and was among few Indians who at that time had a motor car. Each day while driving to work, Laxmichand would stop at a temple in the Madhavbagh area of the city to worship. On the way out of the temple, he would offer alms to any holy men or beggars sitting on the steps. One morning after worship, he'd given money to a group of beggars when he noticed a man leaning against a pillar a bit distant from the others who looked to be an ascetic.

Approaching the man, Laxmichand offered him some money, which the man refused. An awkward conversation ensued in which Laxmichand politely pressed the man to accept his alms and the ascetic affirmed his complete sufficiency and lack of need. Laxmichand explained, "Almighty God has graced me with abundant wealth, and it won't run out if I offer some of it to the poor and the beggars. With this understanding, I donate to whatever extent possible. Kindly take it." To which the ascetic replied, "If you have an abundance of riches go straight to your home and save your son with it."

Laxmichand was puzzled by this response and asked, "What are you talking about? I don't understand. It is my routine to come here on the way to my office." The ascetic answered, "Yes but today you should go back home immediately." Laxmichand ended the conversation by saying, "All right," but thinking the man eccentric, drove to his office anyway. As he got out of the car, the manager of the firm ran to him. "There was a call from your wife telling you to go home at once. She did not say why." The apprehensive Laxmichand hurried home to find that his only son had fallen from the top floor of the house. The eight year-old boy was lying unconscious on the ground, attended by two neighborhood doctors, who told Laxmichand that neither breath nor heartbeat was discernible. They feared that nothing could be done to save him.

Grasping the gravity of the situation, Laxmichand rushed back to the temple and found the ascetic where he'd left him. Falling prostrate at his feet, Laxmichand cried out in an emotion-choked voice, "Forgive my blunder, Mahatmaji. It will be unbearable for me to lose my only son. Have mercy on me and do something! I humbly implore you, please revive my son and I shall be forever indebted to you." Looking compassionately at the businessman, the ascetic asked if Laxmichand had a container. Running into the temple, Laxmichand returned with a small bowl into which the ascetic poured some water from his *kamadal* or water pot. "Give this to your son."

Rushing home, Laxmichand poured a spoonful in the unresponsive boy's mouth. Within a few moments, the boy's eyes opened. After drinking the rest of the water, he was able to sit up and talk. Examining him closely, the bewildered doctors could find no sign of injury. Laxmichand rushed back to Madhavbagh yet again. Grasping the ascetic's feet, the overwhelmed business man said, "Oh great Mahatma, you have saved my son. I beg you to grace our home and give us an opportunity to serve you." The ascetic replied, "I don't require any service, and I don't like going to anyone's home. It is enough that you have realized who is the beggar."

Laxmichand continued, "If you don't want to come to my house, I also have another mansion lying empty. Please make it your ashram. I will make all the arrangements. I don't know your name, and I don't know where you came from, but from today you are my guest in this city. Please give me and my family an opportunity to render our hospitality and service." Hearing Laxmichand's heartfelt plea, the ascetic responded, "All right, as you wish; I have come to stay for a time in Bombay. If you so desire, I will live in your vacant mansion."

Laxmichand took him to the property, which starting that day was converted into the ashram of the ascetic he knew only as *Mahatma*. Laxmichand and his wife took the Mahatma as their spiritual preceptor, receiving mantra initiation and becoming his first disciples in Bombay. They were friends with a Gujarati millionaire, Govardhanbhai Seth, who learned of their son's momentous fall and miraculous recovery. Meeting the Mahatma, Govardhanbhai was charmed by his charismatic personality. He also became a disciple, as did many other prominent citizens. Within two weeks, the ashram was buzzing with activity and its community soon swelled to several hundred with many coming regularly to receive darshan (audience) and render service.

On Thursday evenings everyone would gather for the Mahatma to deliver a short spiritual discourse. It was only eight weeks after the resurrection of Laxmichand's son that the Mahatma told everyone in attendance that he'd come to the city and established the ashram to train a penniless young man who would arrive four months hence and become his foremost disciple.

******

On the surface, this story explains how Swami Kripalu's guru came to occupy his stately, seaside ashram. Delving deeper, it conveys the idea that a spiritually-realized being is more powerful than a worldly man with wealth and status. But the story does more than answer the question: "Who is the real beggar here?" When the two powers align, with the material serving the spiritual, things come together quickly and our purpose in life can be accomplished. This story is presented here not as factual history, but as part of the mythological milieu in which Swami Kripalu was steeped.

1-2: Bankimbabu Meets His Guru

Living in the ashram, Swami Kripalu grew curious about his teacher's past. When questioned, his teacher would only say, "It is not proper to ask an ascetic about his prior life. Having renounced everything, he does not have any relationship with his past." This left Swami Kripalu no option but to set aside his curiosity and hope that answers would come eventually. A few months later, a gentleman came to meet the Mahatma, whose fame was spreading among Bombay's prominent citizens. Entering the audience room, the gentleman was surprised to recognize him as a boyhood chum. Swami Kripalu learned a great deal about his teacher's early life from this chance visitor. Afterward it catalyzed a conversation in which his teacher disclosed that he was given the name *Pranavananda* upon becoming a swami. Before that, he was a successful businessman named *Bankimbabu*. This story provides a sketch of Bankimbabu's householder life that highlights his first encounter with the mysterious guru who would eventually initiate him into the practice of yoga.

******

Bankimbabu and his wife, Ashadevi, lived in Calcutta. Well placed in society, the couple had only one regret: they were childless. Neither of them had a brother or sister, which added to their loneliness. A pious friend suggested they make one of the most arduous of all Hindu pilgrimages, traveling by foot to Kedarnath Dham, a remote Shiva temple in the Himalayas. Bound to his work and skeptical of such notions, Bankimbabu was not interested. Time passed and Ashadevi grew depressed, aware that any likelihood of her motherhood was quickly waning. Giving in to her repeated requests, the two traveled to Rishikesh. Donning the dress and demeanor of pilgrims, they set out unaccompanied into the rugged mountains.

Bankimbabu and Ashadevi had overcome many difficulties when they completed their climb and entered the temple. Enveloped by its holy atmosphere, they humbly offered their prayers and gifts to the jyotir lingam (radiant sign of Shiva) that it housed. Exiting the temple, a sense of accomplishment and hope filled their hearts. But during their return, calamity struck in a desolate spot when Bankimbabu was seized by a sudden illness. After debilitating diarrhea and vomiting, he collapsed and lost all consciousness. Ashadevi held her husband's head in her lap. She tried to revive him but could not and soon felt his body growing cold. Watching the life ebb out of her husband, she became desperate. Crying out for help, she was amazed to see a radiant monk step from the brush into the clearing carrying a kamandal (water pot).

The monk sprinkled Bankimbabu's face with water and then stared steadily into his unseeing eyes. In a short time, Bankimbabu was alert and back on his feet. Ashadevi narrated the events of his collapse and recovery to Bankimbabu, who fell at the feet of the monk, saying, "We are greatly indebted to you, but how can we repay you in this barren place? Kindly come with us to Calcutta and give us an opportunity to serve you there." The monk responded, "Son, I shall keep that in mind and come to Calcutta someday." Turning and walking back into the brush, he was gone as suddenly as he had appeared. Surprised by his abrupt departure, Bankimbabu and Ashadevi were not able to offer him any reward or tell him their address. There was nothing left to do but proceed on their way.

One morning three months later, Bankimbabu was greeted by the monk, who was standing outside the entrance to his house. He immediately called Ashadevi, who escorted the monk into the sitting room, where Bankimbabu and Ashadevi sat at his feet. Bankimbabu said, "In our parting, we were negligent in failing to give you our address." The monk replied, "Son, the names and whereabouts of all persons in the world are known to me." Seeing more evidence of his extraordinary powers, Bankimbabu replied, "We are blessed to have you visit our home. You are welcome to stay as long as you like. Too indebted to ever repay you, we surrender at your holy feet."

Ashadevi brought fruits, sweets, and milk and offered them to their guest. The monk explained, "I shall only stay with you for a day, and this body does not require food." Ashadevi was dismayed at not being able to provide hospitality to a guest in her home and said, "How can one live without food or water? You must take food sometimes. If it does not suit you now, please take it whenever you like." The monk responded by taking a single basil leaf, which he put into his mouth. "I have accepted your hospitality through this leaf. Don't worry about my food, and you should also observe a fast today."

Bankimbabu explained, "We are not worried about our food, but only want to please you and spend time conversing. By what name shall we call you?" "You may call me by any name. Address me as convenient, and I will not object to any name you choose to call me," replied the monk. "Then I shall call you Bhagwan (Lord)," said Bankimbabu. The conversation continued and Bankimbabu indirectly mentioned the couple's secret desire. "Bhagwan, we undertook the Kedarnath pilgrimage to fulfill one desire. Although it may or may not be fulfilled, it has certainly benefited us by providing an opportunity to meet you, especially now that you have favored us with a visit to our home." The monk raised his hand, "Son, one year from now you will have a child." Both husband and wife were overjoyed, and Bankimbabu gratefully said, "Thank you, and kindly bless us with guidance for our spiritual progress, according to our capacity."

"It is enough for householders pursuing a path of success in life to regularly recite the name of God, and I will give you mantra initiation in the evening. Another initiation is required to tread the path of liberation." Bankimbabu said, "I would very much like to try for liberation but am not aware of my competence. If you find me qualified, I will pursue the path of liberation." "The path of liberation requires special effort and the abandoning of worldly duties," said the monk, looking pointedly at Ashadevi.

"No woman wants her husband to become an ascetic. Yet I am not so selfish as to hinder the welfare of his soul," said Ashadevi. "Your thoughts are noble, and I am pleased with you," said the monk. "Bankimbabu shall do mantra recitation while leading his householder life. This will weaken his attachments and prepare him for the path of liberation. In due time, I will give him yoga initiation." The monk drew their conversation to a close by saying, "It's time for me to sit in meditation. You carry on with your routines. Half an hour before the sun sets, I'll get up and have a bath. Then I'll give you mantra initiation, which is why I asked you to fast today."

Ashadevi arranged a carpet in the guest room where the monk could comfortably sit. The couple went about their daily chores, eagerly awaiting the appointed hour. As evening approached, they bathed and waited for the monk to rise from meditation. He came out with his water pot in hand, and Bankimbabu led him to the bathroom, where two large buckets of hot water were waiting. The monk instructed them to bring a large tub and place it in the center of the room. With this done, the monk said to Bankimbabu, "I'll sit in this tub and you two will bathe me. Ashadevi will pour water on my body, and you will rub it clean. Do not be frightened or stop if anything strange happens during the bath. Use all the water from both buckets. When you are finished, pour the collected water into my water pot. Fill it up to the brim and bring it to my room." The monk then sat in the tub, crossing his legs in lotus posture. As the couple began the bath, he closed his eyes in meditation.

Ashadevi poured the water, and Bankimbabu started rubbing his body. They were startled to discover that his skin began to peel off, revealing white underneath like a boiled potato. Although frightened and astounded, they continued as instructed. With all the skin removed, the monk's body resembled a marble statue, but it was soft like a banana. As they continued, the white of the body started melting in the poured water, leaving a round white ball, which finally dissolved completely into the water.

Except for the monk's prayer beads and loin cloth, the tub was now full of water that appeared like milk. Continuing as directed, they began pouring the water from the tub into the water pot. Much to their surprise, they were able to pour all the water from the large tub into the small water pot. Taking the water pot, beads, and loin cloth to the guest room, Bankimbabu and Ashadevi were astonished to find the monk sitting there on the carpet, eyes closed in meditation. They sat close and bowed in reverence.

The monk opened his eyes and with a smile said, "My children, you inquired about the needs of my body this morning, so I made you witness this strange bath in order to give you some idea about it. I hope now you have rightly perceived its nature." He lovingly placed his hand upon their heads and said, "Now I will give you mantra initiation." Regaining their composure, they sat before the monk, who then conferred the twelve-syllable Krishna mantra, *Om Namo Bhagavate Vasudevaya*. (I bow to the Lord in the form of Vasudeva's Son)

Bankimbabu became inquisitive and asked, "Bhagwan, earlier you promised to guide me in the pursuit of liberation. When will I be so favored, and what is the nature of this pursuit?" "Liberation is accomplished through yoga, and it is not proper to give yoga initiation to one who has not qualified for it. Mantra recitation will purify your body and mind, and you will be qualified when they are sufficiently purified," answered the monk. Reflecting on their initiation, Ashadevi said, "We have been calling you Bhagwan, and now you are our guru. So hereafter we shall call you Guru Bhagwan." Bankimbabu nodded his assent.

After a while, Guru Bhagwan said, "It is late now, please go to bed." When Ashadevi began making a bed for him, he stopped her saying, "My child, this body does not require sleep, so do not trouble yourself. I will be sitting here in meditation." Guru Bhagwan had already departed when Bankimbabu and Ashadevi awoke early the next morning. Gone were his *padukas* (wooden sandals) and kamandal. One year later, Ashadevi gave birth to a daughter they named Kamlesh.

Bankimbabu was deeply impressed with Guru Bhagwan and the inspiration to take sanyas (renunciation) and seek liberation became fixed in his heart. He eventually left home with Ashadevi's blessing to pursue the path of yoga. Encountering Guru Bhagwan a second time, he was ordained as a swami and given the name *Pranavananda*, which means *one who attains bliss by activating the life force.*

******

This strange tale is an example of a teaching story with multiple levels of meaning. It uses a simple yet effective ploy to conceal its deeper significance. Where the story line is about miraculous events and mantra initiation for householders, a key piece of its content describes the yoga pointedly declared to be secret. The result is that readers taking the story at face value are distracted from probing more deeply, while those awake to symbolism can decipher a message needed to go further in their practice.

The story opens with a classic theme: when the student is ready, the teacher appears. In this instance, the guru not only appears in the nick of time to save Bankimbabu's life. He goes out of his way to visit their Calcutta home. This expresses the view that a person focused on fulfilling his or her duties in life will be called to the spiritual path when the time is right. The story continues by affirming traditional distinctions between men, women, householders, and renunciates. The guru grants a boon by blessing their efforts to conceive a child. Motherhood, along with mantra initiation, represents the fulfillment of Ashadevi's life as a woman. Bankimbabu aspires to walk the path of liberation, which ultimately will require him to abandon his family.

Readers may find it surprising that married aspirants were not encouraged to practice the physical disciplines of yoga. They were advised to live an energetic, virtuous, and successful family life. Householders wanting to grow spiritually were given mantra initiation and told to practice recitation each morning and evening. Swami Kripalu expanded upon this, permitting earnest householders to practice asana, pranayama, and meditation for up to two hours per day. This represents an extension of the traditional approach.

The story continues to paint a fascinating picture of depth spiritual practice. In the bathing scene, the three participants enact what occurs in yoga sadhana. With transformation traditionally seen as a process of purification, bathing is a fit metaphor. Sitting in the bathtub, the guru is the person doing the practice. He crosses his legs, closes his eyes, and sits in meditation. Ashadevi and Bankimbabu represent the process itself, one of removing the layers upon layers that obscure the Self. As the bath continues, they are astounded to find that there is no personal self. All that remains is a milk-like liquid, a symbol of the vast, undifferentiated, and primordial awareness that is our true nature.

The story's conclusion beautifully expresses the paradoxical nature of deep meditation experiences. After realizing that one is nothing other than the transcendent Self, daily life goes on. Somehow all that awareness fits into the water pot of the bodymind. Carrying the pot into the next room, the guru is there as before, embodied and interacting through the vehicle of a personality and character. Yet the guru is different from the student; he knows who and what he truly is, and that knowing expands his capacities and informs how he lives.

It is noteworthy that the guru is able to provide accurate and detailed instructions to Ashadevi and Bankimbabu. The value of such competence, which can only be acquired by personally going through the transformative process, cannot be underestimated. The words of Guru Bhagwan are worth remembering for any spiritual practitioner: "Do not be frightened or stop if anything strange happens. Use all the water from both buckets." A spiritual practice must be carried through to completion to effect its intended effects, and this always entails passing beyond comfort zones to confront the unknown and unexpected.

The historical implication of this story is clear. Kedarnath Dham is not just a remote pilgrimage site. It is one of the twelve prominent Shiva temples that surrounded Kayavarohan and housed an idol made of meteorite or *jyotir lingam*. Guru Bhagwan is a radiant being who carries a water pot, never tells anyone his name, and appears at opportune times to bring people back from the brink of death and usher fit souls onto the path of yoga. The reader is left to figure out the obvious: Guru Bhagwan is none other than Lakulish, the 28th incarnation of Shiva. This links Pranavananda and Swami Kripalu to the same root teacher and lineage.

The full version of this story can be found in *Infinite Grace: The Story of My Spiritual Lineage* by Swami Rajarshi Muni. It does not include any account of the second meeting of Bankimbabu and Guru Bhagwan and the yoga initiation that presumably took place then.

1-3: The Dreadful Fast Day of Bhima Ekadashi

In this humorous anecdote, Swami Kripalu uses an incident from his early life to introduce us to his family and describe the loving bonds they shared. But he tells the story for a reason, as it also suggests how difficult it must have been for him to complete a 41-day water fast.

******

From earliest childhood, I used to go to my mother – morning, noon, and night – with only one prayer: "Please give me something to eat." Once fed I would go out to play but soon become hungry and run back for yet another snack. Hunger stalked me constantly, making me voracious with the fire of an appetite that never subsided, and apt to eat anything left unattended. Our household consisted of six people at that time: my mother, brother, paternal aunt, two sisters, and me. Because of the constant threat that I would take food without asking, my mother had to guard our pantry in order to feed everyone else.

I was born at a time when Brahmin parents often inspired their five or six year-old children to undertake fasts. My mouth, however, just kept moving like a millstone. As a result, I had not yet fasted at the age of 10. This caused my mother to frown at me. At the table, I would always beg to eat a little more but mother would raise up and say, "Look how much you are eating! That's enough. Get up!" Occasionally she would take pity and serve me an extra piece of bread, but at other times she would hit me with her stick.

One day when I was absent, my mother proclaimed to the others, "Saraswati Chandra has never fasted, and I am determined to have him fast on the auspicious day of Bhima Ekadashi." In Hindu mythology, Bhima is the elder brother of Arjuna, a great warrior, who was also known for his voracious appetite. My sister Indumati was two years my elder and often teased me by hurling the name "Bhimado" at me. Hearing my mother's proclamation, Indumati cheered her idea by saying, "Yes, we must make the Bhimado observe the upcoming fast day!" But Indumati was clever and advised my mother, "If you really want him to fast, you will have to lock him in his room. Otherwise, instead of his normal four times a day, he will eat five times to mark the fast day." Knowing it was necessary, everyone kept this plan a secret from me.

When the day of Bhima Ekadashi dawned, I arose and performed my normal routine. Afterward mother said, "Come upstairs with me." "What do you want?" I asked. "Would I ask you to come without a reason?" she replied. So I followed her to my study room on the second floor. The moment I entered, she locked the door from outside and announced, "Today is the auspicious day of Bhima Ekadashi and you must observe the fast. I will call you when it is time for fruit."

This unexpected attack caught me by surprise, yet I replied as casually as an accomplished faster. "If I am fasting, why do I need fruit? I will be locking the door from the inside, so please be sure that no one disturbs me while I sit for japa (mantra recitation)." Our entire household did japa daily, but there is a tremendous difference between japa and fasting. Japa means to sit on the floor; fasting means to climb the walls! Anyone else would have been fooled by my reply, but my family was all too aware of my mannerisms and pampered appetite.

As soon as mother went downstairs, hunger came upstairs and my mind became restless and angry. First came thoughts like, "How can I ever make it through this fast day? What if I have to go to bed hungry? How will I sleep with an empty stomach? If I cannot get food today, just wait and see what I eat tomorrow!" But soon I began to plot: "How can I get some food into this locked room?" At first it seemed impossible but all of a sudden a bright idea filled me with enthusiasm.

I knew the schedule of the entire household. My mother would go into the kitchen around 9:00 to start preparing lunch for my elder brother, who was already out. Before that she would run errands or do chores around the house. My aunt would be sitting for morning worship in the front room, and my two sisters would soon be playing with their girlfriends. So right at 9:00 when my mother entered the kitchen, I could sneak into the kitchen courtyard pantry.

The next half hour dragged on but then I heard sounds coming from the kitchen. Tiptoeing quietly onto the balcony off my study, I looked and listened to make sure that all was still. There was a garment drying on the balcony, which I lashed to a pillar and quietly hang-jumped into the courtyard. Peeking through a window, there was no one around to see me. My mission now was to creep into the dimly lit pantry and find any food that might be stored there. Mother kept the milk, butter, and other perishables in the kitchen, out of reach of the cat. But even the dry goods she had to protect, changing her hiding places constantly, to forestall the nimble forager hunting for food at this very moment.

Without a sound, I explored every can, jar, pot, and pan. When a bag of rice flakes came into my hand, I gripped it between my teeth and scrambled up onto the balcony the same way I had climbed down. Safely back in my room, I thought to myself, "Now I can spend the whole day eating these rice flakes!" But I was even more gleeful at the thought that I had defeated my family's scheme. Those dry rice flakes were tough, and chewing them up would have been a tiring chore for anyone else. Easily able to gobble up a two-pound sack like this, I warned the rice flakes that they would be polished off by evening. Fortunately, my mother kept a pot of water in my study room, so I commenced my 24-hour fast eating rice flakes and washing them down with water.

At lunchtime, I heard a knock at the door. It was mother who said, "Open the door, I have brought you fruit." After chewing the rice flakes in my mouth, I stated imperiously, "I am not hungry and will not die if I do not eat for one day!" Mother replied sweetly, "That is true, my wise son. Just knock on the door if you get hungry later." A little later, my younger sister Kundanbala came up. We loved each other very much. She beseeched me, "Oh brother, please eat a little. You know you cannot stand hunger." I comforted her by saying, "Today I have firmly decided to observe Bhima Ekadashi. You are younger than me but routinely fast every 11 days. Don't you think I should fast at least one day a year?" She walked reluctantly down the stairs as I went back to my arduous chewing.

My elderly aunt was also very affectionate. She came upstairs but I would not open the door, saying, "Don't worry, I won't be hungry today. I am practicing japa." My elder sister, Indumati, was astonished when she heard that I had professed a lack of hunger. She knew me very well. She too came to my door and said, "Open the door! I have brought some fruit for you." But I would not and she stamped away.

When I came down the next morning, my mother and aunt praised my accomplishment. Showering me with affection, my aunt said to my mother, "Mangalabahen, prepare lunch early today because Saraswati Chandra fasted on only water yesterday." Indumati did not like to hear me praised; she was searching for some explanation. About two weeks passed before my elder brother came home one afternoon and told mother, "I am very hungry." Mother replied, "Son, I have no snacks prepared but if you can wait a moment I will make you something from the rice flakes I have in the pantry." She went directly to the pantry but could not find the sack of rice flakes. She remembered exactly where she had hidden it, but it was gone. She began searching everywhere and when she didn't return Indumati went to help. Mother told her, "I put the rice flakes here, but I cannot find them anywhere." Indumati immediately expressed her suspicion. "Your pampered younger son must have eaten them." Mother agreed and they both came to me as I sat with my elder brother on the swing. Indumati fondly twisted my ear and asked, "Where is that sack of rice flakes?"

I laughingly pointed to my stomach and admitted, "The Bhima Ekadashi ate up all those rice flakes!" She angrily slapped me and said, "I knew you didn't fast on Ekadashi. I just knew it! You fraud!" Astonished, my mother exclaimed, "But I locked him in his room." "Well, mother," said Indumati confidently, "Then you don't really know the Bhimado. This monkey must have lowered himself into the courtyard and climbed back up to the balcony with the rice flakes. I suspected him that very day." Everyone broke into laughter.

******

This tale is told with a whimsical tone that is noteworthy, given the deprivations that we know were endured by the family after his father's death. Swami Kripalu concluded it by saying, "If a person could not tolerate hunger when he was 10 years old, just imagine how much less he would be able to tolerate hunger when he was 19! While each of the people I described was part of my loving family, Gurudev was a great man. Even though fasting for two or three days was the limit of my capacity, I was able to finish a 40-day fast due to his grace. Even today, when I think back, I feel that he loves me most of all." The full version of this story appears in *Pilgrimage of Love, Book Two*, pages 226-232.

1-4: Names are Many, Truth is One

India's religious landscape is extremely diverse and generalizations of all kinds prove false. With that caveat, this story is best introduced by stating the majority Hindu view on what Western religions call *God*. *Brahman* is the highest principle, the absolute reality that is unchanging but also the cause of everything relative and in flux. Brahman is a formless unity devoid of all attributes and therefore utterly beyond the polarizing mind. The godhead of Brahman comes into form through three primary energies called *Trimurti* (three forms) that carry out the cosmic functions of creating, sustaining, and destroying the material universe. These energies are subtle and difficult to grasp conceptually, so they are personified as a triad of gods that can be imagined, invoked, and worshiped: Brahma the creator, Vishnu the sustainer, and Shiva the transformer/destroyer. Feminine energy is not absent from Trimurti, as each god is associated with a goddess, and it's the two taken together that comprise the deity.* All the many gods and goddesses of the Hindu pantheon are best seen as symbolizing spiritual energies and the forces of nature.

Although there are a trinity of Hindu gods, there are only two dominant sects. Brahma's role in the triumvirate was to bring the universe into creation, a task long since accomplished, which is one reason he is so little worshipped. Only a handful of temples are dedicated to him in the whole of India. *Vaishnavs* are the majority sect and worship God in the form of *Vishnu* (All Pervading). *Shaivites* are the largest minority and worship God in the form of *Shiva* (Auspicious). Swami Kripalu was raised in a Vaishnav family devoted to Lord Krishna, an incarnation of Vishnu. After leaving the ashram, Swami Kripalu's guru took him on a pilgrimage to the Vrajbhumi region of north-central India considered sacred by Vaishnavs that contains over 6,000 temples. In accord

---

*Scholars identify four denominations of Hinduism including *Shaktism* (sect of feminine power), which offers an alternative to Trimurti. But by number of adherents, the Vaishnavs (70%) and Shaivites (26%) make up the majority.

with traditional rules, the two traveled by foot, eating once a day, and speaking only in the evening on religious topics. The pilgrimage took seven days as they embarked at Krishna's birthplace of Mathura and proceeded to his boyhood haunt of Vrindavan, visiting as many holy places as possible along the way.

******

After a long day's walk, the two pilgrims made their way into Vrindavan. It was time for the evening ceremony of light called *arti*. Swami Kripalu entered a nearby temple and was surprised to find it adorned with a Shiva lingam. When the ceremony ended, Swami Kripalu came out and sat down next to Pranavananda in the temple courtyard. Night had fallen and conversation was permitted, so Swami Kripalu was able to ask his guru, "Since Vrindavan is Lord Krishna's abode, why is there a temple for Lord Shiva here?"

Pranavananda responded, "Are you talking in your sleep?" Swami Kripalu pressed, "I asked and will ask again, why is this temple dedicated to Lord Shiva?" Pranavananda sounded exasperated, "You seem to be under some delusion about the deity." Swami Kripalu was confounded, "No sir, I had a proper look and even questioned another devotee attending prayers. It is a Shiva temple."

Pranavananda offered an obvious way to resolve the dispute, "Go inside and have another look so that you might come out of your delusion." Swami Kripalu went inside the temple and beheld an idol of Lord Krishna. After rubbing his eyes to make sure he was not imagining this, he went back out to his guru. Pranavananda asked with a smile, "What did you see?" With some embarrassment, Swami Kripalu said, "There's an idol of Lord Krishna in there."

Laughing, Pranavananda said, "Swami, you are not making any sense. Please go in again and remove your delusion." As directed, Swami Kripalu went inside a third time, where he found an idol of Krishna and a Shiva lingam, installed side by side. He came out quite dazed, and sat down before Pranavananda, clasping his head in both hands, totally speechless. Pranavananda asked him: "Did you see properly this time? What is it, an idol or a lingam?" Swami Kripalu could only stammer one word, "Both."

Pranavananda's eyes twinkled, "You say something different each time. Has something gone wrong with your eyes?" Swami Kripalu retorted, "My eyes are perfectly fine, but you seem to have cast a spell on them because I keep seeing different things at different times." Hearing the annoyance in Swami Kripalu's voice, Pranavananda affectionately stroked his head and said, "All right, go inside a final time. Whichever form of God you see, take it to be the presiding deity of this temple."

Reluctantly, Swami Kripalu went inside a fourth time. There was only the lingam that he had seen initially. The temple priest was there, whom he asked to make doubly sure. Returning to Pranavananda, Swami Kripalu said, "I was right. A lingam is installed in this Shiva temple." Immediately Pranavananda asked, "Then how is it that you saw the idol of Lord Krishna? And once you even said that both an idol and a lingam were inside the temple. How did that happen?" Swami Kripalu answered, "I've no explanation. Please do me the favor of explaining this phenomenon."

Pranavananda replied, "Swami, when you first went inside the temple, you saw Lord Shiva there. The next time you saw Lord Krishna. And the third time you saw both of them side by side. What does this indicate? It shows that one form of God is not different from another. Nor is any form of God superior to others. All forms of God are of equal importance. I am enunciating the principle of monotheism for you today, so you do not get entangled in the web of sectarianism. Victims of narrow sectarianism can never acquire real devotion or true comprehension. Since you were born and brought up as a Vaishnav, I've asked you to keep Krishna as the main deity on your altar. However, you should also consider Shiva as the deity and respect the lingam. It can be said that Hara (another name for Shiva) and Hari (another name for Vishnu) are one and the same. I made you witness this miracle so you could acquire an unshakable faith in the principle of monotheism."

Swami Kripalu asked, "Upon leaving Bombay, why did you select this area for our pilgrimage?" Pranavananda replied, "Because of you." "Why because of me?" Swami Kripalu said with surprise. "Because I wanted to strengthen the inherited and existing traits in you," answered Pranavananda. Swami Kripalu continued his inquiry, "What if I had inherited Shaivite traits instead of Vaishnav traits?" "In that case I would have taken you on a pilgrimage to Kashi, Haridwar, and Rishikesh, the places holy to Lord Shiva," answered Pranavananda. Hearing this response, Swami Kripalu protested, "But doesn't this amount to strengthening sectarianism? To strengthen the spirit of monotheism, shouldn't a person with my traits be taken to the land of Shiva?"

"While intellectually noble, your idea is not correct. To practice yoga, it is helpful to have unflinching faith in your chosen form of God. Faith in the form established as an emotional bond in childhood can easily be made stronger. Although effort can rouse faith in a different form, it is less likely to prove strong enough to survive the rigors of sadhana. So the best approach is to build upon one's existing faith. As true comprehension arises with spiritual experience, an objective viewpoint is developed and no form of God will be considered inferior. Remember, faith based on a narrow sectarianism is not true faith. It is a blind faith which arouses fanaticism and intolerance.

One who truly knows God considers all religions, sects, and human beings as equal. This is true monotheism."

******

Hinduism is often considered a pantheistic religion because of its multiple gods. As illustrated by this story, it is actually grounded in a profound monotheism that embraces unity and diversity. The outer meaning of this story is apparent in its moral of religious inclusivity and tolerance. The inner meaning is less obvious. Yoga is a search for Brahman, the unitary power and intelligence underlying existence. When a yogi begins to meditate deeply, he or she will inevitably have what Swami Kripalu called "false experiences of the Absolute." The primordial oneness at the heart of creation will appear in various guises including pure awareness, universal love, and spiritual light. While these are positive experiences, they are only windows providing a glimpse into the temple of Truth. The guidance to an advanced practitioner is to persevere in your practice until you directly experience the singular and unchanging Reality, the true deity, and your real identity. The full version of this story appears in *Infinite Grace: The Story of My Spiritual Lineage* by Swami Rajarshi Muni.

2-1: A Meal at the Muslim Hotel

Along with conveying Swami Kripalu's love of literature, this anecdote paints a picture of the cultural conditions in which he grew up and how his rebellious nature led him to clash with them.

******

In my youth, I had a great ambition to be a literary man and actively wrote poems, short stories, dramas, and novels. There were more Muslims than Hindus in my literary circle and back then we had to comply with strict rules of etiquette and food preparation. We met on a regular basis to feast upon the delights of literature, but we had to go to separate facilities for tea and snacks. My Muslim friends would go to a Muslim hotel, and I would go with my Hindu friends to a Hindu hotel. Our mutual love for each other made such restrictions unpleasant. Annoyed, we would criticize them in bitter words. "How can these practices be called religious when they segregate human beings from one another and erect a wall between them? The supreme dharma is the law of love. We should accept only that principle."

Courage is an integral part of love and one day I made a suggestion. "There are 10 of us. Three of us are Hindus and the rest Muslims. Usually we have to separate for refreshments, but today I have decided to come to your Muslim hotel. I'll have refreshments brought from the Hindu hotel so we can eat together." In those days, the Brahmins were considered the superior caste, and they were not permitted to eat food prepared by the other castes. If a Brahmin was even caught drinking water provided by a lower caste Hindu person, he would be ostracized. It was considered improper to even stand next to a Muslim, so it would naturally be a big offense to sit inside their hotel eating refreshments.

My Muslim friends were very aware of the Hindu mentality. They did not like my proposition and one of them said, "Although it is acceptable for you to have refreshments brought into our hotel so you can eat with us, onlookers will believe that you are eating food prepared by Muslims. It is not appropriate to deliberately provoke a conflict." My friends were afraid for me. Unconvinced, I continued, "I appreciate your concerns, but I want to carry out this experiment."

Reluctantly, my friends consented and news of this revolutionary act of mine spread through the neighborhood and incited a public controversy. One elder Brahman, twisting my ear, scolded me, "You rascal, why do you behave in such a wanton manner?" When I presented my case he gave me a rap on the head and completed his assessment, "Don't consider your misdeed to be an act of courage; it's sheer foolishness." Soon the elders of the caste gathered and sent for me. They scolded, "You have become absolutely corrupted and seem bent upon destroying the Brahmin caste." "I am a Hindu," I declared. "I don't desire to be a Muslim, but why should we follow restrictions which don't serve any useful purpose?"

This trivial incident disturbed the entire community, and eventually I had to take an oath in front of everyone promising not to behave like that again. Afterwards my Muslim friends pleaded with me, "From now on, please don't come into our hotel!"

******

Despite the pressure brought to bear upon him, Swami Kripalu retained his progressive spirit. In adulthood he was an outspoken advocate for religious tolerance and an early proponent of what came to be called *interfaith spirituality*. While displaying a reverence for the age-old wisdom distilled in the Hindu and yogic traditions, he consistently acted in ways that showed his willingness to let go of restrictive social norms that no longer served a viable purpose.

3-1: Lord Buddha Demonstrates the Dharmic Life

Swami Kripalu was a lover of Gautama Buddha and well-schooled in his teachings. This is one of many stories that feature the great master Swami Kripalu always called "Lord Buddha."

******

It was the time of Lord Buddha, when his personality and charisma had spread throughout the land. Just hearing his name, people would lower their heads with respect and awe. One day Lord Buddha was teaching, and a large crowd had gathered to hear his sermon. When he finished, the gathering slowly dispersed, except for one man who was a religious opponent. Drawing close to Lord Buddha, he didn't bow down. The loving, compassionate eyes of Lord Buddha quietly rested on the man, who erupted into anger. His body trembled; his eyes flared with animosity, but there wasn't the slightest disturbance in the heart of Lord Buddha, nor was there any change in his loving gaze.

Perhaps the man felt that his anger would make an impression on the mind of Lord Buddha and render him unsteady? When this didn't happen, the man became even angrier. He stepped toward Lord Buddha and spit in his face with great hatred. Lord Buddha's self-respect wasn't wounded in the slightest way by this bad conduct. He wiped the spittle from his face with his shoulder cloth. Getting up to leave for the monastery where he was staying, he said to the man, "Beloved brother, if you've finished your statement, may I go now to my residence?"

"My statement!" the man replied. "But I haven't spoken a single word to you!" "That's true," Lord Buddha said. "But you made your statement through your actions, and I've listened carefully to your silent statement." The man said nothing and Lord Buddha left, assuming the encounter was over.

Going home, the man could not sleep that night. The impression Lord Buddha had made on his mind was far deeper than he had received from reading his own scriptures. Reading scripture now seemed ordinary, for today he had encountered the actual practice of the spirit of dharma. The whole night the man lay awake. He analyzed his bad behavior and was ashamed of himself. The dharmic actions of Lord Buddha had changed his heart.

The next day the man returned to the same place and listened to Lord Buddha's sermon again. But this time the man was able to listen with a steady, loving mind and ponder the words of Lord

Buddha deeply. When the crowd left, the man went up to Lord Buddha with downcast eyes. He put a garland of flowers at Lord Buddha's holy feet and cried for fifteen minutes unable to stop, looking with sorrowful eyes into Lord Buddha's gentle face.

Once again love flowed compassionately from the Lord Buddha's eyes. He waited until the man was completely done crying and then he stood up and said, "Beloved brother, if you've finished your statement may I go now to my residence?" The man bowed down and touched the feet of Lord Buddha and whispered, "Yes."

******

Swami Kripalu ended this story by saying that only a true master can accept insult and praise with equanimity. Were someone to ask him, "Can you accept insult and praise equally?" he would have to reply, "No, up to now I have not attained to that stage, but I am working toward it."

3-2: Come With Me to the Home of the Lord

Swami Kripalu believed that all teachers were responsible to ardently practice what they preached, hold themselves to high ethical standards, and act to serve the best interests of their students. This is one of many stories he told that speaks to the issue of hypocrisy in teachers.

******

Once in India there was a great saint named Narad who was a rishi and highly developed yogi. Narad was walking into his favorite town, where the Lord Himself lived, and it was a beautiful place. "Whenever I come here I feel so peaceful," he told everyone he met. "Then why do you leave?" they asked him, "Why don't you stay?" "I want to bring everyone here," Narad answered. "Come with me to the home of the Lord, that is what I want to tell everyone."

The Lord overheard this conversation. "Narad," the Lord said, "By all means go and tell everyone about my beautiful town. Bring them all here. We'll wait for you."

"I'll leave right away!" Narad said with great excitement. "But, Lord, your town is too small. I'll come with thousands of people! Make your town a little bigger first and then I'll go." "Actually, my town is a little too big already," the Lord said. "But please, Narad, go and bring us more people. Bring everyone and then I'll make it bigger."

"I'll be right back!" Narad said, standing up immediately, "with thousands!" Narad picked up his tamboura, the instrument he played constantly, and left the beautiful town. He walked until he came to the next town and called together a large group of people. "Come with me to the home of the Lord!" he said. "It's beautiful! I'll be leaving soon. Don't you all want to come with me?

Narad was a great yogi and the town's people answered, "Yes! Yes!" Narad was pleased because it was a large group. "Remember," the leaders of the town said. "You've promised to take us to the home of the Lord, right? Let's leave soon so you don't forget the way." "I won't forget," Narad said.

The people got together and decided on a date for their departure. Word went out and when the day arrived Narad was extremely pleased. There was a huge crowd. Narad chanted and played his tamboura, leading everyone in prayer. Then they left.

On the way they came to a deep woods. As the great crowd entered the forest, golden coins fell from the top of the trees. Everyone got excited and got busy collecting the coins. Stop!" Narad said, but no one listened. "Guruji," the leaders told him. "We're definitely going to join you, but we'll be just a little bit late."

"All right," said Narad. "Those who want to collect golden coins can stay here. But I'm leaving and those who want to accompany me must continue with me." Now the crowd was cut in half. Narad continued walking and those who remained with him started talking among themselves. "Narad is a great yogi," they said. "If we follow him we'll acquire yogic powers. And look, because of him golden coins fell from the trees. Surely if we continue with him even greater things will happen to us." Just as they were saying this, diamonds fell from the sky.

The people became giddy with joy and rushed to collect as many diamonds as they could. "Foolish people," Narad said, "Let them be!" But no one heard Narad. They were all too busy collecting diamonds. Now only four people remained. "Brothers and sisters," Narad said. "Come with me to the home of the Lord. It's very close now." "No," they said. "Look at all these people collecting diamonds. They've forgotten about the Lord. If we go with you, they'll forget entirely. We'll stay here and become their teachers."

Narad was a great yogi and knew their minds. "How cunning," he thought. They've seen everyone else collect the gold coins and diamonds. Now they can gain wealth from them through donations as spiritual teachers." Narad was walking alone when he came to the home of the Lord. The Lord was standing at the beautiful gate to the city waiting for him. Narad was so tired that he could hardly raise his head to gaze at the Lord. The compassionate Lord took his hand and gave him a seat close to Him.

"Narad?" the Lord said softly. "You were going to bring a large crowd. What happened?" Narad burst into tears. "I told everyone about You and Your beautiful home. I chanted and prayed and played my tamboura, but in the end nobody came with me. They all had their reasons why they wanted to stay."

If we don't loosen the attraction of worldly things, how can the love of God be born in our hearts? When our only desire is love for the Lord, then our progress back to His home will be quick. May this love be born in us all.

******

As far as I can tell, Swami Kripalu always taught free of charge, never expecting donations in return. He was supported by his followers, a fact that led him to say, "While I have tried to remain absorbed in service, without any wish for its fruit, society has taken the greatest care of me and my body, giving me milk instead of water, and velvet seats to sit upon."

4-1: Eklavya, Student of Archery

After his experience of pranotthana, Swami Kripalu began to recognize references to this inner form of yoga instruction in various stories and scriptures. This story was prepared and presented as part of a formal discourse. It includes key pieces of the commentary offered by Swami Kripalu during its telling.

******

Maharishi Dronacharya was a powerful master and the guru of the five Pandava princes. As a teacher of archery, he was famous the world over. Thousands of kings and princes would come to Drona's lotus feet from great distances just to learn the science of archery. Eklavya was the son of a *nishada* (hunter tribe) chieftain. He had a great love for archery and had heard about the fame of Drona. Eklavya dreamed of becoming Dronacharya's disciple, but his mother told him that as a shudra or person from the lowest caste, it was futile to dream of such a privilege. Still, with much enthusiasm, Eklavya went to Drona's ashram. When Eklavya arrived, Drona was returning to his residence, surrounded by a crowd of students after completing his teaching for the day.

Eklavya recognized Dronacharya immediately and bowed down with love. Drona asked, "Whose son are you and why have you come?" He responded, "I am Eklavya, the son of Nishadraj Hiranyadhanu, and I have come to learn the science of archery from you." Drona gazed at Eklavya without blinking, then looked around at the surrounding crowd of kings and princes. Suddenly, just for a second, there was a sign of grief on his face, but no one noticed it.

Eklavya was standing there humbly and respectfully, with his hands folded. Drona could see that, although a shudra by birth, Eklavya was in fact a prince. At that time, Kshatriya (the warrior caste) princes were considered superior. They never let shudras study with them. When Eklavya asked this question, the ears of all the princes perked up to listen closely to how their teacher would reply.

With great affection, Drona said, "Son, as a river full of water never disappoints a thirsty man, an acharya who is full of knowledge never wants to disappoint an eager student. While I am an acharya, I am not free. I am bound to serve only Kshatriya princes, because I am paid to do so by their kingly fathers. Due to the caste system, I cannot teach you." The Kshatriya princes were satisfied with this response.

Sometimes social custom imposes impenetrable restrictions even for great masters.

There was a terrible pain of anguish on the shy face of Eklavya, who was very enthusiastic to learn archery. He thought, "Is it such a crime to be born in the lower class?" Eklavya's mental suffering touched the heart of Dronacharya and at once there was a flow of compassion between the two. Drona continued, "My son, I bless you. May you become the best archer."

New inspiration flowed into Eklavya, exhilarating his whole body. The expression on his face changed to one of ecstasy and humble joy. Eklavya bowed low and touched the lotus feet of his guru. With tears in his eyes, he humbly expressed his gratitude. "Gurudev, may you always be victorious. Today you have bestowed upon me the highest grace. Your infallible blessing is my wealth. The archers of the entire world will be jealous of what you have given me today." The princes did not like this last sentence of Eklavya. They thought him conceited and whimsical. Drona, however, understood his inner process and took him seriously. In that moment, he saw unusual genius in Eklavya, who believed his blessing to be the boon of God.

In the heart of the true disciple, the guru assumes the highest place. That is why Eklavya recognized Dronacharya's blessing. The disciple who does not understand the value of the guru is not a true disciple. Even if clever and learned, his heart is not pure and thus he can never receive the blessing of anyone.

Eklavya left the town with infinite enthusiasm and joy. After selecting a residence in a secluded spot in the woods, he worked day and night to make a clay idol of his beloved Gurudev. The image of his guru poured out from his memory, mind, intellect, eyes, and fingers and was faithfully reproduced in the clay. Eklavya made another Dronacharya, and there was no impression in any corner of his mind that it was merely made of clay. By making this statue of his guru, he became one with his guru.

After installing the idol of his gurudev, Eklavya began his study of archery. He slept very little and ate sparingly. Each morning he arose early. After finishing his routines, he would pick flowers and present them to the idol. He would bow down, pray, and bow again. Then drawing on the presence of his guru, he would ask "Gurudev, how should I begin my study of archery today?" As he felt his guru's presence, an answer would come from his inner conscience. Time passed thus with Eklavya lost in his study and practice.

One day, the Pandava princes went to the forest to hunt and Drona was with them. The royal servants were walking behind the chariots carrying the things necessary for the hunt. Looking for wild animals, the entourage included a hunting dog who strayed near the spot where Eklavya was practicing. On seeing his dark skin, and the way he wore his hair piled on the top of his head, the dog began to bark loudly. Not liking this interruption of his studies, Eklavya immediately shot seven arrows into the mouth of the dog to silence him. Though uninjured, the dog was frightened and ran back to his masters.

Arjuna was the best archer among all the princes and the first to see the dog. Astonished, he called to his brothers and said, "Come and look. Imagine the quickness and accuracy of the archer who could silence the sound of a barking dog by filling his mouth with arrows. His skill far surpasses that of mine. He must be in this vicinity, so let us search for him."

Immediately, Arjuna and his brothers began to search for the brave archer dwelling in the forest. They soon came to the place where Eklavya was practicing. Although they had all seen him before, no one recognized him because his appearance was totally different. Arjuna was the first to speak, "May I have your introduction please."

He replied, "My name is Eklavya. I am a disciple of Dronacharya and a practitioner of archery."

After praising Eklavya's skill, effort, and love for archery, the princes left. Returning to the city, they recounted the whole story to Drona. Although the other princes left to go home, Arjuna remained standing besides his guru with a shy expression on his face. Drona understood his reason for standing, and yet he said, "My son, do you want to ask me anything?"

Arjuna sat on the ground, holding his guru's feet, and started crying. After a few moments he was able to express his feelings, "Guruji, you have given me a blessing. Embracing me to your heart, you said that you would make me the best archer among all your disciples. How is it that Eklavya is more talented than me?"

Drona remained silent for a few moments. Taking his disciple's two hands, Drona raised Arjuna up and embraced him. "Come, take me to the place where Eklavya is practicing." Arjuna walked ahead, and Drona followed him. As they drew near, the sound of the bowstring became very clear. When Eklavya saw his guru in the distance, he was happy and hurried towards him. He bowed low, and a river of tears flowed from his eyes. Sobbing, he said "Gurudev, why have you pained your holy feet to give me your darshan (audience)?"

Upon seeing such devotion, the eyes of both Drona and Arjuna also filled with tears. Drona thought to himself, although Eklavya is a shudra in this birth, it is possible that he was a Brahmin, Kshatriya, or Vasya (merchant caste) in a previous lifetime. Although he has outstanding qualities, he is still a shudra nonetheless and must be regarded as such.

Eklavya brought them to his hut, and Drona looked at his image. Aware of the devotion of this disciple for his guru, love flowed from his heart toward Eklavya. Eklavya worshiped his guru according to the tradition, and bowed down before Dronacharya, who said, "My son, be blessed." After remaining silent, Drona asked, "Do you believe that I am your guru?" Eklavya said, "Yes." Dronacharya continued, "Then it is time to give me your guru dakshina (initiation gift.)" Hearing his guru's words, Eklavya was overwhelmed. "Gurudev, what can I sacrifice. Be gracious and give me your command. There is nothing I will not give to you."

"Cut off the thumb of your right hand and offer it to me as your guru gift," instructed Dronacharya. The atmosphere became very still. Even the leaves on the trees stopped moving. Arjuna was stunned to hear the demand of his guru. To ask for the thumb of an archer was equivalent to killing him. Yet hearing this order, Eklavya felt no hesitation or turmoil. With an expression of joy on his face, he cut off his thumb and placed it at his guru's feet. Witnessing this act, Arjuna felt small and stunted. There was no doubt that his guru brother, Eklavya, was far superior in his knowledge, skill, and guru bhakti (devotion). Yet Arjuna's position as top archer was now secure. Eklavya quickly stopped the flow of blood by bandaging the wound.

Drona asked, "Son, has this command caused you any pain?" Eklavya was silent for a moment as he decided whether or not to speak his mind. Then he said, "Guruji, I will only speak the truth in your presence. I have experienced infinite suffering. I offered my entire body to you, and you only asked for the thumb from my right hand. By severing my thumb, I have not offered you a true guru gift. You have given me my whole life, and I have given back only a minute portion of it. Upon your command, I will deposit the rest of my body at your holy feet." Drona stood up and embraced Eklavya, lovingly patting his head. Before he left, Dronacharya demonstrated to Eklavya a way to grasp the arrow and draw the bowstring using his middle fingers and pinkie. After this incident, Eklavya continued to practice daily, but he was not able to shoot as fast.

In this story, Eklavya's infinite faith in his guru brings the inanimate idol alive. Eklavya's devotion towards the idol allows him to enter a stage of meditation beyond the senses where one can one attain supreme knowledge. Through his love, Eklavya feels his guru's presence and is skillfully instructed in the science of archery. To understand how this could be, let us look at today's psychologists who have also conducted surprising experiments. A hypnotist can place a piece of ice in a subject's hand and suggest that it is a burning coal. Instantly, the subject throws away what is believed to be a burning coal and a blister becomes visible in his palm. This blister is also the result of a steady faith. Eklavya was receiving inspiration from within, yet his experience was that he was being told what to do by the idol. Due to the firmness of his faith, he became a yogi open to the suggestion of the divine. His idol worship was not ignorance; it was meditation and the science of yoga.

Did Dronacharya do an injustice to Eklavya? No, when one is about to receive a blow to his head, he stops it with his hand. Whether the blow strikes the head or the hand, the pain is the same. When a hand suffers a blow on behalf of the head, it is not dishonored. The status of the hand actually increases. In order to protect his guru's virtue, Eklavya sacrifices his thumb and prowess. In willingly doing so, he retains his faith and devotion as a disciple, which is of paramount importance to the consummation of his yoga.

****

Symbolically, Eklavya's right thumb represents his ego. After his guru takes his thumb, Eklavya goes back to his practice. It is easy to imagine the rest of his story. While losing his position as the world's best archer, he attains to the highest spirituality. Arjuna grows up to become a great warrior and play a major role in the Mahabharat. As a close devotee of Krishna and the world's foremost archer, circumstances unfold in which Arjuna and Drona are on opposing sides and Arjuna must kill his beloved guru. Viewed in the entirety of this epic work, the sting of Eklavya's fate is lessened.

4-2: The Crow and the Swan

In his early life, Swami Kripalu often referred to himself as a haughty crow and this story points out the facet of his personality that it appears he struggled most to overcome. He introduced it by saying, "In India, a white swan is considered the best among all the birds. While also a bird, the crow is looked down upon for always being after impure things. These ideas are reflected in this story, which illustrates how conceit and egotism block the path to acquiring true knowledge."

******

It was evening time when a flock of swans came down to rest under the canopy of a giant tree after flying a long distance over the ocean. In the rays of the setting sun, the combination of their glistening white bodies and peaceful demeanors filled the atmosphere with beauty.

Just then a crow landed on a branch of the tree. Spying the swans and jealous of their beauty, he did not like the arrival of these newcomers. Swooping down from the branch, he landed on the ground and strutted proudly towards the swans. Then standing still, he steadily gazed at the swans, looking each one over head to tail. When done, he asked in an unfriendly tone of voice. "Where did you all come from?" Beholding his proud walk, impolite behavior, and crude speech, the swans were amused but did not express it on their faces. Out of good manners, they lowered their eyes so the crow would not see their smiles.

One young male swan could not tolerate this unfriendly crow and his rude conduct. He came in front as if representing the group and said, "Dear friend, we have come a great distance and are resting, please join us." The crow disregarded the invitation to get closer and said, "I am all right where I am." The young swan said, "Okay, but please tell us why you have approached us." The crow responded, "Looking down upon you from the tree, I saw that you were beautiful, but one other thought also occurred in my mind. Can you fly?"

Seeing an opportunity to teach the haughty crow a lesson, the young swan said, "You must be the famous guru who gives flying lessons. Could this be the auspicious day when I will learn to fly?" The foolish crow was extremely pleased to hear this. With a smiling face he said, "Dear boy, your guess is correct." The swan continued with his act. "By God's grace, I am fortunate indeed. If you would accept me a disciple and give me private instruction, I would be very grateful." The crow was delighted to receive the young swan as his disciple, and the two of them stepped away from the group.

The young swan acted as if he could not contain his curiosity. "Gurudev, please tell me how many flying techniques you know?" The crow answered with pride, I know all of the 52 flying techniques. The swan exclaimed, "Are there really that many techniques of flying? I will not be able to learn them all, but could your highness teach me a few of them?" "Certainly," the crow said, "Please watch me carefully."

Saying this, the crow jumped up and flew a few feet in the air and returned to his original spot. Next he flew up, circled to his left and returned back. Then he flew up, circled around to the right and returned to his seat. Seeing the crow demonstrating his flying techniques with great enthusiasm, the swan interrupted him. "Enough, Gurudev, please stop. The techniques you are showing me are complicated, and I am not able to absorb them so quickly. I am seeing that your knowledge is indeed limitless. If I can lift off the ground, will you please show me your fastest flying technique?"

Blinded by pride, the crow answered in a scolding manner, "To fly with me is not child's play, but if you get tired you can ask me to slow down." The swan agreed and gestured in the direction of the ocean. The crow took off with the swan flying after him, pretending that he was working hard to keep up with his teacher.

Seeing that the swan was flying along, the crow flew faster and after a bit asked his student, "Are you getting tired?" The swan replied "No sir, you can increase your speed." So the crow flew a little faster and after a bit asked his question again. The swan answered with the same reply, and this exchange was repeated several times. Overexertion began taking its toll and the crow dipped lower and lower. Finally his body grazed the surface of the ocean. Caught by a wave, he began to drown. Seeing the fallen state of his guru, the swan asked, "What are you doing? Is this the 53rd technique of flying?" The exhausted crow's beak was full of water and he could say not a single word.

Pitying the crow, the swan took him onto his back and started flying toward the shore. When land was in sight, the swan said, "Gurudev, I know of only one flying technique. Please wrap your legs around my neck and I will show you." The crow tightened his grip on the swan, who started flying at such a high speed that the crow became dizzy and his eyes began popping out of his head. Reaching the shore, the crow lost his grip and plummeted to the ground. Landing on his head, he rolled over three times and went unconscious. Here ends the story of the proud crow.

******

Swami Kripalu grew increasingly skillful and adept over the course of his life, but it appears that he took the moral of this story to heart, as everything we know suggests that he also became more humble. This story has a second level of meaning, as it suggests that every yogi must ponder this question: What power is it that can change me from crow to swan? One possible answer is willful disciplines that render the body strong, the mind steady, and the executive function decisive and resolute. Another is conscious contact with a pure awareness that illumines the mind and brings forth higher qualities. Still another is awakened energy able to progressively catalyze healing, growth, and evolution. In different phases of his sadhana, all three of these answers are evident in Swami Kripalu's life.

5-1: The Legend of Vishvamitra's Tapas

Swami Kripalu traced his yoga lineage all the way back to an ascetic named Vishvamitra, who practiced a precursor to yoga called *tapas*. *Tapas* means to *generate heat and light*, a reference to the psychic heat and spiritual radiance generated by austerities like fasting and celibacy. Through prolonged tapas, ascetics like Vishvamitra strengthened their willpower and sought to accumulate psychic power and obtain divine boons. While so engaged, they pioneered many psycho-spiritual techniques that contributed to the development of what we know today as *yoga*. It was Vishvamitra who built the Shiva temple that centuries later would be occupied by Lakulish and called *Kayavarohan*.

******

Before embarking on the path of tapas, Vishvamitra was a king named Kaushika who ruled his subjects well. As was the custom of his day, Kaushika and his army would travel throughout the kingdom to assure the safety of his subjects. Kaushika honored the rules that applied to his station in life, and one such rule was that a king should not pass the hermitage of a sage without stopping to pay respects and ask for his or her blessing. In return, the sage would welcome the king, offering him hospitality and wise counsel. Such was the order of things.

One day Kaushika was passing by the hermitage of a Brahmin holy man named Vashishtha. Kaushika could see a stream wending its way through grounds full of flowering trees and shrubs. Deer and other animals walked freely about, and the air resounded with the music of birds. Coming nearer, the king noticed several sages performing tapas, and others lost in meditation. An aura of peace permeated the atmosphere. It seemed to Kaushika that the realm of the gods was not in the sky, but right here in Vashishtha's hermitage.

Kaushika entered and bowed low before the sage. Vashishtha welcomed him with warmth and fanfare, sending for a seat befitting a king and making Kaushika sit upon it like a throne. He offered the king fruits and milk, which Kaushika received with humility. Then they spoke of general things. Vashishtha asked, "I hope your family is well, and that your subjects are happy under your rule, which I am sure is righteous. Are your servants honest and obedient? Is your army large and powerful? Are your enemies subdued? Is your treasury full?" Kaushika answered in the affirmative, and in turn inquired about the health of the sage, if the residents of his hermitage were able to pursue their tapas without disturbance from bandits or wild animals, and if they lacked for any material goods. Each had respect for the other, and in the midst of these formalities a genuine affection sprung up between them.

After they had talked about many things, Vashishtha said, "You are a righteous ruler and a good man, and I would like to entertain you and your army this evening." Kaushika imagined the simple sage was unaware of the size and appetite of his army. To save Vashishtha from embarrassment, he said, "Your words, full of affection, have touched me deeply. You have given me food and drink, and basking in your presence has renewed my spirit. I will soon be taking leave of you to continue my journey." Kaushika rose up tactfully as if to go, but Vashishtha persisted until courtesy required him to accept the sage's hospitality.

Unbeknownst to Kaushika, Vashishtha had come into possession of a wish-fulfilling cow named Surabhi through his tapas. With a mere swish of her tail, all preparations were made. When the army arrived at the hermitage, each man was entertained in a manner that exceeded the luxury granted Kaushika in his royal court. Kaushika was told of the magical cow and saw she had a lovely shape, a gleaming coat of mottled color, and eyes that were soft and gentle.

Coveting the cow, Kaushika interrupted the gaiety to address all those present, "My lord, never in my life have I tasted food like that eaten by us this night. I am greatly impressed by the power of your cow and want to ask a favor of you. Such a cow should be possessed by the king of a country so her bounty can benefit everyone. Please give her to me, and I will give you a thousand cows."

Vashishtha was taken aback by the words of Kaushika. But he composed himself and softly said, "I hate to refuse anyone anything. But not for a hundred thousand or even a thousand thousand cows will I give up my Surabhi. She is part of me, and cannot be separated from me. I have no use for wealth in any form that you could offer. My answer is no, and that is certain."

Kaushika was stunned. Never before had a desire of his been frustrated. Anger took possession of Kaushika, who ordered his army to seize the cow. With a shake of her body, hundreds of warriors appeared that easily defeated Kaushika's forces. Kaushika's sons entered the fray, quickly thinning out the ranks of the opposing warriors, but the cow just created more. Then Kaushika ordered his sons to attack Vashishtha, who raised his staff skyward and burned every one of them to ash. The king was heartbroken. His army was destroyed and his sons were dead. Like a serpent with its fangs pulled out, or a bird whose wings have been clipped, he was vanquished and humiliated.

Kaushika relinquished his throne and retired to the northern forests to perform tapas. He went without food, water, or feminine companionship. He refrained from lying down and sleeping. In the summer, Kaushika sat in the center of a circle of five fires. In the winter, he sat naked in the snow. Kaushika's thoughts were always hovering around the humiliating defeat he had suffered at the hands of Vashishtha. Inwardly, Kaushika called again and again upon Lord Shiva to appear and grant him a boon.

Many years passed, and the power of Kaushika's tapas grew so great that the ground began to tremble. Mountains spit fire and the seas roiled. Fearing for the earth, the gods gathered and begged Shiva to grant Kaushika's wish and end his austerities. Appearing before Kaushika, Shiva inquired, "Why are you performing this tapas? What do you desire?" Kaushika prostrated and sang Shiva's praises. He then asked to be made supremely proficient in the art of archery and granted every spiritual power useful in combat. Shiva said, "I have given them to you, now go in peace."

Kaushika's pride was restored, and he said to himself, "Vashishtha the great is as good as dead. I will destroy him and bring that cow to my kingdom." Kaushika proceeded directly to Vashishtha's hermitage. Arriving, he raised his bow and let fly a flurry of arrows and the incantations that rendered them powerful. The hermitage was quickly destroyed, its residents fleeing in fear, and even the soil beneath it left bare, salty, and fit for nothing.

His staff glowing red hot, Vashishtha came before Kaushika and said, "This peaceful hermitage is ruined, and I am angry with you." Kaushika had lived this moment many times in his mind and was not afraid. Relishing his revenge, Kaushika loosed his full arsenal against his foe. Amazingly, Vashishtha was able to deflect all Kaushika's weapons by simply lifting his staff. Vashishtha then cursed Kaushika, saying, "You are a disgrace to the warrior caste. Acknowledge the divine power of the Brahmins." Kaushika threw down his bow and exclaimed, "Fie on the power of a warrior. The only power worth having is that of a Brahmin." Inwardly, he vowed to perform tapas until he too became a Brahmin.

Kaushika's hatred for Vashishtha was now immense. He traveled to the southern forests determined to conduct the most demanding tapas. He stood on one foot, never slept, and took air as his only food. It is said that Kaushika's tapas was so intense that wisps of smoke could be seen wafting out of his ears. After a thousand years, Kaushika was glowing like the sun itself, and the earth was in danger of being burned up. In heaven, the heat was upsetting the wives of the gods, whose complaints became intolerable. Indra's throne became too hot to sit upon. In desperation, Indra summoned Menaka, the finest woman in his court, and said, "Kaushika is performing tapas and glowing like the noonday sun. Go to him. With your beauty and winning ways, make him succumb to the weakness in the heart of every man. If he abandons his tapas, I will be pleased with you."

Menaka was afraid and said, "Lord, I have been told Kaushika is very powerful and quick tempered. Think of this combination: anger and tapas. You yourself are afraid of him, yet you want me to face him." Despite these concerns, Indra persuaded her to go. Menaka went down to earth and spent several years in the vicinity of Kaushika, waiting for the proper moment to make her appearance. One day Kaushika got up from meditation and was moving about. Menaka walked by the spot with her eyes looking away from him. Just as he noticed her, a faint breeze blew her shawl aside, revealing her heavenly form. Then she slowly turned her lovely face towards him.

Five years passed, and another five, before Kaushika awoke from this pleasurable dream and remembered his tapas. At first he was angry with himself, but slowly it dawned on him that this was the work of the gods, bent on distracting him. Menaka, holding their daughter in her arms, could see what was transpiring on his face. She was overcome with fear, but Kaushika was not angry with her. Bidding Menaka farewell, Kaushika traveled west and engaged in tapas even more terrible that before. He held both arms aloft and never closed his eyes. Years passed and the gods found themselves once again concocting ways to distract Kaushika.

It came to pass that a disciple of Vashishtha named Trishanku asked his guru for an unusual boon: to be admitted into heaven in his mortal body. Vashishtha denied his request, saying that it was an impious and improper wish. Unsatisfied by his guru's response, Trishanku approached Kaushika, who seized upon this opportunity to outdo and embarrass Vashishtha. Kaushika performed a ritual that called upon the gods to gather. When all the rulers of heaven were present, Kaushika asked them to accept Trishanku into heaven. Seeing an opportunity to exhaust his storehouse of tapas, the gods insulted Kaushika and refused his request. Ignoring their refusal, Kaushika raised Trishanku into the sky with the force of his tapas. A tug of war ensued between the gods and Kaushika, in which Trishanku see-sawed between heaven and earth. In the end, Kaushika was able to grant Trishanku's request by creating a whole new universe, ruled by another set of gods, who accepted him into their heaven. Although Kaushika was victorious, his treasury of tapas was once again empty.

Kaushika traveled east and found a secluded spot. He observed total silence, refused to eat or drink, and even his consumption of air was regulated. After some number of years, Indra grew concerned that Kaushika was going to usurp his status as the most powerful being in the universe. Another of his heavenly courtesans was sent, but Kaushika recognized the ploy. Turning her to stone with a curse, Kaushika realized in the next moment that this display of anger was yet another lapse from his tapas, which he resumed immediately.

Breathing regularly, Kaushika's mind gradually grew peaceful. After spending many years lost in trance, Kaushika was awakened by a young boy crying in his lap. As Kaushika opened his eyes, the boy said, "I have no father, no mother, and no kinsmen. I have been told you are very powerful and very compassionate. You are my only refuge. Please help me." Pacifying the boy, Kaushika learned that he was the middle of three sons. The father was fond of the eldest, the mother was fond of the youngest. Being preferred by neither parent, he had been sold for a few cows to be the subject of a human sacrifice.

Kaushika told the boy, "Go and allow yourself to be tied to the sacrificial post. They will place garlands around your neck and smear sandalwood paste on your body. At that time, begin repeating in your mind this two verse hymn. When the ceremony is at its zenith, sing it out loud." The boy learned the hymn with great care and left Kaushika grateful and confident. The sacrificial chamber fell silent when the boy's words rang out, with his captors at first surprised and then filled with admiration at the nobility of his hymn, which eloquently praised the gods. Empowered by Kaushika's tapas, the hymn caused the gods to appear, grant the wishes of those conducting the sacrifice, spare the life of the boy, and bless him with long life and good fortune.

Although he acted out of compassion, Kaushika's treasury of tapas had once again been diminished. Hearing of the boy's success, he returned to his trance for a thousand more years, steadily deepening his concentration. About this time, the Gayatri mantra was revealed to Kaushika from within, and his practice shifted from tapas to one of the earliest forms of yoga: mantra meditation. Inwardly, Kaushika intoned the prayer to a measured and melodic meter: *Almighty God! Thou art the giver of life, the remover of pain and sorrow, and the bestower of happiness. Creator of the Universe, illumine my intellect with thy sin-destroying light and guide me along the path of righteousness.*

Meditating on this prayer of divine origin, all obstacles fell away and Kaushika realized the Brahman (Absolute). Feeling completely at peace, Kaushika noticed he was thin as a stick. He cooked some rice and prepared to break his fast of many years. Just as he was about to eat, Indra appeared before Kaushika disguised in the form of a mendicant begging for food. Kaushika spoke not a word but happily handed him all the rice.

Seeing that Kaushika looked upon the beggar's hunger as no different from his own, Lord Brahma appeared to Kaushika, and said, "With your own efforts, you have achieved the status of a Brahmin. May you prosper." Kaushika prostrated before Lord Brahma and spoke, "If what you say is true, the great sage Vashishtha should recognize me as such." Vashishtha came forth saying, "There is no doubt about it. You are a great man and a Brahmin." A thin smile lit up the face of Kaushika, who honored Vashishtha with true affection. Because the foremost thought in his mind was to do good to others, he was given the name Vishvamitra which means "friend of the universe."

Vishvamitra wandered until he discovered a suitable location to establish a place of pilgrimage. Through the power of his tapas, he altered the course of the holy Ganges in the north, connecting it with the Rangavati river, which flowed nearby. Using this now holy source of water, he created several deep pools for pilgrims to bathe. The site was completed with the building of the Brahmeshvar temple, which housed a Shiva lingam made of meteorite. The pilgrimage place came to be known as "Medhavati," which means "place of purified intellect." It was from here that Vishvamitra propagated the practice of austerity, Shiva worship, and mantra yoga.

News of Vishvamitra spread far and wide. With characteristic zeal, Vishvamitra resumed his tapas to make his pilgrimage site the most famous in all India, surpassing even Kashi in its glory. Shortly thereafter, Vishnu appeared in the form of an old and deaf Brahmin. Distracting Vishvamitra from his tapas, Vishnu revealed his true form and said, "Great Brahmin, your efforts are not in vain. This pilgrimage site will be an important seat of learning. Those who inhabit this place will quickly become pure of heart and the holy Gayatri mantra will resound throughout the universe. Yet it will not compete with Kashi."

On hearing this, Vishvamitra became despondent. Vishnu empathized, saying, "Do not be disheartened. Your dream will be fulfilled when Shiva himself incarnates in this place as Lakulish." Vishvamitra accepted the divine plan. Living a long life, he inspired many to pursue the path of tapas and yoga. Emanating from Medhavati and other places of pilgrimage and learning, the Vedic culture of India spread throughout the land and remained vital for several thousand years.

******

The story of Vishvamitra's life colorfully conveys the transformative power of self-discipline. Ancient India was a highly structured society built upon a rigid caste system. Although Kaushika was a warrior king, the superiority of the priestly Brahmins – a word meaning born from the mouth of Brahman (God) – was taken for granted. In the context of his time, the assertion that a person could raise himself up to the spiritual status of a Brahmin through personal effort was radical and revolutionary. This is a message that we all have untapped potential lying dormant within us, astounding capacities that can be awakened through focused spiritual practice.

At the beginning of the story, Kaushika is depicted as a virtuous and dutiful king, which signifies the progress he made on the householder path of dharma and his fitness to engage in deeper practices. As is often the case, Kaushika's point of entry comes through contact with a spiritual teacher. Vashishtha's enlightened state is symbolized by his wish-fulfilling cow, which has satisfied all his desires and "is part of him and cannot be separated from him." While there is mutual respect and genuine warmth between the two men at the outset, Kaushika's relationship with Vashishtha quickly turns into a profound and long-lasting struggle. Vashishtha's choice to refrain from killing Kaushika in their two confrontations suggests the sage is aware that Kaushika has the capacity to make the shift from warrior king to enlightened sage. Vashishtha's dinner invitation might have been intended to set this whole chain of events into motion. Consciously or unconsciously, spiritual teachers like Vashishtha often fulfill their role in unusual ways.

Kaushika sets out upon the path of tapas with a truly base motive: revenge. This may seem odd, but in truth everyone embarks on the spiritual path for the wrong reasons. Unconsciously, we want to be loved, find relief from suffering, attain power over others, or simply avoid the rigors of facing life directly and honestly. It is only by walking the path, and wandering repeatedly off it, that our motivations are slowly but surely purified.

Although we may have an intuitive sense of our hidden potential, few embark on the path without considerable baggage and a multiplicity of wrong views. It could be said that the main purpose of spiritual practice is to purify us of whatever self-limiting notions are holding us back. At the outset, Kaushika views tapas as a path to vanquish his nemesis and fulfill his egocentric needs and desires. As he journeys onward, this view is turned on its head, with Kaushika being repeatedly humbled. Realization comes only when he is able to let go of his quest for power and status, and sincerely surrender to a higher power.

The duration and intensity of Kaushika's tapas graphically describe the challenge inherent in the spiritual journey, which involves the interruption of innumerable ingrained habits and self-serving patterns of behavior. As the fire of transformation blazes, internal energies build to the breaking point and external situations invariably arise to block the aspirant from going forward until needed lessons are learned. Instead of being immune to distraction, Kaushika succumbs to every temptation that tests him. Despite falling prey to greed, anger, lust, pride, and sentimentality, Kaushika sooner or later remembers his intention and resumes his tapas. These "lapses" are actually the learning process in action.

While each of us is spurred on by an inner urge to grow, there is a definite cost to speeding up the pace of our evolution. The homeostasis of our life is disturbed, time and time again, as the fire of transformation rages. Kaushika's tapas keeps all the gods on edge, disrupting them from enjoying heaven, symbolizing the socially acceptable pleasures we all use to dull and distract ourselves. This story is a clear warning that the spiritual path is demanding. Tapas is done in all four directions, reflecting a need to uplift every area of our lives, and all three Hindu deities – Shiva, Brahma and Vishnu – are eventually encountered. No stone is left unturned on the road to realization.

As his lower nature is brought into balance, Kaushika is able to make a crucial shift. His tapas of inner struggle ceases, and he lets go of external austerities like sitting near fires and holding his arms aloft. There is a beautiful "story within a story" about the boy sold for sacrifice. As mortals awaiting death, each of us shares his predicament. Looked at in this light, the best we can do is go willingly, singing God's praises.

When Kaushika starts to regulate his breathing, he has commenced the practice of pranayama so integral to yoga. As a result, Kaushika falls first into trance and then into peaceful meditation. Instead of thoughts hovering around hatred and desire, a prayer of reverent worship (the Gayatri mantra) arises within him. With this as his focal point, Kaushika is able to dive deep and realize the Brahman. Returning from trance, he is a truly changed person, his personality and character indelibly stamped by what was traditionally called the Brahmavidya – supreme knowledge of the Absolute.

Kaushika's realization does not go untested. Indra appears in a guise strikingly similar to Vashishtha to eat his rice. This is to ensure that Kaushika has woven the truth of spiritual oneness into the very fabric of his being. Life is full of rice eaters and other aggravations that test our mettle. In the Kripalu tradition, it is not the power of a yoga experience, but its expression in daily life that is the true measure of enlightenment. Kaushika is pronounced a Brahmin only after he treats the hunger of another as equivalent to his own.

Kaushika is given the name Vishvamitra to signify his unconditional positive regard for all beings. If there is any guidance that can be trusted to hold true at any stage of the path, it is this inward stance of being the well wisher of self and others. After realization, it is noteworthy that Vishvamitra remains to some extent his stubborn and ornery self, attempting to make his pilgrimage spot the best of any in India. Yet when Vishnu appears to say this is not in the cards, Vishvamitra is able to let go without a fight.

Vishvamitra goes on to promote a path in which adherents learn to restrain the wayward mind and senses through austerities, internalize awareness through pranayama and mantra meditation, and awaken to the vast ocean of being that underlies the individual waves of bodymind and personality. The goal of this path is symbolized in the Shiva lingam installed as the focus of worship in the Brahmeshvar temple. The lingam represents the Absolute and male principle, which is seen as immaterial and spiritual. In this view, the feminine principle is seen as embodied in creation, matter, and the physical body. Asceticism almost always involves a rejection of the material and feminine in order to realize the spiritual, and that is the case here. The story ends with a hint that there is more to come. While self-discipline can bring many things, the highest is beyond its reach.

Scholars believe Vishvamitra lived circa 3500 B.C.E. Along with Vashishtha, Vishvamitra is remembered as one of the seven great rishis – a word meaning seer – whose collective wisdom established the Vedic culture known today as Hinduism. Of the seven, Vishvamitra was the only one not born a Brahmin. The full story of Vishvamitra's tapas can be found in the *Srimad Bhagavatam*.

5-2: The Legend of Lord Lakulish

The central figure in Swami Kripalu's yoga lineage is Lakulish, the twenty-eight and most recent incarnation of Lord Shiva, the Hindu deity closely associated with yoga and the quest for transformation. Images of Lakulish appear in temples all over India and coins of old bear his likeness, but little is known about Lakulish's life beyond this legend of his miraculous birth and death.

The legend opens with a reference back to the Vedic culture established by the rishis, which has grown stagnant for want of potent teachers and is sorely in need of revival. It closes with a marked shift in narration. With the recounting of the legend complete, Swami Kripalu tells the story of how the statue of Lakulish was found by a Kayavarohan farmer in 1866.

✶✶✶✶✶✶

Lakulish was born in the village that sprang up around Medhavati, the pilgrimage site established by Vishvamitra. His father's name was Vishvarup and his mother was Sudarshana. Descended from a long ancestral line of Brahmins, the life of their household orbited around a schedule of ceremonies, rituals, and other sacred rites.

Shortly after Sudarshana gave birth to a son, Vishvarup prepared to go on a lengthy pilgrimage. Traveling on foot to holy places, his intent was to ask the gods to bestow good qualities upon the boy. Before departing, he instructed Sudharshana to continue the family's religious observances in his absence. She was to prepare the necessary materials each morning, and seek the help of a local priest to perform the ceremonies later in the day.

After three months, a strange event began to occur. Sudharshana would leave the house to fetch the priest and return home to find the elaborate ceremonies already performed. The sacred fire would be lit, with all the ceremonial articles bearing signs that evidenced their proper use. Yet the house was empty except for the infant child sleeping in the cradle. This did not happen only once. It happened on the second, third, and fourth days too. Then it became a daily occurrence. Neither Sudarshana nor the priest could explain this mystery.

When Vishvarup returned, Sudarshana recounted the whole story. Determined to solve the mystery, Vishvarup concealed himself in an adjacent house. While hiding, he was amazed to see his infant son climb out of his crib, carry out the ceremonies with perfection, and then crawl back into his bed. Amazed and overjoyed, Vishvarup and Sudarshana entered the house and hugged their precocious son. Knowing these capacities could only be possessed by a most unusual child, Vishvarup inquired, "Son, tell us who you really are?" The child instantly fainted, and his body became lifeless. All efforts to revive the boy proved futile, and the mood of Vishvarup and Sudarshana shifted from joy to grief.

As was the custom of the time, Vishvarup and Sudarshana laid the child's body to rest in a nearby pond. The unusual events continued, as tortoises appeared to carry the body into the pond's depths, placing it at the base of a Shiva lingam installed there by local holy men. A few months passed, during which Vishvarup and Sudarshana returned to their lives, attempting to make sense of what had happened and not lose themselves in sorrow and grief.

Meanwhile and unbeknownst to anyone, the infant's body was undergoing a profound metamorphosis. Growing into a youth, the boy floated to the surface and was found by local sages playing on the surface of the water with a stick in his hand. Seeing his radiant countenance, the sages asked, "Who are you?"

The boy answered: "I am prana." The sages were intrigued by this response, prana being a yogic term for the life force of the body. Engaging the boy in dialogue, the sages were amazed at his penetrating wisdom. He was called Lakulish (club carrier) because he held a stick in his hand when he was found. Ascertaining his complete mastery of yoga, they determined that he was the incarnation of Shiva the sages had long ago prophesized would be born in this place.

News of the incarnation spread. Sages, royalty, and seekers from far-off places began arriving to receive Lakulish's audience. The name of the village was changed to Kayavarohan, which means "Shiva descended into a body." With Lakulish in residence, the rural pilgrimage site quickly grew into a flourishing city, renowned for the purity and prosperity of its inhabitants. Under Lakulish's guidance, many aspirants became realized yoga masters and powerful teachers. Lakulish directed them to locate throughout the land and rejuvenate India's spiritual culture.

After many years, Lakulish summoned his principle disciples to Kayavarohan, asking them to gather at an appointed hour in the Brahmeshvar temple. Everyone was puzzled by the same question: "Why has Gurudev called us together?" A host of kings, ascetics, and devotees also arrived to participate. Seated up front near the jyotir lingam (radiant sign of Shiva) installed by Vishvamitra ages ago, Lakulish ordered the doors to be shut. Gold and silver lamps were burning, and all round was the fragrance of incense and flowers. Everyone was basking in the atmosphere filled with divine vibrations when Lakulish broke the silence by declaring, "My life mission has been fulfilled, and my time on earth is drawing to a close. I want to say goodbye before merging into the infinite."

As if struck by a thunderbolt, the throng broke into sobs and tears until their throats became choked. There was nothing the grieving group could do. Lakulish's chief disciples performed a ritual worshipping first the jyotir lingam, and then their teacher. Afterwards, Lakulish blessed them all and instructed the group, "Close your eyes for a moment of silent prayer."

Folding their hands, they instantly fell into profound meditation. None could determine how long they had been in that state, but when the gathering came out its collective reverie, they found that Lakulish had disappeared. His figure could now be seen on the front of the black stone idol. He had merged into the jyotir lingam by becoming the Divine Light. The doors of the temple were thrown open and the local people rushed in to bear witness to this miracle.

The Pashupat teachings rejuvenated by Lakulish remained vital for over a thousand years. In the year 1025, the Muslims invaded India when an acharya named Anant Sarvagna was the teacher in charge of Kayavarohan. On a full-moon night, he awakened from his sleep shortly after midnight. When his efforts to sleep again proved in vain, he decided to sit in meditation. Going to the temple, he entered into samadhi and saw a vision of a bright ray of Divine Light shoot up into the sky from the jyotir lingam of Somnath (another holy shrine in Gujarat) and come down to enter the jyotir lingam at Kayavarohan. This vision disturbed his samadhi, so Anant Sarvagna again tried to meditate. Then he saw a similar vision: a ray of Divine Light shooting out of the jyotir lingam in Kashi to enter the jyotir lingam at Kayavarohan. Twelve times this cycle repeated, as the Divine Light left all the other jyotir lingams.

Anant Sarvagna meditated a 13th time and beheld a terrible vision of his disciple, Gang Sarvagna, in the Somnath temple. Next to him stood the victorious Muslim king, Mohammad Gaznavi, who wanted to destroy the jyotir lingam but had granted Gang Sarvagna's last wish to worship the idol. When his worship was over, Gang embraced the jyotir lingam and left his body through a yogic technique. The king ordered Gang to get up, but his lifeless body would not move. In anger, one of the king's men hit Gang on the head with a club. His blood colored the jyotir lingam, which was then broken into pieces by the invaders. Anant Sarvagna's terrible vision continued as he saw innumerable temples ransacked and idols broken throughout the land. The horrific sights and cracking sounds that accompanied this vision disturbed his samadhi yet again.

In his fourteenth attempt at meditation, Lord Lakulish appeared before Anant Sarvagna. Prostrating before him, Anant Sarvagna said, "Lord, you have graced me with a vision of future events. I have seen that the Divine Light has been withdrawn from all the other temples and is now merged into you. What is your command?" Lord Lakulish replied, "Now that the Divine Power has been withdrawn from the other 12 lingams, the invaders will break only the stones. This is the requirement of the time, and yogis shall not resist it. Before dawn breaks, I wish to go underground. Just follow me." Lakulish and Anant Sarvagna walked some distance from the temple and approached a pit, which had already been dug. Lakulish stepped down and sat in the pit, instructing Anant Sarvagna to cover him and then fill the pit with soil. With tears rolling from his eyes, he obeyed the command. Walking back to the temple, he found the jyotir lingam bearing the image of Lord Lakulish was gone. In its place was an ordinary stone idol. That very day, through yogic technique, Anant Sarvagna gave up his earthly body.

Swami Kripalu narrates further: With Kayavarohan being the center of yoga in India for 1500 years, we can imagine that its idol disappeared for a specific purpose. In this idol, the most powerful secrets of yoga are hidden. It was to protect these secrets and preserve the science of yoga that the idol must have gone underground. So now I will tell you the story of how this idol was found.

One day a very innocent farmer went to his field with his bullock plow. He was a devotee of Lord Shiva and as he worked was uttering his mantra: Hara, Hara, Hara (Shiva, Shiva, Shiva). As he was moving forward, his plow stopped suddenly in one spot. So he placed his plow on its side and felt into the earth with his hand. Feeling that there was something there, he got a shovel to and started digging from all sides. Even though it was very big, he was able to easily expose the statue. The farmer had plowed this field many times and thought, "something must have brought the idol to the surface." Seeing that it was too heavy for any individual to move, he wondered what to do next. It was a very beautiful idol, so he looked around and saw a flower vine, which he placed at its feet.

Leaving his field, the farmer walked quickly into town and told everybody that he had discovered a great idol. Kayavarohan is a small town and the message immediately spread all over. Everyone gathered and went there in a crowd, singing with drums and cymbals. When they saw this idol, they were surprised, for it is not made from ordinary stone but the stuff of a fallen star (meteorite), so it had a celestial beauty. Only when you see the statue for yourself will you understand.

The crowd lifted the idol into a wagon, brought it into town, and placed it in a small temple. People heard the news and came from near and far for darshan, but after two or three years, things became quiet. People felt it was a most unusual idol but nobody knew what to do about it. They didn't know that Kayavarohan had been one of the most sacred and revered places in all of India where thousands of pilgrims would come, because it was now a small town and its history had been forgotten.

In America, such a happening is not possible. But today in India there are government archaeologists conducting digs and research throughout the country and finding lost cities buried hundreds and thousands of years ago. In America, it seems hard to believe that a farmer would find a statue and immediately place his faith in it and worship it with flowers. But Indians have those kind of *samskaras* (instilled impressions) and their feelings of devotion to God in the form of a statue is a unique cultural attitude. It cannot be explained in a simple way.

******

This legend and its concluding story complete the tale of Swami Kripalu's yoga lineage and its link to Kayavarohan. 841 years elapsed from 1025, the date the Somnath temple is known to have been ransacked, to the farmer's unearthing of the idol in 1866. The idol would remain in its small enclosure for another 89 years until it was seen and recognized by Swami Kripalu in 1955. The legend is too rich in symbolic meaning to interpret here. For a full commentary, see *Swimming with Krishna, Teaching Stories from the Kripalu Yoga Tradition*, pages 28-36.

6-1: The Businessman's Silence

Swami Kripalu believed that yogic disciplines have universal value and can be applied in daily life by householders. This story illustrates the usefulness of restraining your speech when facing a difficult situation.

******

Once upon a time an orphan boy named Mohan lived in a poverty stricken section of Bengal. Mohan's parents had died when he was just a little boy, and he was raised by all his neighbors who pitied him. As Mohan became a young man, he found work as a laborer. He was industrious and everyone loved him because he was generous, polite, tolerant, honest, and soft-spoken. Saving his wages, he opened a small shop in which he sold roasted chickpeas, which enabled him to get married and have three children. Mohan's good qualities enabled him to escape poverty and become a prosperous businessman.

Every Sunday there was an open-air market in his section of the city. Mohan would sit there with bags full of roasted chickpeas and always make a good profit. One Sunday he was going to the market as usual, with his cart loaded with bags of chickpeas. The market was especially crowded that day, so he pushed his cart slowly while shouting, "Hey, brother! Please let me by! Hey, sister! Please make way for me! Oh, mother, please allow me to pass!"

At one intersection, the crowd was dense and pressing. He continued to crawl forward, still shouting, when suddenly a child ran right in front of him and was crushed to death under his cart. People gathered around screaming. The police came. Mohan was terribly upset. He spoke to the police and explained that it was an accident. Although he was innocent, the child's mother claimed otherwise. The two gave differing reports to the police and eventually a day was fixed for his trial.

The day before his trial, Mohan went to the Sunday market with his bags of chickpeas as usual, but his mind was worried and unsteady for tomorrow he must stand trial. There were dark lines of grief on his face and he tried to appease his worry by continually praying to God. Then a sanyasi appeared. Many times this sanyasi had gratefully received roasted chickpeas from Mohan on Sundays at the marketplace. The sanyasi was free of worldly desires, and Mohan and the people of the city loved him dearly. Today, like always, he lovingly accepted alms from Mohan. But seeing Mohan's sad face, he asked, "Brother, why are you so sad today?"

Mohan steadied his shaking voice and told the sanyasi the story of his cart accident, concluding with the news that he must stand trial the next day and face the angry mother. The sanyasi listened carefully and then asked a few questions about the incident. After thinking for awhile, he asked Mohan, "During the trial, will you behave as I advise?" "I trust you as I would my own my father," Mohan replied. "Then tomorrow when the prosecuting attorney interrogates you, observe silence and reflect upon the Lord."

"I will follow your instructions," Mohan said humbly. The sanyasi blessed him and departed. The next day Mohan went to court. First, the woman whose child had died recounted her version of the whole incident. Her lawyer then interrogated Mohan, who remained silent. Keeping his kind composure, he wouldn't answer a single question. Unable to tolerate Mohan's silence, the woman lost her temper. Interrupting her attorney, she loudly snapped, "When you were on your way to the market in your cart, your voice was certainly loud enough! You could speak then! You could have broken someone's eardrum shouting, 'Make way! Make way!' Why are you playing dumb now? Why won't you speak?"

Mohan's lawyer immediately jumped to his feet. "When Mohan was shouting so loudly for the right-of-way passing through the pressing crowd, why didn't you hold your son?" he asked the woman. "Clearly you heard him shouting! Why didn't you keep your son from running so freely?" The mother had no answer.

After hearing all the testimony, the judge declared Mohan innocent and set him free. Afterwards, Mohan's attorney asked him privately, "Why did you observe silence?" "A sanyasi living in our city advised me to observe silence and reflect upon God when the prosecuting attorney interrogated me," Mohan said. Mohan's lawyer inquired about the name of the sanyasi and said, "Mohanbhai, you may not know it, but that renunciate was a famous trial lawyer before taking his vow of sanyas. His advice helped clearly demonstrate your innocence today."

Although Mohan had observed silence for just a few moments, they were just the right moments to stay quiet. Conversely, although the irate mother had let her tongue loose for just a few moments, those were just the wrong moments to let it loose.

******

Although this story involves a businessman's trial in a court of law, Swami Kripalu taught that the ability to curb the tongue was even more critical in our everyday family setting, where bitter speech, fault-finding, and quarreling can destroy the close bonds that make a family happy and resilient.

7-1: Two Great Swamis Come to America

Swami Kripalu felt that his journey to America was a trick of fate arranged with little to no forethought. Yet these stories show that a foundation had been laid in his mind by two renowned and very different swamis who had come before him.

******

Once there was an Indian boy named Narendra Kumar. From birth he had a good character and his early life was happy. His keen intellect helped him receive a good education. But then his comfortable family situation changed. The experience of poverty made his mother unhappy, as she had to feed Narendra and all his brothers and sisters. Seeing his intelligence, Narendra's school teachers helped him qualify to attend the university, a distinction that helped his mother hold onto her high expectations.

More and more, his mother looked to Narendra for help. This son of hers was unusually bright and extremely capable. Certainly he would complete his studies, find a good job, and save their family. She estimated that within a year all her problems would be removed. Then he would marry, his wife would come to live with her, and with God's grace she would see the face of her grandchild. And then, as she neared death, she would say to her son: "Narendra, because of you, my unhappy heart has received peace. I give my full blessings to you and your family. My last desire is to go now to the holy place of Kashi and leave my body there." That was her dream.

But Almighty God had a different plan for Narendra. The events that his mother envisioned were ordinary, but the gracious Lord planned to bestow a greater happiness on her different from what she imagined. So God called the Angel of Struggle. Struggle came and God gave some secret commands, then Struggle walked away.

At this time, Narendra Kumar was just finishing his degree. While at the university he had studied complicated philosophies and scriptures like the Upanishads. He had also come into contact with numerous saints. He was more attracted to the spiritual than the material, but upon completing his studies he began to search for a job. He was confident that he could find one quickly. When this didn't happen, he became frustrated. As his failure dragged on and on, he became ashamed of himself and lost all self-confidence. Here he was with a university degree, yet no one would hire him. What was wrong with him, he asked? He was earning no income, nothing at all, and his family had no savings to rely on.

One day Narendra discovered that there had been no grain in the house for the past three days and his mother was going hungry in order to feed him. This was intolerable. So he renewed his job search with even greater determination. Living in Calcutta, there was no lack of public transportation or restaurants. But poor Narendra did not have enough money in his pockets for even a snack. So each morning he left home early to walk the city. Whenever he felt hungry, he drank water.

Each evening he returned to his house dejected. But before entering his home, he rested his sore feet for a moment, wiped the look of failure off his face, and walked in the door only when he felt strong again. Then in a sweet voice, full of love, he told his mother the same lie. "Mother, sorry I'm late. I met an old friend who invited me to his house for supper, so don't worry about me, my stomach is full. Everything will be fine, don't worry. I visited several good places today. We must be patient a little while longer. I'm going to my room to read for awhile and then go to bed." For one or two days, his mother believed him but she soon found out that he was lying so she would eat.

These were unhappy days for Narendra Kumar. The Angel of Struggle had firmly shut all the doors to material prosperity. God, Himself, had ordered this. The only door left open was the spiritual path. One day Narendra reached the holy feet of Sri Ramakrishna Paramahansa. Narendra had heard about Ramakrishna but never met him. Finding peace in the presence of Ramakrishna, Narendra asked him the same question he'd asked numerous other saints but never found satisfaction in their answers: "Have you seen God?"

Ramakrishna's face lit with a sweet smile and the nectar of compassion flowed from his eyes. With pure love, he answered Narendra's question with another question. "Do you desire to see God?" "Yes, please," Narendra replied. "This is the best desire," Ramakrishna said. That day, Narendra received perfect comfort from his conversation with Ramakrishna. He went back to him regularly and grew in spiritual knowledge and detachment from the world. One day he took sanyas initiation, total renunciation with perfect brahmacharya, and Sri Ramakrishna gave him the name Swami Vivekananda.

Today millions of people know of Swami Vivekananda. Anyone can read his biography and discourses to become acquainted with his unique personality. Yet when he was asked to go to Chicago and address the Parliament of World Religions, no one at all knew him. Rising from his seat with only 15 minutes to speak, the audience was spellbound by his sweet and distinctive speech. From there his popularity spread all over America. It's hard to imagine this is the same person who felt useless as a young man, unable to get a job, walking the streets of Calcutta, and lying to his mother. If Struggle had not closed every door to his material success, but had given him a nice job instead, the direction of his mind may have been diverted and the world would not know the greatness of Swami Vivekananda.

Everyone desires to live happily up to the time of their death with struggle never entering into their life. But this desire has no value. It is a fact that food will not digest without exercise. In the same way, life will not develop properly without struggle. When happiness is experienced at the end of profound unhappiness and struggle, its sweetness is indescribable.

Years later Swami Vivekananda influenced another Indian saint to come to America while visiting the state of Punjab to make a speech. At that time, Swami Ramathirtha was a professor of mathematics and still in householder clothes. He was a loyal follower of Vedanta and putting a great deal of effort into seeing God everywhere, which is an essential element of its spiritual philosophy. Moved by Vivekananda's speech, he approached him afterward and the two chatted briefly. As Swami Vivekananda turned to leave, Ramathirtha wanted to give him something, so he took off his beautiful gold watch and placed it in Swami Vivekananda's hand.

Swami Vivekananda gazed at this professor more closely. Recognizing his saintly nature, Vivekananda felt that he would be a swami someday in the future. Vivekananda looked at the watch for a long time. He turned it over several times and admired it's elegance, and then he placed it back into Ramathirtha's pocket. "You don't want it?" Ramathirtha asked politely. "All is God," Swami Vivekananda said sweetly. "There's no difference between you and me, even though we're dressed differently. What difference does it make, then, whose pocket the watch is in?" Ramathirtha was deeply impressed and shortly thereafter took his swami vows.

But Swami Ramathirtha's trip to America was very different. He wasn't invited to speak anywhere and no one was sure why he went. He had no plans; he was just intoxicated with love for God. He boarded a steamer with no warm clothes, no blankets, and no possessions other than his Indian clothing and an extra dhoti (piece of cloth) he kept wrapped around his neck. One night he was out on the deck of the ship. A man from America saw him and was attracted by his unusual dress. The two of them began talking and the man was taken by Ramathirtha, who spoke sweetly and with so much love, as if they had been friends for a years and years.

As the evening grew late, the conversation turned to practicalities. "Where are you going?" the man asked. "To America," Swami Ramathirtha replied. The man continued, "Which city are you going to?" Ramathirtha answered, "To your city." Surprised at what he thought was a coincidence, the man asked further, "Do you know anyone there?" Ramathirtha responded, "Yes, I know one person." "And who is that?" the man asked. "You!" Swami Ramathirtha replied, and they both laughed.

Swami Ramathirtha had come to America only to love others. He had no purpose beyond that, yet his journey took shape and was successful from that very conversation. Remember this life principle: wherever you go, spread your love. Just keep the candle of your love burning and whenever you find an unlit candle, light it up. There's no higher purpose or answer beyond that.

******

The many parallels between the early lives of Swami Vivekananda and Swami Kripalu are apparent, as is the fame they gained in adulthood as orators. Less obvious is his camaraderie with Swami Ramathirtha, which sheds light on how Swami Kripalu could uproot his life and travel all the way to America and say, "I have not come to propagate Indian religion or even spread yoga and meditation. I have simply come to meet you."

8-1: The Death of Lord Buddha

Swami Kripalu was intimate with the life of the Buddha, as reflected in various talks he gave while in America. This story departs from the established Buddhist lore, which suggests to me that Swami Kripalu was interpreting it based on his own experience.

******

One morning Ananda, the disciple of Lord Buddha, was meditating. As his meditation drew to a close, he had a vision of the sun setting. The sun sets every day, and such a vision would not normally be upsetting. But seeing this vision, Ananda's body shook. Trembling all over, tears poured from his eyes. That scene disappeared but the vision continued, and Ananda saw the light of a lamp going out because its ghee (fuel) was all gone. Then the entire scene of his vision became pitch black, and there was darkness everywhere.

Ananda was an unattached monk, and restraint was his temperament. Lord Buddha himself had given him his name, Ananda, which means bliss. After meditating for many years under the direction of such a great master, few things could disturb his mind. By what secret door had this disturbance entered the impenetrable fortress of his mind? Ananda was only able to imagine that it was a premonition, but he was not sure to what it was related. His intelligence instructed him to discuss the matter with Lord Buddha.

But today was Ananda's day to visit the city for a special task and he had little time. Seeing Lord Buddha for morning darshan, he decided to wait until he returned to ask about the disturbance in his meditation. Getting up to leave, his feet froze in place. Once again his entire body shook, and his heart screamed out a silent scream of intolerable pain. Clouds of tears poured from the sky of his eyes. He never kept anything secret from his guru, yet he still wished to maintain silence about these disturbances until he returned from the city. As Ananda walked toward the door, his heart begged him to once more look upon the face of his teacher. He turned and stole a quick look at the compassionate eyes of Lord Buddha. Then with sad steps, Ananda left for the city.

Meal time came and Lord Buddha left to collect alms. That day a poor person offered him food that mistakenly contained poisonous mushrooms. After finishing his lunch, the Lord returned to his residence. Within two hours, the poison had spread throughout his entire body. The pain became intense, yet the Lord's face remained tranquil. He was a stoic; therefore he silently welcomed the pain.

It was obvious now to his disciples that Lord Buddha had been poisoned. The news spread like wildfire throughout the city. Thousands of feet ran toward their dying teacher, thousands of hearts lamented, thousands of eyes filled with tears. The poor man who had offered Lord Buddha the mushrooms also heard the news. Panting as he ran, he collapsed at the lotus feet of his Lord and uttered a heartrending cry, repeatedly begging forgiveness and cursing himself. Lord Buddha comforted the man with total affection. Being omniscient, he must have desired to withdraw himself from God's divine play, otherwise such an accident could never have happened.

Ananda, too, heard the news while he was still in the city and rushed back to where the Lord Buddha lay dying in seclusion. Other disciples were guarding the door to his room to keep the grieving people away, as everything was in chaos. Ananda was a close disciple, so he entered the room to serve his master. He bowed with great reverence and now understood the significance of the setting sun and extinguishing flame in his meditation.

He sat in front of his dying guru and tried not to cry, but he broke into racking sobs of despair, as if he was crying for all the grieving masses outside the monastery. Lord Buddha allowed him to cry with great patience. When Ananda finally had no more tears, their eyes met. Ananda saw that Lord Buddha's face was radiant. In that moment, a huge ocean of love poured from the Lord's eyes, as if the entire heart of the Buddha had migrated into his eyes. "Ananda," Lord Buddha whispered with such sweetness that the memory of that word and the way it was spoken would forever be with him. "Lord," Ananda whispered back, still grieving, "What happened? Part of me says that this was just an accident, that there was no enmity in the heart of the person that fed you. Yet, I am not convinced."

"The deed was not intentional," the Buddha said, "and it isn't my task to ponder his part. I'm only evaluating my part. I firmly believe that this incident is the result of my karma. Only after I have suffered through it will I be free of it. So hold no hatred towards him. If you hold hatred, new karma will be created in a vicious circle, and it will be an obstacle on the path to your own liberation." Equanimity is the foundation of greatness, and those who like Lord Buddha are able to behave favorably in even unfavorable situations are indeed great men.

Ananda, however, was still a disciple, not a master, so he had doubts. "My Lord," he said. "I understand the truth in your words, yet my heart is still angry. This is such a vicious incident. Isn't anger and bitterness a natural reaction?" Fierce flames from the poison burned in every atom of the Buddha's body, but the Lord was in deep contemplation. He was a great stoic and his mind and body were capable of tolerating any type of pain. Such masters don't allow their minds to go unrestrained toward either pleasure or pain. Instead, they turn it to some other thought.

"Ananda," Lord Buddha said. "It's natural to hold onto hateful feelings when they arise. To suppress such feelings and keep them from arising is also wrong. Learn to tolerate the situation, believing it to be the result of previous karma." Ananda bowed down at his master's holy feet with faith and devotion. Years ago he had offered his life to the Buddha and today he offered his life again, but this time with greater understanding. He never even considered saying, "Please bless me." He had developed complete faith that the Lord's strong grace would always be with him.

Ananda left the room, allowing Lord Buddha to rest in silence, but he felt as he walked out that Lord Buddha was walking with him. A few minutes later, Lord Buddha left his body and entered Parinirvana (the death of someone who attained nirvana during his lifetime).

Three days later, Ananda awoke suddenly with no memory of his previous days or nights. He looked around and realized that he had been lying on the banks of a river for a long time. In the distance, he could see a chain of mountains studded with a canopy of green trees. Streams wound down the mountains to the river in divine beauty. It was dusk and the sun glowed with a deep red hue. Beholding the scene, he remembered the sunset that had appeared as a premonition in his meditation. The sun was gradually descending from the sky. Was it truly the sun? No, Ananda thought, it's my Lord gradually withdrawing his radiance.

Tears filled his eyes and he slipped into meditation. "Ananda?" he heard the familiar voice. "Yes" he replied quickly as every atom in his body recognized the voice and surged with a reply. "Do you believe me dead?" "My Lord, permanent separation from the body is called death, is it not?" "Ananda, you haven't yet become truly Ananda, true bliss. Only a genuine monk can be considered Ananda. You have remained worldly, grieving my death, and that's the reason you are lamenting. Give up your despair." "I hate the word death!" Ananda shouted back, "That's the reason for my despair!"

"Dear monk, you haven't yet realized the final truth. Listen! As long as my yogic principles live, as long as my system of sadhana lives, I will also live. Death of the truth is my death. Since truth is eternal, I am also eternal. I, the Buddha, was merely a seed. Now a huge Buddha tree has sprouted from this seed. On its countless branches and sub-branches, innumerable Buddha seeds have budded. In the future, Ananda, huge forests of Buddhas will flourish. I believe this occurrence to be the cause of my immortality. This is not ego. One in whom ego resides can never be called a yogi."

Ananda almost drowned in the torrent of Lord Buddha's teachings. "Lord," he whispered, "my aching heart has received complete consolation. Now I will be able to walk upon the path lit by you for countless years to come. With your grace, I'll reach the final destination."

******

Swami Kripalu told this story in January 1981, after he had been suffering symptoms for many months, and less than a year before his passing. While practicing in a lineage that sought to overcome death, Swami Kripalu was clearly reflecting on the Buddhist view that death is inevitable. In this story, the Buddha is cast as being eternal despite having suffered his bodily death.

8-2: The Old Man Chooses a Dentist Here is a story of Swami Kripalu's that I don't believe has ever before been presented. I found it in a few hard-to-decipher sentences written on his slate that got transcribed. Once I realized it was a metaphor for choosing a spiritual teacher, its storyline jumped off the page for me.

******

Once an old man was sorely troubled by a bad tooth. His friends offered to help him consult with a good dentist. While agreeing, the man said definitively: "Okay but I will be the one who selects the doctor. Only then will I let him treat me." Instead of arguing, his friends accepted this condition because the man was known to be very smart.

So the whole group drove to the dispensary, with only the old man going in to see the dentist. While the dentist was examining his mouth, the man was examining the dentist to see if he wanted to be treated by him. After hearing what procedure the dentist thought was needed, he returned to his friends and said, "Not this one." Three more offices were visited with this same scenario repeating itself. The friends were taken by surprise and exclaimed, "There are only five dentists in town. We don't understand. What is it that you are looking for?" The man would only say, "I'll let you know in the end."

Finally they arrived at the fifth dentist, who was also old but still well-regarded. Sitting down across from each other, the dentist opened his mouth to speak but was immediately interrupted by the man, who began to ask him questions. Early in your life, did you have a full set of teeth? How many teeth have you lost? At what age did you lose them? What was the cause of your disease? What pains did you suffer and has removing the tooth remedied them?

The old dentist wasn't at all insulted by these questions. He answered them with a great smile and in a way that demonstrated his competence. Returning to his friends, the man happily made an appointment to have his tooth pulled the next day, explaining, "How can anyone with all his teeth be my dentist?" Now his friends understood, he was looking for help from someone with personal experience who had himself walked the path of losing teeth.

******

Swami Kripalu met many young foreigners who came to India with a shortlist of famous teachers and a dream of finding their guru. He was incredulous to watch them get initiated after staying in a guru's ashram for only a day or two. He felt that students should take a guru only after knowing him or her for a substantial period of time. This allows the student to assess the teacher's true character by seeing it demonstrated in action, and for the foundation of a loving and supportive relationship to be laid.

In today's world, people often want a celebrity guru who appears to have it all and be blissfully free of all ailments and problems. This story sends a very different message. Perhaps what we should be looking for in a teacher is someone who has been through life's difficulties, felt the pain of losing a tooth or two, and still has a nice smile.

Bibliography

Works by Swami Kripalu:

Asana and Mudra. Rhinebeck, NY: Red Elixer, 2018.

The Illusion of Conjugal Sadhana. Kayavarohan, Gujarat, India: Sri Dahyabhai Hirabhai Patel, 1978.

Kripalupanisad. St. Helena, CA: Sanatana Publishing Society, 1979.

Letters from Swami Kripalu: Personal Correspondence from HH Swami Kripalvanandji to Yogi Amrit Desai, 1966-1973. Salt Springs, FL: Yoga Network International, 2017.

The Passion of Christ: A Discourse. Summit Station, PA: Kripalu Publications, 1983.

Premyatra: Pilgrimage of Love, Book I. Summit Station, PA: Kripalu Publications, 1981.

Premyatra: Pilgrimage of Love, Book II. Summit Station, PA: Kripalu Publications, 1982.

Premyatra: Pilgrimage of Love, Book III. Lenox, MA: Kripalu Publications, 1984.

Prerana Piyush (The Nectar of Inspiration). Stockbridge, MA: Kripalu Center for Yoga & Health, 2013.

Revealing the Secret: A Commentary on The Small Burning Lamp of Sun-Moon Yoga (The Hathayoga Pradipika). Merimbula, N.S.W. Australia: H. C. Berner, 2002.

The Sadhak's Companion: From the Words of Swami Kripaluananda. St. Helena, CA: Sanatana Publishing Society, 1977.

Science of Meditation. Kayavarohan, Gujarat, India: Sri Dahyabhai Hirabhai Patel, 1977.

Yoga and Celibacy. Kayavarohan, Gujarat, India: Sri Dahyabhai Hirabhai Patel, 1978.

Works by Other Authors, Compilers, and Editors:

Levitt, Atma Jo Ann (compiler and editor). *Pilgrim of Love: The Life and Teachings of Swami Kripalu.* Rhinebeck, NY: Monkfish Book Publishing Co., 2004.

Mundahl, John (compiler and editor). *From the Heart of the Lotus: The Teaching Stories of Swami Kripalu* / as spontaneously translated and spoken by Yogi Amrit Desai. Rhinebeck, NY: Monkfish Book Publishing Co., 2008.

—————— *A Sunrise of Joy: The Lost Darshans of Swami Kripalu* / compiled and edited by John Mundahl. Rhinebeck, NY: Red Elixer, 2012.

—————— *The Swami Kripalu Reader: Selected Works from a Yogic Master* / by John Mundahl. CreateSpace, 2014.

Swami Rajarshi Muni. *Infinite Grace: The Story of My Spiritual Lineage.* Vadodara, Gujarat, India: LIFE Mission Publications, 2002.

—————— *Light from Guru to Disciple.* Sumneytown, PA: Kripalu Yoga Ashram, 1974.

Additional Resources

Readers wanting to continue their study can find the majority of Swami Kripalu's written works and a wealth of other information on the Pashupat lineage of Lord Lakulish available for download free of charge at the website maintained by the Foundation for Natural Meditation: naturalmeditation.net

Starting in 2020, a treasure trove of photographs and other information related to Swami Kripalu's life and teachings will become available free of charge on the website of Umesh Eric Baldwin: swamikripalvananda.org

Joel Feldman is one of Kripalu Center's founding residents and a teacher in the Kripalu tradition who maintains an active Facebook page named Swami Kripalu-Bapuji: facebook.com/groups/324315144380/

Photo Credits

All photographs contained in this book (unless otherwise noted) are from the archive of Umesh Eric Baldwin, who is also the primary source of some photographs I obtained from and cited to Kripalu Center. For more see swamikripalvananda.org

Page	Title	Source
3	Swami Kripalu at his desk	Kripalu Center
4	Mataji Desai serving Swami Kripalu	Kripalu Center
11	Sumneytown ashram welcome sign	
13	Four shots of Swami Kripalu circa 1981	
14	Vandana blessing ritual	Kripalu Center
15	Sumneytown chapel	
22	Summit Station Yoga Retreat	Kripalu Center
24	Kripalu Center and its staff	Kripalu Center and Eric Umesh Baldwin
33	A young Swami Kripalu	
44	Rajpipla street scene 1974	
50	Krishnalal Majmudar	
52	Swami Shantananda	
53	Swami Kripalu soon after sanyas initiation	
56	Swami Kripalu in wandering years	
59	Swami Kripalu delivering discourse	
60	Swami Kripalu in blessing pose	
68	Swami Kripalu in sitting meditation	
69	Swami Kripalu on Rajpipla steps	
71	Four shots of Swami Kripalu doing dance-like movements he later called dhyana (meditation) mudras	*Asana and Mudra,* Monkfish Book Publishing Company
73	Four shots of Swami Kripalu doing postures: Ardha Upadhanasa or Half Pillow Pose, Kaksina Hasta Catuskonasana or Four Angle Pose, Utthita Padmasana or Raised Lotus Pose, and Hasta Padangusthasana or Angled Hand to Foot Pose	*Asana and Mudra,* Monkfish Book Publishing Company

Page	Title	Source
75	Four shots of Swami Kripalu doing the three locks (bandhas) in Bhadrasana or Blessed Pose, Parvastasana or Separation Pose, Supta Bhadrasana or Lying Down Blessed Pose, and Visesana or Excellent Pose	*Asana and Mudra,* Monkfish Book Publishing Company
76	Swami Kripalu in early phase of his kundalini sadhana	
78	Swami Kripalu in matsyasana (fish pose)	
88	Four shots of the statue of Lord Lakulish in the Kayavarohan temple	Kripalu Center and Umesh Eric Baldwin
95	Four shots of Swami Kripalu doing the bodily mudras: Pasvini Mudra, Yoni or Womb Mudra, Maha or Great Mudra, and Tadagi or Tank Mudra	*Asana and Mudra,* Monkfish Book Publishing Company
96	Swami Kripalu in the Malav ashram	Kripalu Center
103	Five shots of Kayavarohan temple and installation ceremony	Kripalu Center and Umesh Eric Baldwin
106	Lakulish statue being lowered into temple	Kripalu Center
113	Swami Kripalu at JFK airport in 1977	Kripalu Center
115	Swami Kripalu speaking to group	Kripalu Center
117	Swami Kripalu in 1977	Kripalu Center
119	Four shots of Mukitdham	Kripalu Center and Umesh Eric Baldwin
120	Writing chalkboard message	Kripalu Center
121	Four shots of Swami Kripalu doing dhyana mudras	Kripalu Center and Umesh Eric Baldwin
124	Four shots of Swami Kripalu near the end of his time in America.	
126	Swami Kripalu at last gathering in USA	
130	Four shots of the burial and memorial service	
132	Swami Kripalu mandir or shrine	Floyd A. Rivera
139	Blessing	Kripalu Center

Acknowledgments

Anyone who has written a book knows that it's not an individual effort, and this one is no exception. Extra special thanks are due to Umesh Eric Baldwin, someone who truly serves in the spirit of Swami Kripalu. Along with endless patience in helping me compile the photographs needed to bring this biography to life, Umesh was a walking gold mine of back-in-the-day stories and fresh insight that carried my understanding of Swami Kripalu into new realms. Coming from different ashram eras, we became friends while doing this work, something I cherish.

Sati Mona Sosna is a student of Yogeshwar Muni who recently accomplished the herculean task of finishing the stalled translation work and interfacing with Monkfish Books to publish Swami Kripalu's encyclopedic textbook of yoga, *Asana and Mudra,* in English. After providing this enduring service to the lineage, she was willing to lend her skills to my little project. Sati's close reading and insistence on accuracy made this book considerably better.

Lawrence Noyes is a dear friend and spiritual teacher who pulled me out of the doldrums when my spirits were sinking. But his encouragement and support were matched with discerning analysis, overarching views on critical issues, and detailed input. I so hope that Lawrence writes a sequel to his first book on the Enlightenment Intensive, as his life has brought him to a place where what he has to say is precious.

As the book makes clear, Yoganand Michael Carroll and I go way back. But our friendship remains current, and his willingness to read anything I sent him, reflect upon it, and always teach me new things is deeply appreciated.

Satyajit Kevin Foran or Moose is another friend who made a difference. In his role as Kripalu Center historian, he was able to dig up some pivotal photographs. The same goes for Vandita Kate Marchesiello, who is giving me the opportunity to launch the book with a keynote talk to the annual conference of Kripalu Yoga teachers in October 2019. Truly, I thank spirit for all six of the above individuals, each one a lineage holder carrying on the tradition of Swami Kripalu in their own distinctive way.

I also have a Kripalu Board of Trustees grants committee to thank. In accord with nonprofit conflict-of- interest rules, I was kept entirely out of their inner workings. The result is that I'm not even sure who served on the committee. I believe that a deep bow of gratitude is due to my close colleague and former Kripalu CEO David Lipsius, Micah Mortali, Joan Kopperl, and my steadfast friend Marcy Balter. If there were others, so sorry to have failed to recognize you. To Kripalu Center's current CEO, Barbara Vacarr, I salute you for taking the institution and its staff into the 21st century and know from experience that leading a spirited organization like Kripalu is never easy. And to graphic designer Dana-keli Derek Hansen, thank you for not only taking this project on but seeing it through to a beautiful outcome.

I also have another heartfelt Board friend and personal mentor, Justin Morreale, to thank, but I am saving his kudos for the next book in this series. Stay tuned for more on Justin.

I can't end without some mention of my best bud Sudhir Jonathan Foust. Early versions of the book included some funny stories about him that ended up on the editing room floor. Hopefully they will make it into the next book, as anytime the big guy is around there's fun close by.

To Danna, my amazing wife and partner, whose creative touch is apparent on each page of this book and in every wondrous day of our life together for the past 36 years, I thank God for you daily.

And to all you readers, who care about these matters enough to study and practice them, it's you who make the difference as only together can we be a real force for good in this world.

About Kripalu Center

Kripalu Center for Yoga & Health is the largest yoga-based retreat center in North America, a distinction it has held for almost 40 years. Nestled in the beautiful Berkshire mountains of western Massachusetts, it attracts more than 50,000 people a year for programs that feature world-class teachers on topics that include mental, physical, and spiritual health. Kripalu is known world-wide as a premier destination for those seeking a joyful, compassionate environment for connection, learning, and retreat.

Located 2.5 hours north of New York City and west of Boston, Kripalu's campus offers exquisite views overlooking the serene Stockbridge Bowl. The expansive grounds include beautiful gardens and wildflower meadows, an apple orchard, labyrinth, walking trails, and private lakefront area. To participate in a Kripalu program is to enjoy an in-depth immersion experience offered in a vibrant, holistic environment. Whether you come for a program on yoga, self-discovery, or health enhancement, seek professional training or certification, or explore Kripalu R&R with its flexible schedule of daily workshops, classes, and outdoor activities, Kripalu makes lifelong learning accessible and fun.

Kripalu is a tax-exempt 501(c)(3) nonprofit educational organization whose mission is to empower people and communities to realize their full potential through the transformative wisdom and practice of yoga. For more, see kripalu.org

About the Author

Richard Faulds (Shobhan), MA, JD, has practiced yoga and meditation in close association with Kripalu Center for nearly 40 years. A chance 1981 encounter with Swami Kripalu shifted the trajectory of his life. Joining the ashram community and eventually the residential staff, he was Kripalu's legal counsel for 25 years. He left the residential community in the mid-1990s and earned a master's degree in counseling and human development. He returned as Kripalu's president from 1998 to 2001 and was one of many dedicated staff who helped Kripalu move beyond the guru-disciple paradigm to become a national retreat and program center. He has also served as Kripalu's Board Chair, CEO, senior teacher, and author of *Kripalu Yoga: A Guide to Practice On and Off the Mat (Bantam 2006)*. His wife, Danna Faulds, is a longtime Kripalu Yoga and meditation practitioner who delights in being the "poet-at-large" of the Kripalu tradition. Together, their books include:

Richard Faulds:

Sayings of Swami Kripalu: Inspiring Quotes from a Contemporary Yoga Master (2004)
Swimming with Krishna: Teaching Stories from the Kripalu Yoga Tradition (2006)
The Enlightenment Teachings of Yogeshwar Muni: Self-Inquiry and Surrender Meditation in the Kripalu Yoga Tradition (2009)

Danna Faulds:

Go In and In: Poems From the Heart of Yoga (2002)
One Soul: More Poems From the Heart of Yoga (2003)
Prayers to the Infinite: Yoga Poems (2004)
From Root to Bloom: Poems and Other Writing (2006)
Limitless: New Poems and Other Writing (2009)
Into the Heart of Yoga: One Woman's Journey: A Memoir (2011)
Breath of Joy: Poems, Prayers and Prose (2013)
What's True Here: New Poems and Other Writings (2019)

Shobhan and Danna live in the Shenandoah Valley of Virginia where they practice yoga, write, and tend an organic vegetable garden that mostly feeds their rodent and insect friends. They also continue to teach a mix of programs at Kripalu Center.